FISHING ARIZONA

**Your Guide to Arizona's Best Fishing
Featuring over 100 great locations!**

(Includes all of Arizona's Urban Lakes plus a bonus
section on popular Mexican lakes!)

by G. J. Sagi

**GOLDEN
WEST ☼
PUBLISHERS**

Front cover photograph by G. J. Sagi.

Back cover photograph provided by Gregg Munck

Dedication

To my parents, who took the time to teach me
what a wonderful world we live in. Without their
help and support, this book would have never been
undertaken, much less completed.

Library of Congress Cataloging-in-Publication Data

Sagi, Guy J., 1957-
    Fishing Arizona: the guide to arizona's best fishing / by G. J.
Sagi.—Rev. ed.
    p.   cm.
Includes index.
ISBN 1-885590-92-X : (pbk.: alk. paper)
1. Fishing- -Arizona- -Guidebooks.   2. Arizona--Guidebooks. I. Title
SH469.S24 2003
799.1' 2' 09791 - - dc21
2003002771

Printed in the United States of America

Revised Edition © 2005

Information in this book is deemed to be authentic and accurate by author
and publisher. However, they disclaim any liability incurred in connection
with the use of information appearing in this book.

Golden West Publishers
4113 N. Longview Ave.
Phoenix, AZ 85014, USA
(800) 658-5830

For entertaining excerpts and complete Table of Contents for all
Golden West titles, visit: **goldenwestpublishers.com**

A note from the publisher

Thank you for purchasing this updated and expanded version of *Fishing Arizona*. In an effort to make the book even more valuable to you, we are presenting double the number of listings of fishable bodies of water. We have even included information on Arizona's urban lakes and some of the popular lakes in Mexico.

While a lot of the information presented in earlier editions of *Fishing Arizona* has been retained, author Guy (G. J.) Sagi has updated not only the information on the lakes, rivers, streams, reservoirs and water holes, he has also provided resource listings, with phone numbers and websites.

This book is intended to be a guide to Arizona's many spectacular fishing opportunities. Keep in mind that fires, floods and droughts wreak havoc on Arizona's natural resources, and a lake that is fishable one day may literally not be usable or accessible the next. In addition, road conditions can change very quickly as well as water conditions and facilities. Take advantage of modern technology and access the many websites listed throughout the book, they are your best source of updated information (see pages 245-247).

While many of the lakes and rivers in Arizona are well-known, we hope, by increasing the number of sites discussed in this book, to expose you to some new adventures; maybe you'll go to some places you hadn't considered before, or maybe this will help to open up some new fishing and travel adventures for you and your family.

At press time, some lakes in Arizona were experiencing mercury warnings, others were having their stock shocked and transported for survival purposes, limits on others were being scaled back, or increased. Arizona's waterways management is a fluid operation, so use this book as a guide to where the places are and use your computer and telephone to stay updated on latest developments.

This book may not answer all of your questions or give you the magic formula for catching the biggest fish. It will, however, serve as a useful guide to exploring the wonderful fishing opportunities that await you in Arizona!

Fishing Arizona

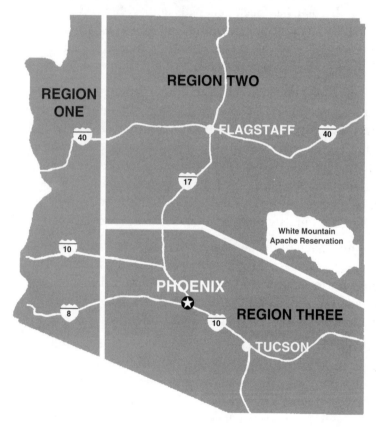

Table of Contents

Table of Contents *(continued)*

Introduction

Arizona's mountains soar to more than 12,000 feet, while other areas of the state plunge to nearly sea level. In higher elevation waters, you'll find Arctic grayling that thrive in the oxygen-thin air above 10,000 feet, along with Apache, rainbow, brown, cutthroat and brook trout. At lower elevations largemouth bass, carp, channel and flathead catfish, sunfish, bluegill and even tilapia flourish.

This wide range in elevations translates to comfortable, year-round fishing. Tired of summertime heat? Pack your favorite rod and head for the White Mountains. Suffering from cabin fever? Head for Lake Havasu and fish for largemouth bass in the shadow of London Bridge. With more than one hundred fishable bodies of water, Arizona allows savvy anglers to fish in comfort year round, while enjoying spectacular scenery, colorful history and almost on-demand solitude—a unique experience I call "Fishing Arizona."

Arizona is home to more than 85 species of fish, including largemouth and smallmouth bass, black and white crappie, northern pike, walleye, striped bass, white bass, channel and flathead catfish, bullheads, bluegills, redear sunfish, carp and even the exotic tilapia. Add yellow bass, black and bigmouth buffalo, yellow perch, Arctic grayling, blue catfish, mullet, warmouth and even the occasional Pacific tenpounder that winds its way up the Colorado River, and you can see why our state offers some of the world's most diverse angling.

True to its desert image, water can be a scarce commodity in Arizona though. Drought can result in lake levels low enough to prevent boat launching, severe drawdowns and on occasion the temporary disappearance of entire waterways. Water shortage, coupled with the latest phenomenon—wildfires capable of consuming entire cities and defoliating whole forests—has made it more important than ever to check conditions prior to heading out.

While you may be among those who consider drought to be

some sort of disaster, most droughts are simply a component in any lake's lifecycle. Every time a waterway recedes, even a few feet, nutrient-rich brush begins to grow. Once water levels return to normal and the new growth is inundated, spawning fish have added timber for cover. Survival rates improve, and even larger fish, like the predatory smallmouth bass, soon take advantage of the new ambush points. Along with the nutrient loading fresh timber adds to a waterway, and it's little wonder gamefish growth and catch rates typically accelerate even after short periods of drought.

During the summer of 2002, Arizona fell victim to a potential catastrophe, one whose impact might be felt for generations to come. The 462,606-acre Rodeo-Chediski Fire, charring more than 500 structures in the state, generated an economic loss of $320 million and garnered national attention during the precautionary evacuation of Pinetop-Lakeside. While Show Low, Payson and Pinetop-Lakeside were spared the fire's full wrath, cities like Heber, Overgaard and Pinedale weren't nearly as lucky.

Much to the shock of the public, whole forests were temporarily closed. Worse yet, concerns quickly grew that the scorched landscape would yield the kind of blackened, potentially suffocating, monsoon runoff that would seriously impact all downstream waterways—including Roosevelt Lake and others along the Salt River chain of lakes.

Aggressive monitoring began immediately, and despite the water's slight darkening, as of this printing, none of the ominous fish-kill predictions have come true. Although the fire left devastating consequences, it appears to have also returned tons of valuable nutrients to the watershed, holding the promise of accelerated fish growth rates for decades to come.

As a result, fishing in Arizona has never been better. And the future is even brighter.

Although designed to help you catch more fish, or maybe discover a hideaway or two of your own, bear in mind this book is only a snapshot at best. Arizona's ecosystem continues to evolve, and renewable resources like fish and wildlife are cyclic in nature. Calling ahead, checking websites and taking full advantage of meteorological conditions and management decisions are some of the most powerful tools in your angling arsenal. While every effort has been made to provide accurate, up-to-date details on the lakes included in this book, information for a few is extremely limited, and as is always the case, management plans continue to evolve.

While Arizona is home to more than half a million anglers—a number that grows every year—the winds of political change also impact angling opportunities. Tucson debated an end of its involvement with urban angling in January 2003, and lakes like Rucker Canyon Lake—once a popular destination in southeastern Arizona—remain a dry, voiceless victim of federal mandates.

Make your voice heard by elected officials, and work hard at keeping each body of water clean. Pack out all your trash; cut discarded line into small pieces before throwing it away or recycling it (fish and birds can become entangled in the longer line and die); and consult a set of current regulations and religiously adhere to them.

Remember too, almost every trout caught in Arizona has been reared in one of our state hatcheries. If you aren't going to eat the fish, let it go for the next angler to enjoy.

To release any species of fish successfully, the Arizona Game and Fish Department recommends:

- Play and land the fish as quickly as possible to minimize exhaustion stress, especially in warm water.

- Handle the fish gently and keep it in the water as much as possible.

- Remove the hook gently. If the fish has swallowed the hook, cut the line. The hook will decompose, but pulling it out can kill the fish.

- Use barbless hooks, which make hook removal much faster. Use needle-nosed pliers to flatten barbed hooks.

Finally, don't forget to take the time to share this wonderful heritage. The sights, smells and sounds of that first fishing trip will remain crystal clear in a youngster's memory, no matter how old they become—it is the rarest of all treasures, one capable of transcending time and binding family and friends for generations to come.

I sincerely hope this book enhances your pleasure of one of the purest, most enjoyable, family-oriented sports around today—fishing Arizona, where everyone has the same chance of landing a lunker, regardless of social status, physical limitations or economic challenge.

Tips & Tricks for Arizona's Unrivaled Fishing

Those who think Arizona's fishing is less than spectacular are wrong.

Fishing Arizona offers something totally different. It's not your typical angling adventure, one whose success is measured in pounds and ounces. It's a total package that includes an occasional lunker, near-perfect weather—regardless of season—history, scenery, solitude and so much more.

Lake Ontario has some great walleye fishing, but gorgeous sunsets are rare. Show Low Lake's walleye fishing is pretty good, but most nights feature a specular sunset.

Which is better? While a matter of taste, I can tell you this much for certain: There are plenty of fish to catch in Arizona, especially when you know which techniques have been working.

Even before Roosevelt Lake's dam was improved and its water level raised, Arizona Game and Fish biologists estimated it was home to no less than 3 million crappie. Add aggressive habitat improvement to the promise of an incredible nutrient load from the Rodeo-Chediski Fire's aftermath, and it's little wonder most are claiming Roosevelt Lake is on the verge of reestablishing itself as the Southwest's premier crappie fishery.

I hope readers understand why the decision was made not to note "record" fish in this book. Instead, large catches are noted, without identifying the records of the time. You can consult a current set of regulations to determine which were or are records; however, as nutrients migrate into the state's lakes, odds increase considerably that records will be regularly rewritten.

Arizona's fish are a wary breed. Landing a lunker here often requires that you adjust your technique and learn a few new tricks—otherwise you might as well resign yourself to coming home with little more than a serious case of frustration.

Lakes Mead and Powell are particularly challenging. One good look at the gin-clear water tells you exactly why. The fish take advantage of the increased visibility, and while you might be accustomed to another state's muddy waters camouflaging your lure, hook and line, you don't have that luxury here most of the time.

If you use 15-, 20- or higher-pound test line on Mead, you might as well be tossing anchors. Clear, light line is mandatory anywhere in Arizona—the lightest line you can get away with. On more than one occasion, I've watched anglers fishing side by side, using the same bait. If one routinely lands more fish than the other, more often it has always been because of the difference in test line. In Arizona, less is best.

Summer heat can also force many fish species to depths most anglers are unaccustomed to working. Because it's a lot harder to detect a strike after a long cast in deep water, sensitive rods, high-quality reels and staying in touch with the bait (even on the drop) are the remedy. You would be shocked at the number of bites most anglers miss in deep water.

Since nearly all of Arizona's impoundments are manmade, always take a good look around the dam. Most of the state's record walleye have been taken in the deeper water near Show Low Lake's dam, and you can expect cold-water species, like walleye and rainbow trout, to concentrate in those cooler, shadier areas of the lake, especially during the summer months.

Historically, some of the biggest catfish caught in Arizona have surrendered to a live bluegill rig. A bluegill rig is a system that allows a bluegill to swim around while a bobber floats topside serving as a strike indicator and a huge sinker helps get the bait down to catfish-holding depth. Be sure to consult a current set of regulations to determine if live bait is allowed on a particular waterway, as Arizona's management scheme is constantly evolving.

Arizona's largemouth bass are particularly finicky, although when water clarity is low, which does happen from time to time, it's wise to change to baits that either make a lot of "noise," or vibrate their way through the water. Bass sense the vibration in their lateral line, and a little advertising never hurts.

At most other times, think split shotting (using a light line with a split shot several feet above the grub or worm) or Carolina rigging (worm several feet below a slip sinker and swivel). Both systems are designed to allow the bass to pick up the bait without feeling pressure, thereby allowing an extra second or two to successfully set the hook.

Spinnerbaits are great for quickly locating aggressive bass, and small grubs are always a good bet. Remember, Arizona's bass often lay in ambush along shadows, considering themselves "covered" in seemingly featureless lakes. Working main and secondary points of any waterway can also be a formula for success. Sight fishing for bedding bass is an annual spectacle, although the right tube jig and a good pair of sunglasses are a must, and don't forget to help preserve the resource by practicing catch-and-release, particularly during the spawn.

Unlike impoundments elsewhere, Arizona's lakes rarely have any serious flooded timber. Instead of looking for that occasional stick-up when in pursuit of largemouth and small-mouth bass, watch your graph or study the shoreline to locate submerged boulders or thick beds of rocks. If you do find woody structure in the water, so much the better, but start with the rocks.

Drift fishing or trolling mini-jigs (or live minnows when legal) are great methods for locating thick schools of crappie. Once you're on a school, keep tossing in until the action stops. Be sure to remember the depth you caught the fish at, since every crappie in the entire lake will be within a foot or two of that depth. Arizona's crappie are typically a little more wary than their Midwestern counterparts, thanks again to water clarity. However, that means, armed with a good pair of polarized sunglasses, you can often relocate the school by simply looking while you troll.

Some of Arizona's trout easily surrender to corn, while others prefer small Mepps or Z-Ray spinnerbaits. Super Dupers have always been a good bet, as have marshmallow-style trout baits, Velveeta cheese and salmon eggs.

And never be afraid of trying something new. Years ago, I spent a lot of time at Hawley Lake, and one day, either out of curiosity or frustration, I baited up with corn and added a miniature marshmallow for good measure. I'd like to tell you I was deliberately floating the bait off the bottom, but I really don't know what compelled me to experiment.

That day, my father, my mother, my best friend and I all limited-out. Since then I use the technique regularly, especially when all else fails. Since miniature marshmallows are available in a wide variety of strange colors, it's an easy system to dial into any waterway's color pattern!

The best insurance for catching fish in Arizona is to call the nearest Arizona Game and Fish Department office. The department accumulates reports weekly from throughout the state, and although you never know where the fish are going to be hitting, Arizona Game and Fish often does. You can also visit www.azgfd.com or call 602/789-3701.

Keep in mind that although some lakes—like Picacho Lake and a few others—were dry at the time this book was printed, they were still included for future reference, making those last-minute phone calls even more important. Drought and oxygen-starving heat can also affect conditions, causing partial or full kill-offs, so inquiring about conditions is the best way to ensure success.

Jerkbaits like this are a sure hit when largemouth topwater action turns on!

Region One

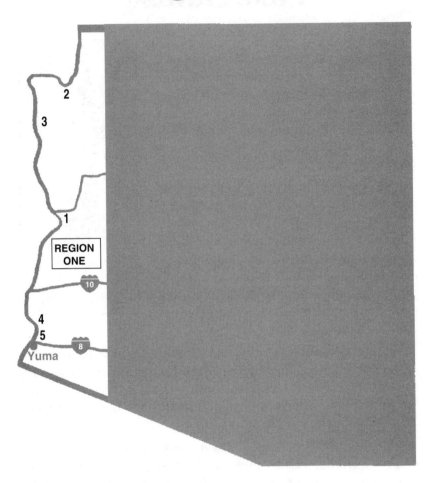

Region One

Note: Maps are not to scale.

Lake Havasu

Lake Havasu is a sprawling 19,300 surface acres and averages 35 feet in depth. Perhaps the only drawback to the waterway is its low elevation—480 feet—which means it's very hot during the summer. Lake Havasu is one of those fishing destinations that isn't hard to sell the rest of the family on.

Situated on the on the Colorado River at the California-Arizona border, its beaches and watersports will keep everyone happy. Add the kind of habitat projects that continue to improve fishing, and Lake Havasu is a special destination in its own right. To get to the lake, take I-40 west out of Flagstaff, and just before the California border, turn south on State Route 95.

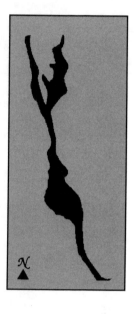

Lake Havasu was once one of the Southwest's premier largemouth bass fisheries, until the lake started to show its age. Much of the submerged structure that lent itself to lunker largemouths had decomposed, and those once-heavy stringers almost disappeared during the 1980s.

Fortunately, the Arizona Game and Fish Department and several local bass clubs undertook an aggressive habitat improvement program. Now your boat graphs routinely show large clumps of submerged trees and, if you know what you're looking for, an occasional synthetic bass bungalow (tires bound together), crappie condo (snow fencing) and catfish bungalow (bundled corrugated plastic pipe). Really, I'm not making these names up, they're exactly what the Arizona Game and Fish Department named these artificial structures.

Most bass fishermen head north into the Colorado River. But watch out for the notorious sand bar, shallow enough for "beach volleyball," which migrates with the seasons. The sight of people standing in waist-deep water, in the middle of the lake can be a little disconcerting, particularly if you're about to run up on the bar. Of course, when someone puts up a volleyball net, the sand bar is hard to miss.

Once you get by the infamous sand bar, it's relatively smooth sailing as you head north. The canyon soon narrows, and both sides of the river are covered with tules. Here, some bass fishermen will literally jump their boats into many of the backwaters and sloughs to flip and pitch the thick structure. There are also plenty of channels to work.

If you keep going, you will come to an area affectionately called the "Canyon." Here, rock walls rise in sheer cliffs on either side of the water, shading it for most of the day. The water turns swift here, and when Ted Miller of Apache Junction won a Bass Anglers Sportsman's Society (B.A.S.S.) tournament on Havasu, he spent part of his time working the rubble collected below each of these walls.

South of the main boat launches near Lake Havasu City, the Bill Williams River arm of the lake has always been a proven bass producer. The shoreline there is thick with tules, although there are enough deep rocky bumps to keep any fisherman happy. Consider, too, that Miller credited fishing the marinas for ultimately winning the B.A.S.S. tournament, and you can see that largemouth can literally be found anywhere on the lake.

During the summer, when recreational boaters typically crowd the lake, topwater action seems to dominate, especially early in the morning. When striped bass were added to Havasu, many anglers were concerned it might ruin the largemouth bass fishery. Although they were wrong, common wisdom today has it that there are no "deep" largemouth left. After watching several tournaments on this water, at different times of year, I agree. Fishing is still good, as evidenced by the 2001 catches of a 7.32-pound largemouth (January 20), a 9.34-pound largemouth (March 10), a 7.67-pounder (May 15) and the June 29, 2002, 8.64-pounder, although it's still best to start in relatively shallow water.

In March 1979, the state record carp was caught at Lake Havasu. As of this printing, the 42-pound monster still stands unbeaten among Colorado River waters.

Striped bass are also one of the area's most popular species. When they start "running," the water is literally cluttered with boats trying to get into the thick schools. From 1962 to 1964, the California Department of Fish and Game loaded Lake Havasu with 83,000 fingerlings and nearly a thousand year-old stripers. Many thought the experiment would not work, but a 59-pound, 12-ouncer caught south of Bullhead City in March 1977 proved otherwise. At the time it was a world record for land-locked striped bass, and it stood as the state record up until August 15, 1997, when a 67-pound, 1-ouncer was caught at Willow Beach on the Colorado River.

From October to March, the stripers generally stay in relatively open water, although in the spring they begin their annual migration toward the tailwaters of Davis Dam. Expect them to remain there until June when they again move downstream and scatter.

When the fish literally stack up below Davis Dam, proficient striper fishermen will anchor and throw heavy spoons or crankbaits. Oftentimes, the most productive method is to create a "chum" line with anchovy oil. Obviously, when you strategically place your hook baited with an anchovy nearby, hold on to your rod!

One of the best ways to locate a school of stripers is to closely watch your graph. Usually the shad stack up in a vertical line on the depth finders, and large blips at the bottom are often stripers. If you don't have a graph, watch for shad jumping on the surface while you troll the lake. Their hurried efforts at escape signal a feeding frenzy is underway somewhere below.

Crappie, an occasional rainbow trout lost from upstream, bluegill and sunfish also call Havasu home.

On June 15, 2000, a 3-pound, 8.64-ounce redear sunfish caught here shattered the state record. The previous redear sunfish record for the Colorado River waters was also caught at

Havasu, a 2-pound, 14-ouncer, caught on June 24, 1995. Green sunfish aren't exactly a slouch in Havasu either. On July 16, 1997, a 1-pound, 5.28-ouncer was caught here to set what was then the Colorado River record as well. A 2-pound, 12-ounce black crappie caught at Havasu Springs on March 11, 1996, held the Colorado River record for that species.

Just below the canyon, boats will often anchor and probe the depths for catfish. In fact, even during the summer heat catfishing remains good. On June 23, 2000, a 15-pound, 6-ounce channel catfish was caught at Havasu.

There are a number of state parks near Lake Havasu City, each sporting well-developed beaches and boat launches. Lake Havasu State Park encompasses 45 miles of shoreline and includes 132 campsites at Windsor Beach and another 225 at Cattail Cove. For details on this and other state parks, visit www.pr.state.az.us or call 602/542-4174.

Perhaps the best known attraction in the Lake Havasu area is London Bridge. That's right, Lake Havasu City, Arizona, is now the home of the London Bridge—not just an inexpensive look-alike, but the real thing.

The bridge was purchased in 1971 at a cost of $7.5 million. When it was disassembled in England, each outside brick was numbered to ensure accurate reassembly once it reached the United States. The bridge spans a finger of water that was diverted specifically to run under the bridge. London Bridge alone is worth a trip to Lake Havasu.

Notable

>   January 23, 1978, 9-pound, 13-ounce razorback sucker
>   March 1979, 42-pound carp
>   June 24, 1995, 2-pound, 14-ounce redear sunfish
>   March 11, 1996, 2-pound, 12-ounce black crappie
>   July 16, 1997, 1-pound, 5.28-ounce green sunfish
>   June 15, 2000, 3-pound, 8.64-ounce redear sunfish
>   June 23, 2000, 15-pound, 6-ounce channel catfish
>   March 10, 2001, 9.34-pound largemouth bass
>   July 30, 2001, 2-pound, 14.88-ounce hybrid sunfish

Lake Mead

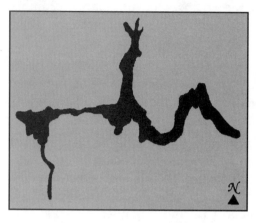

Lake Mead deserves a book by itself. This is one of the largest, most diverse fisheries in the nation.

Impounding Lake Mead 726 feet above desert bedrock is Hoover Dam, the highest concrete dam in the Western Hemisphere, completed in 1935.

At 110,000 surface acres, Lake Mead is also the largest manmade reservoir in the United States. It is 105 miles long with more than 800 miles of shoreline. The average depth of this huge lake is an incredible 280 feet. Although Lake Powell has more surface acres, Lake Mead's deeper water makes it the volumetric victor. Lake Mead is just 1,200 feet above sea level, so expect hot temperatures during the summer.

Head west toward the gambling Mecca of Las Vegas, and you can't help but drive over Hoover Dam and wind up at Mead. Take U.S. Route 93 northwest out of Kingman and the lake is just about 90 miles away. There are very few developed camping areas on the Arizona side of the lake. Temple Bar is one of them. It features a number of both tent and trailer camping sites. It has a dump station, drinking water and bathrooms. To reach it, take the well-marked turnoff along Route 93 about 40 miles before you reach Hoover Dam. There is also a resort at Temple Bar with full RV hookups, a restaurant/lounge, motel, boat rental, and much more. For information or reservations call the Seven Crown Resort at 800/752-9669 or go to www.sevencrown.com.

Camping is permitted at a number of other sites on the

lake. For more information, contact the National Park Service at 702/293-8907 or 702/293-8990. You can also visit the Lake Mead National Recreation Area website at www.nps.gov/lame.

There are more campsites on the Nevada side of the lake, including Overton Beach, Echo Bay, Callville Bay and Las Vegas Wash.

Species available at Lake Mead include largemouth bass, crappie, sunfish and channel catfish. Be prepared to work hard here, especially if you want to catch bass, since the clear water makes catching a limit quite tricky. Long casts are usually necessary, and alert bass fishermen often spot their prey before they ever land them.

Lake Mead also has a population of striped bass, although their numbers have been reduced since the early 1990s (bear in mind though, striped bass populations are cyclic, so expect numbers to rise again). The best places to look for stripers are Las Vegas Wash, Government Wash and the areas uplake, from Temple Bar to Callville Bay. Lake Mead's stripers are typically deep in the winter, rising a little in the spring and quite often on top in the summer and fall. Stripers were originally stocked here in 1969.

Watch the surface of the water during summer and fall when striper schools often herd threadfin shad to the surface in a feeding frenzy. Boils like this may last only a few seconds, so be ready to make a cast at a moment's notice.

The most popular spots for catching largemouth bass are from Temple Bar to Granite Wash. Remember that this kind of water clarity makes light lines a necessity. During the winter when action often cools off, try spooning or jigging deep drops. Big catches in this area include a 7.36-pound largemouth caught on April 14, 2001, and a 5.90-pounder on May 5, 2001.

If you're looking for non-stop crappie action early in the year, probe the areas of the Overton and Virgin rivers. The murky water there usually provides the earliest limits of the speckled beauties.

Catfishing on Lake Mead is usually best from May to

October. Expect to find the whiskerfish at night in depths of about 20 feet. Frozen anchovies, waterdogs and stinkbaits are perennial performers.

After the completion of Glen Canyon Dam upstream, the phosphate levels in Lake Mead were severely depleted. As a result, the micro-organisms and food base that game fish depend on to grow—and grow large—started to deteriorate slowly.

To help alleviate the problem, a huge experiment was undertaken in the late 1980s. Two hundred and fifty boats flooded 30,000 surface acres of the Overton Arm and 11,000 surface acres of Gregg Basin with 100 tons of a special fertilizer designed to artificially elevate phosphate levels. During the same period, experiments conducted on stripers revealed that some of the population was actually eating zooplankton instead of their usual meals of shad. After the fertilization, algae production increased threefold in 2 days. The algae being produced, in turn, increased the shad population for the stripers to forage on. In other words, things are looking up on Lake Mead, as evidenced by the 36-pound striped bass caught in September of 2002 by an angler near Gregg Basin.

The largest bluegill caught along the Colorado River was landed at Mead on May 27, 1989. It tipped the scales at 2-pounds, 11.5-ounces.

For current fishing conditions call 602/789-3701 or visit www.azgfd.com.

Notable
May 27, 1989, 2-pound, 11.5-ounce bluegill
April 14, 2001, 7.36-pound largemouth bass
December 2002, 36-pound striped bass (near Gregg Basin)

Lake Mohave

Lake Mohave is on the Colorado River near Bullhead City and Laughlin, Nevada. The easiest way to reach Lake Mohave is to take State Route 68 west from Kingman.

Lake Mohave was created in 1953 when Davis Dam was completed, impounding a total of 26,500 surface acres at an average depth of 75 feet. The lake runs for some 63 miles upstream before it encounters Hoover Dam. Lake Mohave has a total of 237 miles of shoreline, and at an elevation of only 645 feet you can expect hot summertime temperatures.

One of the most popular fishing destinations on Lake Mohave is Willow Beach, which is the most upstream camping area. To reach it, take U. S. Route 93 toward Las Vegas out of Kingman and follow the signs. It is managed as part of the Lake Mead National Recreation Area. For more information on the area call 702/293-8907 or 702/293-8990. You can also visit www.nps.gov/lame.

Willow Beach Resort, which is located there, offers campsites, fresh drinking water, a dump station for RVs and restrooms. There are relatively few campsites, so be sure to contact the National Park Service well before your visit.

Willow Beach is home to some of Arizona's biggest striped bass. Catches of 30-pounders are often reported and occasionally a 40-pounder is caught, like the one weighed at the marina in May 2000. The Colorado River waters record for Arizona was also caught here—a 67-pound, 1-ouncer that was brought ashore on August 15, 1997.

Heavy striped bass at Willow Beach are hardly news. When the state of Nevada did an electro-shocking survey near there in the early 1990s, one striper convincingly bottomed out a 50-pound scale. Instead of further exposing the fish and getting another scale, the surveyors released it. In 1990 a 49-pound, 8-ouncer was caught here as well.

For best results near Willow Beach use Bomber Long As. Although a striper migration doesn't typically occur on Lake Mohave, in August 1991, the Arizona Game and Fish Department reported stripers were indeed herding toward the dam. Although stripers prefer threadfin shad for food, they also consume rainbow trout, so the upper end of the lake where trout are stocked is where you can usually find many stripers.

Don't forget the crappie fishing here. On April 4, 1977, the then Colorado River waters record was caught on Lake Mohave. The 2-pound 11.3-ounce monster surrendered to a minnow in an area nearly 12 miles north of Katherine's Landing in a large basin that opens near Al's Point. Largemouth in the lake can be pretty big as well, with a 5.09-pounder caught on March 20, 2002, and a 6.25-pounder the next month.

Catfishing is also good, and the reef at the north end of Telephone Cove regularly produces more than its fair share of the whiskerfish. Both channel cats and flatheads call Lake Mohave home.

The state Colorado River waters rainbow trout record was also taken here. The 21-pound, 5.5-ounce fish was caught in September 1966 near Willow Beach. Most anglers go slightly upstream from the camping area there and work spoons. It is not uncommon to catch 2- and 3-pounders.

For more on Lake Mohave and Lake Mead, which are part of the Lake Mead National Recreation Area, visit www.nps.gov/lame. For current fishing conditions call 602/789-3701 or go to www.azgfd.com.

Notable

September 1966, 21-pound, 5.5-ounce rainbow trout
April 4, 1977, 2-pound, 11.3-ounce black crappie
August 15, 1997, 67-pound, 1-ounce striped bass

Martinez Lake

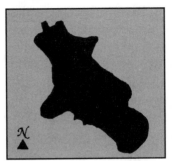

Martinez Lake, north of Yuma on the Colorado River, has laid claim to some huge bass and catfish over the years. At an elevation of only 200 feet above sea level, I don't recommend visiting during the dead of summer though.

Species available here include largemouth bass, a few smallmouth, white bass, crappie, bullheads, channel and flathead catfish, tilapia, redear sunfish, bluegill and, of course, carp.

If a non-fishing spouse prefers a few hours of wildlife viewing, particularly waterfowl, Imperial National Wildlife Refuge rests on the north shore of the lake. In other words, Martinez does have something for everyone.

The lake averages 640 surface acres, though its size and depth varies by year and with the amount of water allowed to make its way toward the Mexican border. There are well-developed boat launches and no motor restrictions.

To get to Martinez Lake, take U.S. Route 95 north from Yuma (you can find a number of shortcuts on a good map). Then take the Martinez Lake road heading west, and you'll see the lake in 10 more miles.

The lake is definitely worth a visit. For example, in the early '90s a pair of catfish were caught here that tipped the scales at 46 and 20 pounds. Both were caught on live goldfish.

If largemouth bass are more your style, consider the 4.9-pound and 5.6-pound bass caught the same month on crawdads. Perhaps the 8-pound lunker caught on an anchovy in May 1993 is a little more exciting or another 8-pounder caught off the docks in April 2000 or the April 13, 2002, 6.12-pounder.

Go to www.martinezlake.com. For current fishing conditions call 602/789-3701 or visit www.azgfd.com.

Mittry Lake

Mittry Lake is just off the Colorado River, about 17 miles north of Yuma. To reach the lake, take U.S. Route 95 east from Yuma, turn left (north) onto 7E. and follow the signs. The lake is only 185 feet above sea level, so expect some downright

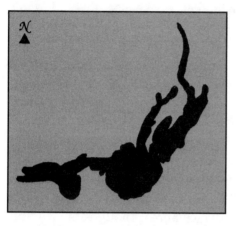

inhospitable temperatures in the summer. Visit during the winter though, and you'll be glad you did!

On January 3, 1991, what was then a new state record tilapia for Colorado River waters was caught near Mittry. It was 17 inches long and weighed 4 pounds, 11.04 ounces. Mittry had previously held the record, with a 4-pound,

5.33-ounce lunker caught September 17, 1984. Unfortunately, that mark was first shattered by a 5-pound, 8- ouncer caught at Saguaro Lake in 1996 and again by a 6-pounder, also caught at Saguaro, on April 7, 2000.

Although it looks much like a sunfish, this exotic fish, *tilapia Mozambique*, which was introduced from Africa, has thick lips that allow fry to seek shelter from danger in an adult's mouth. Tilapia have been at home in Arizona for the last 50 years.

An electro-fishing survey in the late 1980s indicated Mittry's predominate species are largemouth bass, bluegill, tilapia and carp, with smaller amounts of redear, warmouth, black crappie, channel catfish, flathead catfish, yellow bullhead and even goldfish. The chief forage species in this lake is threadfin shad.

Creel surveys by the Arizona Game and Fish Department show some interesting results on Mittry. August was the most productive month to fish here, with a 56-percent success rate. So you might actually want to brave the heat. December was the worst month, with only an 11-percent success rate. According to the study, anglers catch 0.32 fish per hour and keep 0.08 fish per hour fished. Apparently the fisherman who caught a 12.4-pound largemouth in late February 1993 wasn't paying much attention to those statistics.

Mittry Lake is about 500 surface acres, although it has only an 8-foot average depth. Any size motor is allowed here and the boat launch is good.

For current fishing conditions call 602/789-3701 or visit www.azgfd.com.

Notable

September 17, 1984, 4-pound, 5.33-ounce tilapia
January 3, 1991, 4-pound, 11.04-ounce tilapia
February 1993, 12.4-pound largemouth bass
April 28, 2002, 1-pound, 11.52-ounce bluegill

WEEDLESS RIG

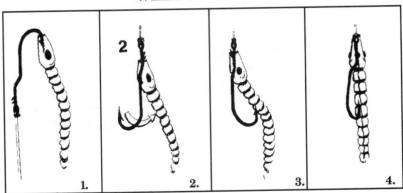

1. Slip hook through head of worm and out. This distance will depend on size of worm and hook used. **2.** Pull shank of hook through worm. Before the slices and eye enter the worm, rotate the hook 180°. This will prevent reaming out the worm head. **3.** Pull slices and eye into the worm head. **4.** Place the point in the **side** of the worm. This allows a quicker, easier exit when setting the hook. The worm should hang straight down on your line.

(Line art courtesy of Tru Turn, Inc.®)

Region Two

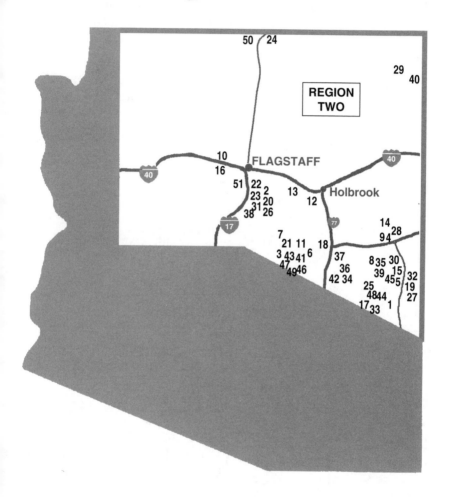

See **Region Two Index** next page.

Note: Maps are not to scale.

Region Two—Lakes & Reservoirs

Region Two—Creeks & Rivers

Ackre Lake

Ackre Lake's strategic location, only two miles south of Hannagan Meadow, makes it one of the most important bodies of water in the area. In fact, it's the only real impoundment for miles.

At two surface acres the chief attractions at Ackre are grayling and Apache trout—plenty of them. It seems many people weren't too appreciative that the Arizona Game and Fish Department enacted an artificial fly and lure-only rule in the early 1990s and an on-again, off-again catch-and-release rule subsequently (consult a current set of regulations for up-to-date information).

Of course, that means reduced pressure and a more secluded atmosphere. Add the fact that State Route 191 isn't the easiest way to get into Arizona's lake-infested White Mountains, and the solitude alone makes it worth the trip.

Ackre Lake stands at a chilling elevation of 8,600 feet and is skirted by Douglas fir and blue spruce. It's an ideal location to combine a day picnic and fishing trip.

There are a number of campsites nearby, though none directly on the lake. For more information on camping in the area, contact the Apache-Sitgreaves National Forest by writing P.O. Box 640, Springerville, AZ 85938. You can also visit www.fs.fed.us/r3/asnf or call 928/333-4301.

To get to Ackre Lake, take U. S. Route 191 north out of Clifton. Then take Forest Service Route 24 west from Hannagan Meadow for two miles.

For more information on fishing regulations contact the Pinetop regional office of the Arizona Game and Fish Department at 928/367-4281, or visit www.azgfd.com.

Ashurst Lake

Ashurst Lake, about 19 miles southeast of Flagstaff at an elevation of 7,110 feet, is one of Arizona's few lakes where a wintertime freeze can make it safe for ice fishing. At 229 surface acres, there's enough water to prevent a kill-off, although the lake's average depth is 20 feet or less. Ice fishermen should visit Ashurst in January or February. A phone call first to Arizona's Game and Fish office in Flagstaff at 928/774-5045 is a good idea. You can also visit www.azgfd.com or call 602/789-3701.

From Flagstaff, take the Lake Mary Road, go beyond Upper Lake Mary and follow the signs that lead along Forest Service Road 82E.

The lake is managed as a coldwater fishery, which means you can expect to catch pan-sized rainbow trout with an occasional brookie to spice up the frying pan. It is stocked a dozen times a year, usually from the first week in April until late August. There is also a sizeable northern pike population, as evidenced by the April 8, 2002, 20-pound, 0.18-ounce northern caught here. You'll also find catfish and crappie.

The high altitude also translates into cool summertime camping. For more detailed information on camping, contact the Coconino Forest's Mormon Lake Ranger District, 4773 S. Lake Mary Rd., Flagstaff, AZ 86001, 928/774-1147. Or, go to www.fs.fed.us/r3/coconino.

Ashurst lake has a boat launch, but motors are limited to 8 horsepower (consult a current set of regulations for more details).

Most anglers work the lake's three miles of shoreline with corn, cheese, and Berkley's Trout Power Bait. As temperatures increase during the summer, working deeper areas of the lake can be the secret to limiting out, though when I visited during the summer of 1999, youngsters were catching dozens of trout just feet from shore. My long casts and patience didn't produce a thing, while they were having a ball only a few feet away.

Notable

April 2002, 20-pound, 0.18-ounce, northern pike

Bonus Spot!

You might also want to visit Coconino Reservoir—just 1.3 miles beyond Ashurst Lake. There is no camping there, just idyllic scenery and fishing.

There's plenty of elbow room when fishing Ashurst.

Bear Canyon Lake

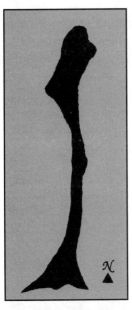

In the fall of 1990, the Arizona Game and Fish Department mounted a desperate effort to save part of the Arctic grayling population then residing in Lee Valley Reservoir. Using seine nets, it captured nearly 2,000 of the high-altitude dwellers and transplanted them to Bear Canyon Lake on the Mogollon Rim, north of Payson.

Arctic grayling are hardly anything new for Bear Canyon Lake. In 1985, when the Arizona Game and Fish Department introduced its coldwater fisheries management plan, it called for an increase in grayling opportunities for fishermen across the state. As a result, Bear Canyon soon received 38,000 fingerlings.

Of course, the bad news was that the lake was too "sterile" to support much of a grayling population, and today few if any remain. Bear Canyon Lake's habitat was also much less hospitable to grayling than Lee Valley, so you really never did hear much about them. Today, most people go to Bear Canyon in search of brook trout and the stocker rainbows that arrive every summer.

During most summers expect Bear Canyon Lake to receive about five rainbow trout stockings. The first usually takes place in early June, with the last coming in mid-August. The waterway also held the state Apache trout record for a 1969 catch just under 2 pounds. Four years later, a 22-incher weighing 3 pounds, 10 ounces came out of the lake—a mark that has been subsequently eclipsed, although at the time it made headlines and rewrote International Game Fish Association record books.

To get to Bear Canyon Lake, take State Route 260 east out of Payson. Once you climb the Mogollon Rim, turn north toward Woods Canyon Lake. It's only a few miles of dirt, and the signs are easy to follow.

Regulations change with regularity at Bear Canyon, which covers 60 surface acres at an average depth of 50 feet, so be sure to consult a current set prior to leaving. Only electric motors are allowed on the water.

At an elevation of 7,560 feet, you can expect cool temperatures year round. Camping is allowed about four miles away, and for more information you can contact the Apache-Sitgreaves National Forest at P.O. Box 640, Springerville, AZ 85938 or by calling 928/333-4301.

For up-to-date regulations contact the Arizona Game and Fish Department's Pinetop office by writing 2878 E. White Mountain Blvd., Pinetop, AZ 85935 or call 928/367-4281. You can also visit www.azgfd.com.

Lightweight spinning reels are ideal for landing Bear Canyon's wary rainbow trout.

Bear Wallow Creek

This little-known waterway on the east/central part of Arizona, is home to one of Arizona's rarest residents—the native Apache trout. In 1984 the Arizona Wilderness Act protected 11,000 acres in the area, and Bear Wallow Creek is the dominant waterway in the Bear Wallow Wilderness. Be sure to check regulations prior to leaving, as any stream, particularly those with Apache trout, are subject to change.

Just how aggressively this particular creek has historically been managed by the Arizona Game and Fish Department is best summarized by the 1979 construction of a "fish proof" barrier to prevent interbreeding between Apache and rainbow trout. The two species exist naturally in various parts of the creek. Unfortunately, sizeable flooding in 1983 destroyed the structure.

To reach Bear Wallow Creek, take U.S. Route 191 toward Hannagan Meadow. A few miles south of the Meadow, take the Forest Service Road 54 west. This small trail will lead you to the headwaters of the creek, and one of the forks is accessible north of this trail if you prefer the solitude that a short hike ensures.

Camping is allowed nearby in several areas. Most of the upper creek's elevations will be around 8,000 feet, and it courses through the Apache-Sitgreaves National Forest until Bear Wallow Creek joins the Black River.

For more information contact the Apache-Sitgreaves National Forest at P.O. Box 640, Springerville, AZ 85938 or call 928/333-4301. You can also visit www.fs.fed.us/r3/asnf. For up-to-date information on whether fishing is open in the area contact the Arizona Game and Fish Department by calling 602/789-3701 or visit www.azgfd.com.

Becker Lake

Becker Lake is one of Arizona's true Blue Ribbon trout fisheries. Lee's Ferry may dwarf it in quality, but located a few miles northwest of Springerville on U.S. Route 60, its 85 surface acres and special regulations highlight just how successful scientifically managing our waterways can be.

Regulations on Becker have varied from the state's only closed season—from November to April—to artificial-lure and fly-only seasons. Historically, the lake also features a reduced bag limit. To check current regulations before going to Becker, visit the Arizona Game and Fish Department's website at www.azgfd.com or call 602/789-3701.

Becker, like many of Arizona's waterways, has a checkered past. Anchor worms infested the lake's fish sometime in the 1980s, and to get rid of the parasite the lake was drained to a tiny pool in 1989. The remaining water was treated with rotenone, but disaster struck again when it was discovered that a host population of golden shiners had somehow survived the poisoning. As a result, Becker was closed for the 1990 season.

It reopened in 1991. At first only rainbow trout were stocked, along with a number of 1-pound incentive fish to "keep things interesting." Becker's average depth is only 10 feet, and it has 1.7 miles of shoreline.

Becker Lake has few facilities except for the traditional toilets and a boat launch that was improved along with the dam's spillway when the water level was lowered. Camping is not allowed, but nearby Springerville has a full range of services. Boaters are limited to electric trolling motors.

At an elevation of 6,900 feet, the real attraction to Becker Lake is the opportunity to escape summertime heat. At that altitude, the lake can freeze in the winter.

Becker Lake (named for Gustav and Julius Becker), is more than 200 years old and Arizona's oldest manmade reservoir. It was originally created when an abandoned oxbow to the Little Colorado River was flooded. The only fish in the water at that time were the Apache trout that came in with the original rush of water. They were thick enough to support a commercial fishing operation until the late 1800s when carp were introduced.

Because of its age, there are a number of "legends" associated with the lake, not the least of which includes several outlaws allegedly buried somewhere beneath the water.

Until the 1950s, the lake was literally infested with carp. By the 1960s, the Becker family, which owned the lake, had eradicated the carp. They purchased fish from private sources, stocking the lake and running it for a time as a free fishery. In 1973, the Arizona Game and Fish Department purchased the lake from the Beckers.

For more information contact the Pinetop office of the Arizona Game and Fish Department by calling 928/367-4281. You can also write to 2878 E. White Mountain Blvd., Pinetop, AZ 85935 or visit www.azgfd.com.

Trout are the main attraction in Becker Lake.

Big Lake

Big Lake is one of Arizona's highest-altitude angling destinations and features fishing that leaves you wondering if it's the 9,000-foot altitude or the fishing that leaves you breathless.

Big Lake came to be in 1930 when a dam was constructed on the East Fork of the Black River. Part of the old Apache National Wildlife Refuge, it was originally intended as a waterfowl project. Because the dam was only 10 feet high at that time, winter kills were common. To remedy the situation, the Arizona Game and Fish Department doubled the height of the dam and by 1965 the lake was full.

The 450-acre lake is not the state's largest reservoir, but some estimates say that about 400,000 trout are taken from its waters annually. It has an average depth of 27 feet and nearly 8 miles of shoreline. Expect Big Lake to freeze over every winter, though you should never assume the ice is safe.

To reach Big Lake, take State Route 260 east from Pinetop-Lakeside. Then turn right on State Route 261 just before you reach Eagar. The road is paved and relatively easy to find. There is another route—State Route 273—that runs past Sunrise Lake. That road is not as good, but it will get you there.

Open from May to November (with snowmobile access most other times), there is a launch area for boats, and motors are limited to 8 horsepower. A store there rents boats and has gasoline and a few grocery items.

Most of the time you can count on landing "stocker" size trout 8 to 10 inches in length. Species available on Big Lake include rainbow, cutthroat and brook trout. If you're working from shore, use those baits most popular with stocker fish, like corn, cheese and salmon eggs. Any of the trout power baits also work well, and a clever angler might float his corn off the bottom with a marshmallow for extra advertising.

Anglers who prefer artificial lures might start with a Z-Ray. Gold or silver finishes with some sort of red or orange coloring work extremely well. When you troll, a limit is almost a certainty if you use a brown Wooly Worm on the end of cowbells. Wet flies are a pretty good bet.

The weedline on Big Lake can get pretty thick, so shore fishermen might have to walk some distance to find a clear area. If you're in a boat, use the weeds to your advantage by working their edges.

Creel surveys by the Arizona Game and Fish Department showed that 3,027 anglers surveyed caught a total of 88,522 fish. Gill-net studies showed 90 percent of Big Lake's population is rainbow trout.

A state record brook trout was caught on Big Lake in May 1986. It weighed 4-pounds, 10.25-ounces and measured 21.5 inches long (the lunker surrendered to a silver Z-Ray). On October 20, 1995, that record was toppled by a 4-pound, 15.2-ouncer caught at nearby Sunrise Lake. Big Lake also surrendered a 4-pound, 8-ounce cutthroat trout (which was Big Fish of the Year for that species) on June 15, 2000. Another 3-pound, 12-ounce monster was caught on August 15, 2002.

There are plenty of campgrounds around Big Lake, but most are open only from May to September. The campsites are managed by the Apache-Sitgreaves National Forest. Write to P.O. Box 640, Springerville, AZ 85938. Call 928/333-4301 or visit www.fs.fed.us/r3/asnf.

For current information on Big Lake, contact the Pinetop office of the Arizona Game and Fish Deptartment, 928/367-4281. You can also call 602/789-3701 or go to www.azgfd.com.

Notable
> May 1996, 4-pound, 10.25-ounce brook trout
> June 15, 2000, 4-pound, 8-ounce cutthroat trout
> June 29, 2001, 8-pound, 1.12-ounce rainbow trout
> August 15, 2002, 3-pound, 12-ounce cutthroat trout

Black Canyon Lake

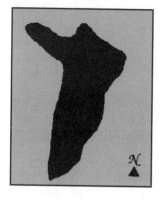

Black Canyon Lake covers 78 surface acres along the Mogollon Rim. At an elevation of 7,100 feet above sea level, it features comfortable summertime temperatures and is managed as one of the state's coldwater fisheries.

Expect to catch brook, rainbow and brown trout at Black Canyon Lake. Most of the fish remain active throughout the summer, as the lake has an average depth of 40 feet. Fingerling and catchable-sized rainbow trout were stocked on November 19, 2002, after water sampling determined the summer's fires had not negatively impacted the waterway.

To get to this lake in the Apache-Sitgreaves National Forest, take State Route 260 east from Payson toward Heber. Turn right on the Black Canyon Lake turnoff (well marked) onto Forest Service Road 300. In just over three miles of dirt, you'll be bearing left, again following the signs, toward the lake. For up-to-date fishing information call 602/789-3701; visit www.azgfd.com or www.fs.fed.us/r3/asnf.

Black Canyon's rainbow trout action can get hot in the early spring.

The Forks
of the Black River

Annually, when Arizona's mercury climbs above the century mark, residents seek shelter in higher elevations. The White Mountains in central-east Arizona and the San Francisco Peaks near Flagstaff offer an ideal refuge, soaring well above 10,000 feet.

For the off-road enthusiast who knows where to go, those areas are also home to some of the most secluded experiences to be found in the entire Southwest. Arizona's Black River runs all the way from near the New Mexico border, to central Arizona, where it finally joins the White River, turning into the Salt River.

Much of the Black River's remote regions wind through both the White Mountain and San Carlos Apache Indian reservations. One particularly scenic section, ideally located on the Apache-Sitgreaves National Forest, could become one of the Southwest's premier angling destinations, depending on efforts currently underway.

On October 17, 1992, the Arizona Game and Fish Commission approved a proposal that made the West Fork of the Black River Arizona's first catch-and-release Blue Ribbon fishery. Every fish caught in the West Fork area had to be released immediately, and only artificial lures were legal.

According to the Game and Fish Department, Arizona's Coldwater Fisheries Management Plan calls for a number of catch-and-release fisheries, and the Black River was the first step in what many are calling the wave of future in preserving quality backcountry outdoor experiences for generations to come. You won't come away with fish for the frying pan, but the reduced pressure ensures plenty of exciting watertop dances from the rainbow and brown trout. Consider too, that four of the river's many tributaries are being managed for native Apache trout, and this may be an off-roader's ultimate destination.

The quickest way to reach either fork of the Black River is to take U.S. Route 191 toward Alpine. A few miles north, Forest Service Road 249 heads west into the Apache-Sitgreaves National Forest. This dirt road is a little hard to see, so be sure to slow down. The sign, located near mile marker 423, indicates it as the route to Big Lake.

Where Forest Service Road 249 turns to the right toward Big Lake, you bear to the left and pick up Forest Service Road 276. In about 12 miles, you'll come to Deer Creek turnoff and the river is visible. Regulations change periodically, so be sure to consult a current set of Arizona fishing regulations prior to leaving. If you continue toward the West Fork, the road will slowly get rougher.

There are a number of water crossings on the way into the West Fork. At times the road can be rough, especially if you visit in the late fall or are lucky enough to be the first visitor in spring. Forest Service Road 276 merges with Forest Service Road 25 at the junction of the West and East Forks of the Black. There you will continue on Forest Service Road 25 and turn north if you want to probe those fish-holding pools in the more remote sections of the river. Forest Service Road 68 will take you north along much of the river and into Big Lake the back way (just in case the fish are uncooperative on the Black).

If you don't mind an occasional truck bouncing by, the river also offers a few of those rare waterside campsites. Firewood is plentiful, and permits are not required in most undeveloped sites, although Arizona's on-again, off-again drought situation means camping and fires can be temporarily banned.

If you're really adventurous, it's possible to take one of these back roads all the way to Whiteriver. Remember, if you plan on entering the White Mountain Apache Indian Reservation you must have a reservation permit.

Though the Black River originates on the slopes of Mount Baldy, the highest point in the White Mountains, most of the fishable sections of the river are at 8,500 feet above sea level. With altitudes like that, the area definitely guarantees refuge from the desert's 100-degree temperatures. Add the number of fishable creeks accessible only by high-clearance or four-wheel-drive vehicles, and the upper reaches of the Black River are an unparalleled summertime getaway.

Sections of this area are restricted from off-road travel. But they are well posted, and you can explore to your heart's content near most of the Black. For more information contact the Apache-Sitgreaves National Forest at P.O. Box 640, Springerville, AZ 85938 or call 928/333-4301. You can also visit www.fs.fed.us/r3/asnf.

The Arizona Game and Fish Department can answer all of your questions about current regulations on the Black River. Contact their Pinetop office at 2878 E. White Mountain Blvd., Pinetop, AZ 85935 or call them at 928/367-4281. You can also visit the Arizona Game and Fish Department website at www.azgfd.com or call 602/789-3701 for fishing conditions.

The Black River is home to a number of pools, like this one, which can yield excellent fishing opportunities.

Blue Ridge Reservoir

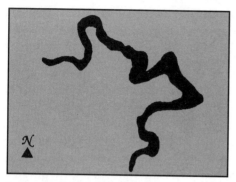

On April 24, 1993, the Arizona Game and Fish Department's weekly bulletin reported a 10-pound brown trout had been caught at Blue Ridge Reservoir. In fact, the bulletin reported that three other anglers who braved the icy road (which had just opened for the season), caught their limits, including 8-, 5- and 3-pound browns.

These fishermen were the first ones to work the lake that summer. While their success may lead you to conclude that arriving early in the season means some of Arizona's best brown trout action, be careful. This high-altitude lake is remote, and even in the early spring most of the lake can be frozen over, and the boat ramp so icy as to be totally unusable. It's not the kind of place you want to get stuck in during winter.

Blue Ridge Reservoir was the seventh impoundment created on the Mogollon Rim, which, other than creeks and streams, once had no fishable bodies of water. The reservoir was created by Arizona's copper mining giant, Phelps Dodge, in exchange for water it used from the Black River at its Morenci mining operation.

Blue Ridge Reservoir covers 70 surface acres and because of the cliffy area it was created in, sports an incredible average depth of 147 feet. It stands at an elevation of 6,720 feet above sea level, making it a sure hit for those of us looking for an escape from summer heat.

Access is limited to the reservoir though, making each trip

a relatively solitary affair. There is a boat launch, though motors are limited to 8 horsepower.

Shore fishermen will also find a number of trails meandering through the countryside that will take them to the water's edge. Be forewarned though, this lake is in some rough country, so traditionally, boat fishermen have enjoyed easiest access.

Species available include rainbow trout (stockings historically begin in mid-April and continue through late summer for a total of about eight stockings), brook trout and those lunker browns.

To get to the reservoir, take State Route 87 north out of Payson, through Pine and Strawberry. Five miles after the paved Clints Well/Happy Jack turnoff, take the gravel road heading east (Forest Service Road 751). The lake is about another four miles on the right hand side of the road.

Camping is available nearby at Rock Crossing Campground which stands at an elevation of 7,500 feet. For more information, contact the Coconino National Forest Mormon Lake Ranger District at 4773 S. Lake Mary Rd., Flagstaff, AZ 86001 or call 928/774-1147. You can also visit www.fs.fed.us/r3/coconino.

For fishing conditions call 602/789-3701 or visit www.azgfd.com.

Notable
April 24, 1993, 10-pound brown trout
November 26, 2002, 7-pound, 0.96-ounce brown trout

*Z-spin—an in-line spinner often works
well on Blue Ridge Reservoir*

Bunch Reservoir

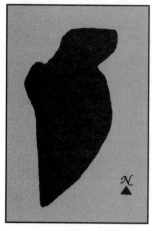

Bunch Reservoir is one of three reservoirs (the other two: Tunnel, p. 108 and River, p. 103) that are just outside of Greer in the scenic White Mountains. Bunch came into being when a dam was created to impound the Little Colorado River about a mile north of Greer.

Bunch Reservoir suffers chronic changes in size and, depending on the time of year (and recent atmospheric conditions), it can run anywhere from 44 surface acres in the spring to 20 by the end of the summer.

As is the case with most lakes in the White Mountains, the best time to prospect the lake for finny gold is in the early spring right after the thaw. Bunch Reservoir is home to a healthy population of brown and rainbow trout, and periodically stories come out of the lake about huge fish.

Bunch Reservoir stands at the chilly elevation of 8,200 feet above sea level. There are nearly 100 campsites nearby, but they are not adjacent to the water. The area fills quickly on busy summer weekends. For more information, contact the Apache-Sitgreaves National Forest at 928/333-4301, or write P.O. Box 640, Springerville, AZ 85938. You can also visit www.fs.fed.us/r3/asnf.

There are a couple of "general stores" in Greer, so campers/picnickers who forget critical items don't need to worry too much. The bed-and-breakfast industry is also thriving in the Greer area, so it's the ideal getaway for a non-fishing spouse.

Boats are allowed on Bunch, and it has a good boat launch. Motors are restricted to electric trolling motors. For bait, start with Super Dupers in yellow and red or Z-Rays in the same colors. If the fish are particularly stingy, add a salmon egg or power-style bait.

Come prepared for the cold though. At this altitude, the days when a stiff breeze isn't blowing are relatively rare, and alpine storms arrive quickly. To find the lake, take State Route 260 east out of Show Low. Take State Route 373 south toward Greer. In about two miles, signs will indicate a small paved road on your left that leads to the lake.

The other two lakes in the area ensure angler success, and if you want to try your hand at some finicky stream trout, the Little Colorado has plenty just waiting for your arrival. For up-to-date fishing information call 602/789-3701 or 602/942-3000 or visit the Arizona Game and Fish Department website at www.azgfd.com.

Yellow and red Z-rays work well in Arizona waters.

Canyon Creek

Editor's note:

The 2002 Rodeo-Chediski fire had devastating effects on Canyon Creek. Surrounding vegetation was destroyed and silt- and ash-infused runoff choked the fish in the stream. Hopefully, with time and volunteers, Canyon Creek can once again become a great trout stream. Be sure to check with Arizona Game and Fish for updates on this waterway! Editorially we felt the information presented by the author, while dated, still makes for compelling reading.

Intense flooding from early rains during the early 1980s literally scoured Canyon Creek below the Mogollon Rim, effectively ruining what was once one of Arizona's premier backcountry Blue Ribbon trout fisheries. Flooding in August 1992 had the opposite effect. When seven inches of rain fell in a single weekend above Canyon Creek, forcing the waterway to rise three feet in most places, "banks were undercut, rather than washed away, creating better trout cover. Pools were deepened by the scouring action of the water, and silt throughout the system was swept away providing better gravel beds for trout spawning and insect reproduction," said then Mesa Regional Fisheries Specialist Jim Warnecke of the Arizona Game and Fish Department.

When the first flood scoured the canyon in the early 1980s, the creek's banks were largely cleared of vegetation, exposing once cool trout-holding pools to Arizona's relentless sun, and huge amounts of silt had ruined the prime habitat.

The Arizona Game and Fish Department, in conjunction with the U.S. Forest Service and Trout Unlimited, first began to repair the fishery in 1986. Boulders were moved to provide trout hiding spots, trees were planted to reinforce the bank and fences were constructed to keep cattle away from vegetation.

"It was a lot of work, but in 1989 we completed the project. From the beginning of the project in 1986 to 1990, the riparian area experienced a rapid recovery. Then in 1990, the Department instituted new regulations setting the limit for trout taken out of the stream at two fish over 12-inches long. What we created was a Blue Ribbon fishery," Warnecke said.

The dedicated efforts of both volunteers and government agencies paid off when the last set of floods hit. A subsequent electro-shocking survey conducted on Canyon Creek graphically proves Warnecke's point. During the survey a 25.5-inch 8-pound brown trout was captured and released. The lunker was living in less than three feet of water! Another 6-pound fish, measuring 23 inches, was found hiding in a hole dug by a beaver in the side of a bank. "What we have now in Canyon Creek is a riparian system where natural forces like flooding create a dynamic, productive system not just for trout, but for all wildlife," Warnecke said.

Canyon Creek's total length is 31 fishable miles, and it covers elevations ranging from 2,905 feet to 5,300 feet. It begins on the White Mountain Apache Indian Reservation, so remember that you must purchase their fishing permits. To reach the area, take State Route 77 north out of Globe, then turn west on Indian Route 12 towards Cibecue. Continue on Route 12, north and slightly west out of Grasshopper. The road will "Y" in slightly over 20 miles. Both directions lead to Canyon Creek.

Canyon Creek is also accessible in the Tonto National Forest by taking State Route 260 east out of Payson. Turn south on State Route 288 toward the town of Young. This direction is dirt for quite a while though, so be prepared for a long trip. The creek is found north of Young after the road turns back into dirt and begins climbing the Mogollon Rim.

Camping is allowed at the creek in the Tonto National Forest. At 6,600 feet, you're ensured cool temperatures, but there are only 15 sites—be sure to arrive early. For more information write the Tonto National Forest at 2324 E. McDowell Road, Phoenix, AZ 85006, or call 602/225-5200. You can also visit www.fs.fed.us/r3/tonto or visit www.azgfd.com. For more information on the White Mountain Apache Indian Reservation write P.O. Box 220, Whiteriver, AZ 85941, call 928/338-4385 or visit www.wmatoutdoors.com.

Carnero Lake

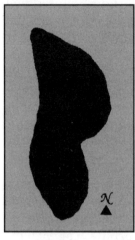

Carnero Lake is one of those wonderfully hidden getaways in the White Mountains. Unless you know exactly where it is, how to get there and have a high-clearance vehicle, forget ever finding its solitude—if it's even there, that is.

When I was a youngster, my parents took me to this scenic lake for the first time. With Green's Peak towering at 10,137 feet, plenty of elk and a waterdog population thick enough to walk on, it's something I'll never forget.

Rainbow and brown trout are all I've ever caught out of Carnero. In fact, during my first visit I threw in from the dam, and promptly had a 3- or 4-pounder break me off (using corn and marshmallows). By the end of summer, the lake, which I estimate to be about 30 surface acres, will be covered in a weedline thick enough to preclude shore fishing. In other words, visit in early spring.

To reach Carnero, take State Route 260 east from Pinetop. Turn north at mile marker 385. The road is about eight miles of dirt on Forest Service Road 118. There are no signs along Route 260, but once you're on the dirt road you will find them.

There are no developed campsites, no toilets, and consider yourself lucky if you locate a bear-proof garbage can or two. Camping is allowed along most of the trail. Check with the Apache-Sitgreaves National Forest for current restrictions by calling 928/333-4301 or visit www.fs.fed.us/r3/asnf.

For up-to-date information on Carnero call the Pinetop office of the Arizona Game and Fish Department: 928/367-4281 or visit www.azgfd.com.

Cataract Lake

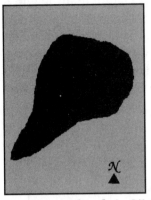

Only two miles from Williams, 35-acre Cataract Lake is one of the area's least known, least used fisheries. To get to Cataract, take I-40 west out of Flagstaff toward Williams. Turn north at Exit 161. It's very close to the interstate.

Cataract Lake stands at an elevation of 6,800 feet, and with an average depth of only 12 feet, it periodically suffers a winter freeze. The lake's maximum depth is 25 feet and has 1.5 miles of shoreline.

The lake was created in 1947 when the city of Williams put a forty-foot-high dirt dam on Cataract Creek to provide a steady water supply.

Coconino County owns the western shoreline of the lake, where it has a vehicle-maintenance storage facility. About 150 yards of shoreline access are owned by private interests, and the rest of the lake lies on the Kaibab National Forest.

Rainbow trout are stocked in Cataract during the summer. According to the regional Fisheries Program Manager, the largest rainbow trout he's heard of being caught at Cataract was a 22-incher. Expect the first stocking truck to arrive early in April (weather permitting), and it will come back a total of seven times (with the last in late August).

The lake is also home to brown trout, channel catfish and sunfish. The largest brown trout recorded for the reservoir was a 6-pounder, and the largest channel catfish tipped the scales at 8 pounds.

The fish in Cataract were poisoned by rotenone in 1956, 1963 and 1971. In 1971 a huge concentration of stunted crappie were negatively impacting the lake, so the poisoning was an effort to improve the fishing. Trap netting and electro-fishing surveys conducted in March and April of 1987 found the lake was holding green sunfish, fathead minnows, brown trout, rainbow trout, black crappie and channel catfish.

In 1993, the Arizona Game and Fish Department began a more aggressive management policy on Cataract. Instead of concentrating exclusively on salmonoids, it began attempts at increasing the lake's bass and bluegill resource. At last report, things were picking up considerably, though the drought of 1999-2002 had a serious impact on the lake.

There is a concrete boat launch, and 8 horsepower or less outboards are allowed. Camping is allowed nearby, and there are 37 sites available on county land, with another 18 sites on the national forest.

For more information contact the Kaibab National Forest at 800 S. 6th Street, Williams, AZ 86046 or call 928/635-2681. For more on current fishing conditions contact the Flagstaff Arizona Game and Fish office by calling 928/774-5045. You can also visit www.azgfd.com.

This Mepps lure can bring excellent results.

Live Baitfish Illustrations

The use of live baitfish in Arizona waters is very restricted. Be sure to consult the Arizona Game and Fish Regulations Manual, or visit www.azgfd.com.

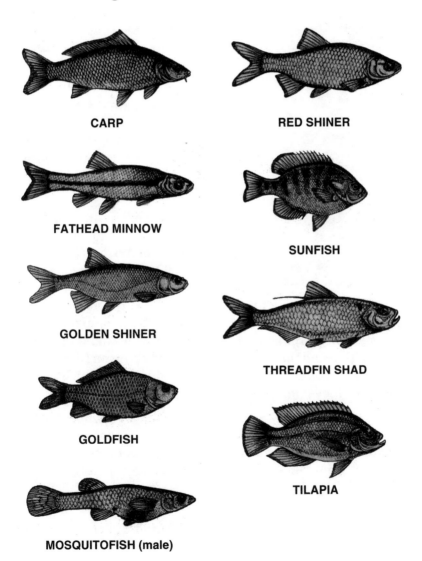

CARP

RED SHINER

FATHEAD MINNOW

SUNFISH

GOLDEN SHINER

THREADFIN SHAD

GOLDFISH

TILAPIA

MOSQUITOFISH (male)

Chevelon Canyon Lake

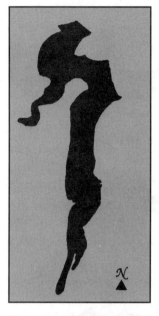

Access to Chevelon Canyon Lake is extremely limited. Although many might consider this, coupled with its remote location, something of a drawback, the combination makes for some of the best trout fishing in the state.

The road that was used for construction of the impoundment has not been maintained since the lake was created in the 1960s. It may be closed, but you can still use it to walk to the water's edge.

Atop the Mogollon Rim, northeast of Payson, Chevelon Canyon Lake is located in some of Arizona's most scenic country. To reach Chevelon, take State Route 260 northeast out of Payson. Be sure to take your time because the ascent up the Rim offers some spectacular views. A healthy population of elk can make nighttime travel something of a challenge. Turn north on the road that leads toward Woods Canyon Lake (follow the signs). Then turn north on a small dirt road, which is well-signed to Chevelon, another 20 miles or so.

This entire area was once popular among trappers before Arizona became the "civilized" place it is today. Chevelon Canyon is named after a beloved early trapper who lived in the area and unfortunately died after eating a poisonous root. When full, the lake impounds 200 surface acres at an elevation of 6,380 feet.

Species available include rainbow and brown trout. The best time to visit is in the spring or fall.

Be sure to check regulations before leaving as the waterway has historically had a slot limit. You can park relatively close to the lake, and outboards up to 8 horsepower are permitted. There are restrooms and picnic tables around the lake.

The entire lake is in the Apache-Sitgreaves National Forest. Developed campsites can be found a few more miles upstream along the road at Chevelon Crossing. For more information contact forest offices by calling 928/333-4301 or visit www.fs.fed.us/r3/asnf.

For up-to-date fishing information call 602/789-3701 or visit the Arizona Game and Fish Department website at www.azgfd.com.

Notable
February 1984, 14-pound, 5-ounce brown trout

Many fishing enthusiasts currently collect antique reels and this one has a special spot in my collection.

Cholla Lake

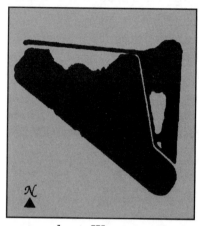

Cholla Lake, is one of Arizona's most important fisheries in the northeast section of the state. It is also managed as a Navajo County park.

To reach Cholla, take I-40 11 miles west from Holbrook toward Joseph City. Take Exit 277 south and follow the signs.

The lake typically impounds 380 surface acres and is a storage facility for a nearby power plant. Warmwater routinely pumped into the reservoir promotes weed growth which translates into a relatively productive warmwater fishery.

Species available include largemouth bass, channel catfish and various kinds of sunfish.

Camping is permitted around the lake. There are good boat launches, and any size boat motor is allowed. Water skiing takes place most of the year. There are 15 campsites available, and RVs and tents are allowed. Expect cool temperatures as winter approaches, since the lake is 5,000 feet above sea level. Access is paved, and you'll find restrooms and drinking water.

Be sure to check ahead as the lake suffered a bad fish kill in the fall of 2002. For more information call the Arizona Game and Fish Department at 602/789-3701 or visit www.azgfd.com.

Christopher Creek

Christopher Creek is the ideal getaway for those of us who enjoy a true flyfishing outing once in a while. It's ideally located northeast of Payson, far away from civilization's hectic pace.

Perhaps the area's only drawback is its vulnerability to droughts, like the recent severe dry spell during which many streams—including Christopher Creek—have at times literally gone dry. Always call ahead to check conditions.

Fishable water runs from an elevation of more than 6,500 feet to below 5,200. The water is rugged in sections, but well worth the effort. Though you probably won't come away with the lunker of a lifetime, you will experience some of Arizona's truly pristine out-of-doors—all within a mile of one of the most traveled roads on the Mogollon Rim.

Species available here include rainbow, brook and brown trout. You can expect the Arizona Game and Fish stocking truck's first run of the year sometime around mid-April, and on the average it will return ten more times until late August.

The waterway is relatively easy to find. Simply take State Route 260 northeast out of Payson. About two miles past Kohl's Ranch Campground, the Christopher Creek Campground will be on the right hand side. Christopher Creek is just over 20 miles from Payson.

From the campground, you can probe the waters either upstream or downstream. Expect most of the lunkers downstream though. You can also follow the stream for some time, until it finally runs into Tonto Creek.

Christopher Creek Campground stands at an elevation of 5,600 feet above sea level. For more information contact the Tonto National Forest at 2324 E. McDowell Road, Phoenix, AZ 85006, call 602/225-5200 or visit www.fs.fed.us/r3/tonto.

For current fishing conditions call 602/789-3701 or visit www.azgfd.com.

Clear Creek Reservoir

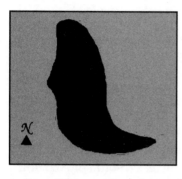

Located south of Winslow, Clear Creek Reservoir features largemouth bass, sunfish, channel catfish, bullheads, rainbow trout and carp. Camping can be found near the waterway at Winslow's McHood Park. There you'll also find ramadas, grills and restrooms. To get to the park take State Route 87 south from Winslow to State Route 99 and turn left. It's about 5 miles from Winslow. For more information contact the Winslow Parks Department by calling 928/289-5714.

The waterway averages 45 surface acres, although it often swells to 85. At an elevation of 4,867 feet, it can be a little cool in the winter or early spring, but it's one of those relatively unknown getaways ideal for the entire family.

For up-to-date fishing conditions call the Arizona Game and Fish Department at 602/789-3701 or visit www.azgfd.com.

There are times when the bass action on Clear Creek Reservoir is incredible!

Concho Lake

Concho Lake, in the White Mountains, was created in the early 1880s by the Concho Irrigation Company when it built a dam near Concho Springs. In 1956 the Arizona Game and Fish Department took over management of the lake, quickly poisoning out the "rough fish" that were residing in the waterway. It was then stocked with rainbow trout. In 1977, brook trout were added to the lake and cutthroat in 1980. In 2000, a survey by the department determined that over the year, anglers caught 0.48 fish per hour, 99 percent of which were rainbow trout (average length of fish kept was 12 inches).

At an elevation of 6,300 feet and impounding 60 surface acres, Concho Lake is 29 miles northeast of Show Low. It is pretty shallow, with an average depth of 8.2 feet and a maximum depth of slightly more than 16 feet. Take U.S. Route 60 and continue on State Route 61 where it forks northeast from the main highway. The entire route is paved and the lake is well marked. You can't miss it off to the right as you head toward St. Johns from Show Low.

Species of fish available at this reservoir include rainbow and brook trout, with an occasional cutthroat. Unfortunately, several years ago someone illegally stocked largemouth bass in the lake, and this promises to have a severe impact on the fishery's future (even though the drought from 1998 to 2002 was much more disastrous, when bag limits were taken off at the waterway due to low water level and quality).

There is a boat launch, but motors are limited to electric trolling motors. For more information contact the Pinetop office of the Arizona Game and Fish Department by calling 928/367-4281. You can also call 602/789-3701, or visit the Arizona Game and Fish Department website at www.azgfd.com.

Crescent Lake

At 138 surface acres, Crescent Lake shouldn't be overshadowed by any body of water, but its nearest neighbor, Big Lake, does exactly that. Crescent Lake offers shore fishermen a total of 4.5 miles of shoreline to work.

Take State Route 260 east out of Show Low, then turn south on State Route 273 toward Big Lake. The entire route is paved, and easy to follow. (Take Forest Service Road 114).

This impoundment is home to rainbow and brook trout. Annually it will receive around three rainbow trout stockings, the first in early May and the last in late June. This lake is something special, and I've enjoyed every day I've spent here.

At an altitude of 9,040 feet, Crescent is also a guaranteed bone chiller, even during the summer. Those times when the wind actually lays down, it's also a great place to flyfish.

Though no camping is allowed right on the lake, there are a number of campsites nearby in the Apache-Sitgreaves National Forest. For information write to P.O. Box 640, Springerville, AZ 85938. You can also call 928/333-4301 or visit www.fs.fed.us/r3/asnf.

Crescent's altitude in the past has led to complete freezes and fish kills, so make sure you check conditions prior to leaving by visiting www.azgfd.com or by calling 602/789-3701. As Crescent has an average depth of only 15 feet, even during relatively warm winters it can suffer a kill-off.

One such winter was 1992-93. But in less than a year, catches were just about back to normal, highlighting the fact that this waterway is extremely fertile.

Dogtown Lake

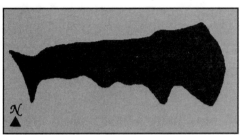

On a good, wet year, you can expect Dogtown Lake to swell to slightly more than 50 surface acres. When the skies aren't as kind, it can dwindle to little more than a big, slightly more than 3-acre cattle tank. Though enough water is almost always present to ensure our finny adversary's survival, during the late 1990s and early 2000, limits were taken off due to concerns regarding total fish kill-offs. It was not stocked for 2002.

The Arizona Game and Fish Department lists the lake as having an average depth of 15 feet. Expect about a mile of shoreline to probe, though again, take into consideration long-term weather's impact.

The Arizona Game and Fish Department has some pretty strict rules about conducting your own stocking program. It's all really simple: you cannot transport fish from one lake to another. It's a good system, one that makes sure the professionals manage the lake properly. Placing a species like catfish in a small tank used to rear the endangered desert pupfish can have tragic results, reversing years of research and work.

Unfortunately, Dogtown Lake is the scene of one such "Bait Bucket Charlie" stocking. In this case it was crappie, and though you can catch them today, the lake wasn't originally managed for that species.

Today, Dogtown offers those desperado crappie, rainbow, brook and brown trout—even an occasional cutthroat. At an elevation of 7,070 feet the trout thrive. But, because crappie are a warmwater species, they rarely get big enough to keep.

There is a boat launch, but motors are limited to electric trolling motors. There are 60 developed campsites at the lake.

To get to the lake, take Perkinsville Road south out of Williams (which is on I-40 west of Flagstaff). Then turn east on Forest Service Road 140. It's six miles out of Williams.

For more information contact the Kaibab National Forest at 800 S. 6th Street, Williams, AZ 86046 or call 928/635-2681 You can also visit www.fs.fed.us/r3/kai.

Be sure to check lake conditions prior to leaving by calling 602/789-3701 or by visiting www.azgfd.com.

Editors note: At time of publication, Dogtown Lake was closed for Forest Service renovation of the campground and picnic areas.

Crappie were illegally introduced to Dogtown.

Dry Lake

Searching for an off-road fishing destination—one with a nearly iron-clad guarantee of privacy and incredible scenery right here in Arizona?

Dry Lake is that destination! Take my word for it, the trip into this small lake (in a good year you can expect roughly 50 surface acres) is an adventure in itself.

To get there, follow the directions to Point of Pines Lake (see p. 99). The road is now paved through the area called Point of Pines, but the last 4-5 miles into Dry Lake are not.

Once there you can literally drive right next to the water and over the dam. The last time I visited Dry Lake it was one of the most enjoyable solitary experiences I have ever had in many years of fishing Arizona.

It's little wonder though. As if the often rugged four-wheel-drive trail isn't enough, add a small log "bridge" (a pair of split logs that theoretically help you negotiate a deep ravine) with a Volkswagen-sized boulder strategically placed in the ideal spot to "turtle" you into the lake when the water's up, and you have all the makings of yet another of Arizona's behind-the-wheel cardiopulmonary workouts. Okay, maybe it's not quite that bad, but it's definitely not a trip for the faint-hearted. Do not try to get in to Dry Lake in the winter, early spring or during the monsoons. You might get in, but getting out is another story.

Rainbow and brown trout were Dry Lake's original attraction. In 1990 however, the San Carlos Apache tribe tried an experimental transplant of 68 sizeable largemouth bass (they were electro-shocked from San Carlos Lake). Unfortunately, someone brought in shiners as bait for the bass and they took

*Dry Lake
is incredibly
beautiful!*

over the lake. At this date, the shiners rule.

Tribal officials state that they have brought on fisheries biologists to work on the problems and plan to dredge the lake deep enough to return it to its original trout fishery status in the near future.

Remember, you need a permit from the San Carlos Apaches to camp, fish or even drive on their land. For more information contact the San Carlos Apache Recreation & Wildlife Department by writing to P. O. Box 97, San Carlos, AZ 85550 or by calling 928/475-2343.

This lake is also prime bear and turkey territory. Keep your ears open, and during certain times of the year you won't believe how many gobblers you can hear. Dress warm, since even in the summer things can get pretty chilly at Dry Lake.

Eagle Creek

Eagle Creek, located south and west of Hannagan Meadow, runs a total length of 48 miles, though the Arizona Game and Fish Department lists only a total of four miles as actually fishable. It varies in elevation from 5,450 feet to 3,250.

To get to the remote fishery, take U.S. Route 191 north out of Clifton toward Hannagan Meadow and the White Mountains. After Pinal Point campground, begin watching on the left side of the road for Forest Service Road 217 (also called Upper Eagle Creek Road). You'll see it in about 6 miles.

Take Road 217, which is dirt, just about all the way to the end, and you'll find Honeymoon Campground. Just before the campsites, you'll also pass the spot where the Arizona Game and Fish Department stocks rainbow trout once a year (usually in late April though it's always best to check ahead by visiting www.azgfd.com or calling 602/789-3701).

The total trip on dirt is slightly more than 20 miles. Though it's a relatively well-maintained road, during rainy season or early in the spring a high-clearance or four-wheel-drive vehicle is a good idea. If you're lucky you'll be the only one in there.

Species you'll find include rainbow and brown trout, which occur naturally. You probably won't come home with a trophy, but you will enjoy one of Arizona's truly pristine areas. Anglers interested in visiting this area should also bear in mind stocking can be cancelled for a variety of reasons and that this creek, as is true of most in Arizona, can fall victim to drought.

There are very few campsites available at Honeymoon. The area is open from May to September. For more information, contact the Clifton Ranger District of the Apache-Sitgreaves National Forest at HC 1 Box 733, Duncan, AZ 85534 or by calling 928/687-1301. You can also visit www.fs.fed.us/r3/asnf.

Fool Hollow Lake

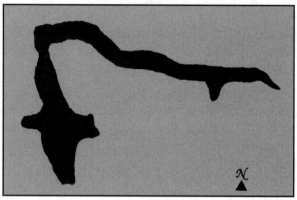

Fool Hollow Lake, in the White Mountains just outside of Show Low, covers 140 surface acres. Average depth for the impoundment is 23 feet, though it does plummet to as deep as 60 feet. The lake offers more than 5 miles of shoreline.

Species available include rainbow and brown trout, largemouth bass, crappie, sunfish, channel catfish, walleye and even an occasional smallmouth bass. The bass fishing is good enough here for a couple of the White Mountain bass clubs to routinely use the waterway for tournaments. In fact, on May 10, 2002 a 5-pound, 14.56-ounce smallmouth bass was caught and released here.

Walleye fishing is pretty good too, as evidenced by the 12-pound, 11-ounce lunker caught here in September 2002 on a Rapala Countdown. Catfishermen won't come away disappointed either. An 11-pound, 5.44-ounce channel cat was caught here on September 28, 2002.

The lake stands at an elevation of 6,600 feet. To get there take State Route 260 west from Show Low, then turn north on Old Linden Road. The lake is about four miles from Route 260.

Fool Hollow is one of the best developed recreation areas in the White Mountains. On July 4, 1991, thanks in part to the Arizona Game and Fish Department, it got even better. The expansion that began that day included a second boat ramp, full-time staff on site (courtesy of the Arizona State Parks Department), an increase in camping areas and more day-use facilities. Since 1958, the Arizona Game and Fish Department owned and maintained the lake. Unfortunately, since that time, use of the lake had outgrown facilities. Things are different now, thanks to the $2.3 million in improvements.

Besides the second boat ramp installed on the western edge of the lake, a 90-unit RV campground (55 units with full hookups) was added. Each loop of the campground also has a modern restroom with showers, and a total of sixteen drinking fountains were installed.

Other phases of the construction included another 71-space RV campground, a 32-unit tent-camping area, day-use area, sand volleyball court, ranger contact station, bicycling and hiking trails and even a host center.

There are two good boat launches at Fool Hollow Lake. Motors are limited to 8 horsepower and virtually every service imaginable can be found in nearby Show Low.

Beyond a doubt, Fool Hollow Lake is now one of the premier angling/camping destinations in the entire state. For more information contact the Arizona Game and Fish Department in Pinetop at 928/367-4281.

The lake is part of Fool Hollow Lake Recreation Area, managed by Arizona State Parks. For more from the Arizona State Parks Department visit www.pr.state.az.us or call the park directly at 928/537-3680. For up-to-date fishing information call 602/789-3701 or visit www.azgfd.com.

Notable
> March 25, 2001, 6-pound, 2.56-ounce smallmouth bass (catch-and-release)
> May 10, 2002, 5-pound, 14.56-ounce smallmouth bass (catch-and-release)
> September 2002, 12-pound, 11-ounce walleye (caught on a Rapala Countdown)
> September 28, 2002, 11-pound, 5.44-ounce channel catfish

Haigler Creek

If you're looking for a classic stream-fishing experience, Haigler Creek, located west-northwest of Young below the Mogollon Rim, is a great getaway. Just how good it can be is best summarized by results from a mid-1990s survey, using a backpack-style electro shocker, from the Arizona Game and Fish Department.

"We found lots of brown trout ranging up to 15 inches, which was good news, but what really impressed me was the number of small rainbow trout. That means the rainbows have been spawning in Haigler," said then Fisheries Program biologist Tom McMahon.

He explained that two years prior to that survey, the department stocked fingerling brown trout in the upper, less accessible reaches of Haigler Creek. "We found lots of 10-, 11- and 12-inch browns, so they have really done well. The 15-incher we caught was probably a holdover from some past stocking," he said. "There are some really big, deep pools along Haigler that you could even work with spinner baits. For those who like fly fishing, Haigler offers some classic reaches to fish."

To reach Haigler Creek take Forest Service Road 291 south from State Route 260 (which heads northeast out of Payson). The turnoff for the road is just before you ascend the Mogollon Rim. It's dirt and can be rough, so go slow. At the junction with Forest Service Road 200 (about three miles), go right and follow it to Haigler Creek. There are two campsites near the area. They are at 5,300 feet above sea level so it can be chilly. You can fish the creek here, though downstream has less pressure because of the deepening canyon.

The stocking truck makes regular summertime deliveries here as well. Expect its first arrival, weather permitting, in early April. It comes back roughly 18 more times through the summer, if water quality holds up.

For up-to-date information call the Arizona Game and Fish Department at 602/789-3701 or visit www.azgfd.com.

Hulsey Lake

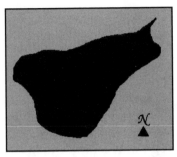

Hulsey Lake is perhaps one of the least known fisheries in the state of Arizona. Beyond a doubt, it's definitely a destination you'll remember for quite a while.

To reach Hulsey, take U.S. Route 191 south from Springerville/Eagar. Then turn east on Forest Service Road 56 (dirt), which is just north of mile marker 421. For up-to-date information call the Arizona Game and Fish Department—Region 1 Office, in Pinetop: 928/367-4281 or visit www.azgfd.com.

Hulsey Lake may not have a reputation for surrendering huge fish, but it does offer a mountaintop retreat, relatively few crowds on most weekends and a shot at a decent number of stocked rainbows and an occasional brown trout.

I still fondly remember one cold, and believe it or not, snowy Memorial Day weekend when I visited. It seemed no matter how much pink trout power-style bait I threw into the lake, each cast was met with another rainbow trout.

Though the lake only covers roughly 4 surface acres, it's extremely pretty and in at least one spot reaches a depth of 24 feet. During the hotter months, expect to be battling a thick weedline, though oftentimes fishing near it for the lunkers is the most productive method.

Expect stocking to begin in late April. Most years the lake won't receive much more than three stockings with the last coming on June 1. The small reservoir heats up by the end of summer, making successful trout stockings nearly impossible.

Parking is limited near the lake, and it's a downhill walk of about 200 yards to the water. Camping is not allowed in the area. The lake is impounded by an earthen dam and stands at a cool elevation of 8,600 feet.

Kinnikinick Lake

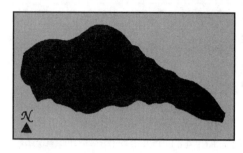

To reach Kinnikinick Lake, take Lake Mary Road southeast from Flagstaff. Turn east on the dirt road across from Mormon Lake and follow the signs. It's only about 10 miles away (rough road!).

Kinnikinick Lake stands at an elevation of 7,040 feet and provides relative solitude and some cool temperatures for the summer visitor. It averages a depth of 22 feet, 126 surface acres and slightly more than 2 miles of shoreline.

Species available here include channel catfish, crappie, rainbow, brown and brook trout, along with an occasional bullhead. A netting survey that took place in April 1992 came up with a 6-pound brown trout, so there are some big fish in Kinnikinick.

On an average year, expect the Arizona Game and Fish Department to stock rainbow trout here a total of seven times, beginning sometime in early April and ending in early August. There is a developed boat launch at the upper end of the lake. Motors are limited to 8 horsepower.

The lake is located in the Coconino National Forest, and there are a few developed campsites. For more information, contact the Mormon Lake Ranger District 928/774-1147. You can also visit the Forest's website at www.fs.fed.us/r3/coconino.

For current fishing conditions call 602/789-3701 or visit www.azgfd.com.

Notable

April 1992, 6-pound brown trout

Knoll Lake

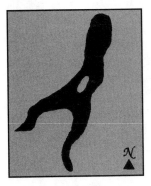

Knoll Lake, atop the Mogollon Rim above Payson, currently boasts a population of rainbow, brown and brook trout.

During the average summer, you can expect the stocking truck to arrive at Knoll Lake with rainbow trout about seven times. Its first trip usually occurs in early May, the last in August.

The lake impounds a total of 75 surface acres, boasts an average depth of 50 feet and is at 7,340 feet above sea level. There is a small boat launch, and boat motors are limited to electric trolling models. There are plenty of campsites in the area. For more information contact the Apache-Sitgreaves National Forest by writing P.O. Box 640, Springerville, AZ 85938. Or, call 928/333-4301 or visit www.fs.fed.us/r3/asnf.

To get to the lake, take State Route 260 northeast out of Payson. At the top of the Mogollon Rim, turn west on Forest Service Road 300 (the Rim Road that goes past Woods Canyon Lake). Turn left at Forest Service Road 34, then left again on Forest Service Road 300. You will follow this for several miles, then turn right on Forest Service Road 295. The lake is a few miles ahead.

Early in the spring or during the rainy season, this road can be a rough one. High-clearance or four-wheel-drive vehicles can be a necessity, so plan your trip accordingly.

Always check ahead by calling Arizona Game and Fish at 602/789-3701 or by visiting www.azgfd.com. The water level was so low in the fall of 2002 that trout limits were taken off, and boaters were being warned that the ramp was a full 30 feet out of the water, making launching all but impossible.

Notable
1983, 12-pound brown trout

Lower Lake Mary

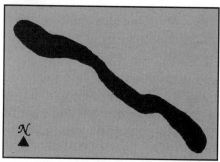

Sometimes you see it. Sometimes you don't.

Lower Lake Mary, southeast of Flagstaff on Lake Mary Road, can swell to as many as 100 surface acres on a good year. During the early 1990s, it was particularly wet, and the Arizona Game and Fish Department resumed aggressive management of the waterway.

In April 1992, the department transplanted a number of redear sunfish and largemouth bass (ranging up to 4 pounds) to the lake. The transplant also included a few crappie and smallmouths. They asked anglers to practice catch-and-release, to enable the fish to reproduce in the waterway.

The lake is only about 13 miles from Flagstaff and stands at an elevation of 6,850 feet above sea level. That translates to cool temperatures during the winter, and, compounded with an average depth of only 12 feet, it means you should always check with your nearest Game and Fish office prior to visiting the lake.

Species traditionally available here (prior to the '92 stocking), include sunfish, catfish, northern pike and an occasional walleye. The lake's thick weedline makes it one of the best northern fisheries around.

There is a primitive boat launch, and there are no limits on the size of outboard you can use. During dry years, like 2002, the lake can all but disappear, during which time limits are often liberalized. Visit www.azgfd.com to check the lake's condition prior to leaving or call 602/789-3701.

Upper Lake Mary

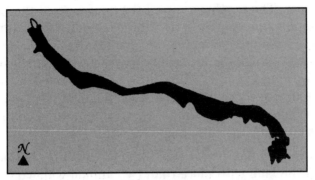

For many visitors to Arizona, which is altogether too often stereotyped as little more than desert, a quality northern pike or walleye fishery seems unlikely. Yet that's exactly what Upper Lake Mary is (8 miles southeast of Flagstaff on Lake Mary Road). In the 1960s, when the lake began to have an overabundance of "trash" fish, the Arizona Game and Fish Department loaded the 600-acre lake with northern pike.

Today, working large red-and-gold spinners (typically larger than bass lures) along the thick weedline can be quite productive. Come to the lake early in the spring or late in the fall when temperatures are still low, and hang onto that rod!

The action never seems to cool off. What was then a state record northern pike was taken here June 4, 1981. It weighed 24-pounds 3-ounces, and measured 47.5 inches long. The lake surrendered a 16-pound, 13.28-ounce pike in 1989, and one of Arizona's greatest angling mysteries began the first weekend of March 1993, when a fisherman using a live waterdog caught and measured a 55-inch northern from Upper Lake Mary. There were dozens of witnesses to the amazing battle with this huge fish, but apparently the angler had no idea he was holding what would have been a new state record. When later he packed up and went back to Phoenix, the lake's legend only continued to grow, and requests from Game and Fish that he come forth with the lunker have gone unanswered to this day.

In May 1999, a 24-pound, 11-ounce state-record northern was caught here, and the next month a 22-pound northern was caught by an angler working a handmade spinnerbait from his small boat. The northern towed the boat around the lake like a toy during the lengthy battle. It took 45 minutes to land a 22-pound, 11.5-ounce monster caught here in April 2000. The angler was using 6-pound test line with a live night crawler for bait. On February 21, 2002, a 21-pound northern pike was caught at the lake by an angler using a Cactus Critter Spinnerbait, and the same day, a 10-pound, 1-ouncer was caught on a plastic frog.

During the late 1980s, the Game and Fish Department also stocked the lake with more than two million walleye fry. Since these fry can grow up to 7 inches a year, Upper Lake Mary quickly became one of the state's premier walleye waters as well.

With an average depth of 38 feet, Upper Lake Mary is also home to rainbow trout, an occasional largemouth bass, sunfish and channel catfish. The elevation is 6,895 feet, so it's also a good place to cool off in summer.

There are no campsites right on the edge of the lake, but Lakeside Campsite is directly across the highway. Contact the Coconino National Forest Mormon Lake Ranger District 928/774-1147 or visit www.fs.fed.us/r3/coconino. Upper Lake Mary has a paved boat launch and several ramadas for use during the day. There are no motor limitations on this lake.

For current fishing conditions call 602/789-3701 or visit www.azgfd.com.

Notable
June 4, 1981, 24-pound, 3-ounce northern pike
May 29, 1999, 24-pound, 11-ounce northern pike (on a
    waterdog near the dam)
June 1999, 22-pound northern pike
April 2000, 22-pound, 11.5-ounce northern pike
February 21, 2002, 21-pound northern pike
April 2002, 8-pound walleye

Lake Powell

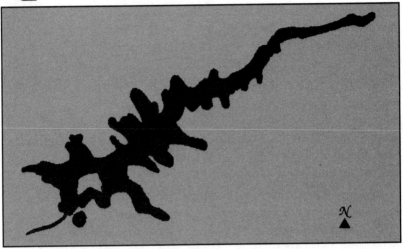

Here's another of those huge Colorado River lakes that is beginning to show signs of age. Glen Canyon Dam was completed as recently as 1963, but the 160,000 surface acres of water it impounds can be extremely stingy, especially for anglers who have never been on the lake.

In all, Lake Powell is 186 miles long with 1,900 miles of shoreline. In other words, no matter how many people are on the water at any given time, odds are pretty good your fishing will be a solitary experience. With largemouth bass, stripers (stocked during the 1970s), crappie, sunfish, northern pike, walleye (which were never stocked, but migrated from upstream), trout and channel catfish lurking in a waterway with an average depth of 800 feet, Lake Powell is one of Arizona's most diverse fisheries. There is also a struggling smallmouth bass population in the lake, and with the rocky banks they could very well become one of this lake's prized possessions in the near future.

State records held on Lake Powell include what was then the Colorado River waters record brown trout, caught on May 1, 1971, near Last Chance Bay, tipping the scales at 17 pounds.

The record walleye was also caught here in May 1977, and weighed in at 8-pounds, 1-ounce.

Getting to Powell is as simple as driving north out of Flagstaff toward Page on U.S. Route 89. During the trip, you'll be treated to some spectacular views. Follow the signs and the lake is only seven miles from the Page turnoff.

Perhaps the biggest "lake resort" operation in the Southwest is Wahweap Lodge, where you can rent boats, stay in the hotel on the water, book tours to Rainbow Bridge (the world-famous arch that's only accessible by boat now) and enjoy world-class cuisine. Plan far enough in advance and you can rent a houseboat for a week, although you should make reservations a year or more in advance.

In one Bass Anglers Sportsman's Society tournament on Lake Powell, the winner was a Phoenix angler who took his boat every day to the San Juan arm of the lake to work a pumpkin-colored tube jig along the rocky drop-offs. In another tournament, the winning weight was comparable, but in this case the anglers used jigs in 20 to 30 feet of water within sight of Wahweap. So you don't necessarily have to go a long way to catch sizeable largemouth bass.

The best time to look for largemouth on Lake Powell is during the spring when they come up to spawn. The rest of the year the fish tend to stay pretty deep, partly because of the lake's incredible water clarity. Recent notable catches include an April 7, 2001, 6.86-pounder; an April 21, 2001, 5.38-pounder; and a May 11, 2002, 6.10-pounder.

Crappie are strong performers here, and in spring they move into the shallows, as they do elsewhere. Small white or yellow jigs are a good way to start prospecting for the speckled beauties. March through May is the best time for crappie on Lake Powell.

Striped bass were first introduced in Lake Powell in 1974. They are one of the most sought-after fish here, and during the summer when most people visit the lake, they are relatively easy to locate and catch.

The striper population is so healthy in Powell that on March 4, 1993, the Utah Wildlife Board temporarily lifted the lake limit on the fish in an attempt to reduce their numbers before they depleted their main food source, threadfin shad. A striped bass contest in November-December 1992, saw a 32.3-pounder take first place honors. Surveys conducted in 2002 showed the striper population was extremely healthy, as were the smallmouth and walleye.

Walleye may never have been stocked in the lake, but the few that migrated from upstream love the clear, cold water and rocky shoreline. Now they are actively reproducing, and you can expect the biggest catches to come in May.

Houseboating on Powell is an experience of a lifetime. I can still vividly recall spending Easter morning in a small, totally isolated cove on the lake. There were plenty of trails to hike, the beaches were ideal for sunbathing or swimming, and every morning I woke up to the sight of a herd of wild burros as they grazed nearby.

At an elevation of 3,700 feet, Lake Powell is pretty comfortable, even in midsummer. Steep cliffs rise literally everywhere around the lake, so finding shelter from the mid-afternoon sun is not difficult.

Lake Powell's length means it offers all sorts of watersports. There are no limits to motor size, and a number of good boat launches can be found. Five marinas serve the lake.

For up-to-date fishing information you can call 602/789-3701 or go to www.wayneswords.com or www.azgfd.com.

Notable
May 1, 1971, 17-pound brown trout
May 1977, 8-pound, 1-ounce walleye
December 1992, 32.3-pound striped bass

Lee's Ferry

It seems Lee's Ferry has been Arizona's true Blue Ribbon fishery for rainbow trout forever. Chunky rainbows in the 5-pound range were almost commonplace, and in the early 1980s, people flocked here from around the nation to enjoy the Southwest's premier trout angling. Flyfishermen in particular find "The Ferry" something special.

Glen Canyon Dam impounds Lake Powell just above the 16 mile stretch of Colorado River known as Lee's Ferry. It was completed by the Bureau of Reclamation in 1963. With Powell on the upstream side and Mead downstream, both being managed as warmwater fisheries, something different happened at Lee's Ferry.

Water entering Lee's Ferry from Glen Canyon Dam comes from a relatively low level in the lake. As a result, year-round water temperatures average between 47 and 52 degrees—ideal for rainbow trout. Quickly, Lee's Ferry became a household name among flyfishermen. With every huge fish caught there, more and more people came, saw and left believers.

Unfortunately, Glen Canyon Dam generates power for a significant portion of the western United States. While this in itself sounds innocent enough, that means huge amounts of water were released into Lee's Ferry during peak energy use times, and water slowed to a mere trickle when excess electricity wasn't needed.

For the trout, wildly fluctuating river levels spelled disaster. Many became trapped and died. Even more disastrous, instantly lowered water levels left many spawning beds exposed.

From 1989 to 1991, a study began assessing the fluctuating flow's impact on the Grand Canyon and the Colorado River. While the study was in progress, Glen Canyon Dam was limited to flows between 20,000 and 1,000 cubic feet of water a second. Drops in flow during that time were required to occur gradually.

The study was to assess the impact of the violently fluctuating flows on the Grand Canyon and the Colorado River. While the flows were down, many of the algae beds in the Lee's Ferry region dried up and died. One of those algaes, cladorphora, is the main food source for one of the Ferry's most important residents—a form of freshwater shrimp. Unfortunately, when cladorphora populations dwindled, so did many of the chunky rainbow trout that relied on it for food.

It was a classic food chain effect, one that greatly impacted every rainbow trout enthusiast across the Southwest.

In 1991, an Arizona senator introduced legislation called the Grand Canyon Protection Act. It mandated higher minimum flows, and in theory would bring back Lee's Ferry. By the end of the year, the Arizona Game and Fish Department was declaring the new, higher flows a success story. Its studies showed trout 12 inches and smaller were "downright fat." Its survey found only 10 percent of the trout looked thin, or "snakelike" as many of the fishermen had been describing them.

With spring traditionally the time of year when a lot of big trout are caught at Lee's Ferry, things were really looking good when an 8-pound rainbow trout was caught in April 1992.

Subsequent stockings increased the number of fish, and growth rates were exceptional. A parasite (nematode) problem took a toll on the fish in the early 1990s; however, a recovery was well on its way within a couple of years.

While fishing at Lee's Ferry has been good in recent years, one unfortunate phenomenon that had been noticed was that over the last few years the fish were getting smaller. To keep the Blue Ribbon experience at highest quality, in 2003 regulations were changed to allow for increasing the harvest of smaller fish, thereby decreasing the competition for food, which should result in larger fish in the future.

Normally, rainbow trout begin to spawn on the gravel bars at Lee's Ferry sometime in the middle of October. During that time, flyfishermen have good luck with pink scuds. Rubber worms and Maribou jigs are sure hits for lure aficionados.

Lee's Ferry also offers so many different fishing situations that you can stay all week and feel like you've never even been on the same water.

For the flyfisherman, bring a 5- to 7-weight stiff rod. Usually an additional weight is added to the leader for long casts. Shallow nymphing can be productive for dry fly anglers, and a four-weight rod will help. Use floating line and a weighted leader.

The fish at Lee's Ferry spawn all the way through March in some years. Usually they occupy a gravel bar in five feet of water or less. A few good places to prospect include: Eight Mile Bar, Powerline Bar, Four Mile Bar, Pumphouse Bar and Dam Island.

For a rainbow trout to spawn on a bar, it takes a particular current speed and gravel size. When they are up on the redds, sight fishing is the ideal way to go. In other words, pack a pair of polarized sunglasses to spot them.

Lee's Ferry is found in northernmost Arizona. Simply take U.S. Route 89 north out of Flagstaff. Turn left on Alternate Route 89, roughly 25 miles from Page.

The waterway is also home to Arizona's Colorado River waters record for brook trout—a 5-pound, 4-ounce monster caught March 6, 1982. For up-to-date information go to www.leesferry.com, www.azgfd.com or call 602/789-3701.

Notable
March 6, 1982, 5-pound, 4-ounce brook trout
April 1992, 8-pound rainbow trout

Lee Valley Reservoir

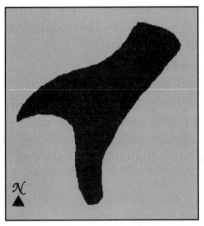

Lee Valley Reservoir, about ten miles from Greer in the White Mountains, is one of Arizona's few true alpine experiences. At an elevation of 9,420 feet above sea level, it is a chilly one, but offers anglers a chance at Apache trout, brook trout and grayling. Beyond a doubt, Lee Valley's finny residents are some of our state's rarest.

Making Lee Valley the quality fishery it is today hasn't been an easy job.

In the fall of 1990, the Arizona Game and Fish Department became concerned about Lee Valley's drought-induced low water level and began an ambitious program to save the lake's grayling population (at the time the lake was down to a depth of 8 feet). Using seine nets they captured 2,000 of the lake's estimated 4,000 to 5,000 grayling. They were then transported to Bear Canyon Lake on the Mogollon Rim.

At the time, the Game and Fish Department was four years into a project designed to elevate Lee Valley's grayling population. It was concerned that low water levels might lead to a hard freeze on the lake, depleting oxygen supplies and suffocating the grayling. As the water situation at Lee Valley improved, the grayling were moved back. In addition, some of the Bear Canyon population was used for brood stock, with their fry later stocked back into Lee Valley (about 10,000 fish).

Arctic grayling were first stocked here in 1968-69, though grayling were introduced to Arizona in a few lakes above the Mogollon Rim in 1965. Ultimately, nearly every specimen of this fish found in Arizona is from Lee Valley, since their eggs have been used as brood stock ever since (with rare exceptions).

Unfortunately, the first stockings of grayling didn't fare too well. In 1985, when the Arizona Game and Fish Department drafted its new Cold Water Fisheries Plan, another 43,000 grayling went into Lee Valley. Today, the population of grayling there is tremendous. Though the fish don't reproduce naturally in the lake, sperm and eggs are routinely collected and used for other stockings across the state.

Lee Valley is also a designated Blue Ribbon fishery. That means anglers interested in catching its rare residents are required to use artificial lures and flies only. Limits are also subject to change periodically, so consult a current set of regulations, or check the sign clearly posted in the lake's only parking lot.

Lee Valley covers 44 surface acres and has 1.51 miles of shoreline. Expect the average depth to be about 10 feet on a good year, and a few "honeyholes" may go deeper than 20 feet.

The lake is usually open to fishing from mid-May to the first of November. Be sure to call the Game and Fish Department in Pinetop at 928/367-4281 for conditions before you plan a trip or visit www.azgfd.com.

You won't find much here, except for a restroom, a few lounging cows in the middle of summer and a paved boat launch. For wildlife enthusiasts, a healthy elk herd usually appears periodically, so keep your eyes open. Boating is allowed, though you must limit yourself to electric trolling motors. This is a fantastic lake for float tubing.

Early in the season, jigs and scuds seem to work best early in the morning. Flyfishermen have good luck with Royal Coachmen and small Wooly Worms. If you prefer to use a spinner, try a Panther Martin. The lake is shallow and waders are a plus. In fact, a few years ago I watched a fisherman catch his limit in just a few minutes wading the northern shoreline.

The lake's shallow profile presents a problem during cold winters when partial fish kill-offs can occur. Remember, small grayling live on plankton. As they age, their diet changes to small insects. Keep this in mind when choosing your lures/flies, and you should have good luck.

To get to Lee Valley Reservoir, take State Route 260 east from the Pinetop-Lakeside area and turn south on State Route 273. Continue on this road to the National Forest boundary where it becomes Forest Service Road 113 (dirt). After about 6 miles, you will come to Road 113E. Turn west and go 1/2 mile to the reservoir.

Arizona's record Arctic grayling was caught here on July 10, 1995. It tipped the scales at 1-pound, 9.76-ounces.

Notable

July 10, 1995, 1-pound, 9.76-ounce Arctic grayling

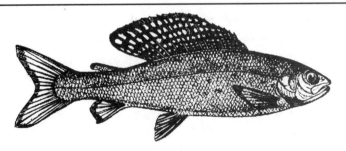

Arctic Grayling

Non-native trout. Dorsal fin is large, dark-gray, blotched with pale spots, with cross-rows of deep blue spots and edged with red or orange. The dorsal fin has 17 to 25 rays. The tail fin is forked. The body has scattered black spots on silver-gray, sometimes pink sides.

Long Lake

Long Lake can be reached by taking I-40 east of Flagstaff to Meteor Crater Road (Exit 233) and travel south. If you decide to take that route, expect to travel a total of 26 miles of dirt road.

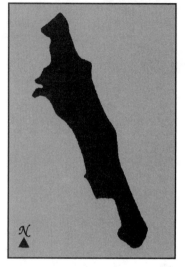

Another way is to go north from Payson on State Route 87 about 50 miles. When you reach Forest Service Road 211, turn north and travel 2 miles to Forest Service Road 82. Follow that road north for 13 miles to the lake.

Although Long Lake is in the Coconino National Forest, there are no developed campsites in the vicinity. According to the Arizona Game and Fish Department, camping is allowed. For more current information, contact the Coconino National Forest by calling 928/ 527-3600 or visit www.fs.fed.us/r3/coconino.

Although the lake stands at an elevation of 6,700 feet and is in a relatively cool portion of the state, it is managed more as a warmwater fishery. Expect to catch an occasional rainbow trout, along with sunfish, channel catfish and largemouth bass. Though trout aren't the main fare at Long Lake, when they do surface, they're usually big. In fact, a 5-pounder was caught with a bass topwater lure.

Expect the stocking truck to arrive here with rainbow trout about three times a year, beginning in mid-April and ending in late September. Occasionally a special stocking will occur, which is exactly what happened in 1993 when the Game and Fish Department added 10,000 Kamloop trout to the lake.

You never know what will answer the dinner bell either. In July 2000, the Arizona Game and Fish Department was advising that the lake's newest inhabitant, walleye, weighing up to 1.5 pounds, were being caught by anglers using night crawlers. On October 26, 2000, a 23-pound, 7.04-ounce northern pike was caught here, and on April 13, 2002, the lake surrendered a 5-pound, 1.92-ounce rainbow trout.

Long Lake occupies 268 surface acres, averages 25 feet in depth and is connected to Soldier and Soldier Annex lakes. Long Lake has more than three miles of shoreline, though there is only a primitive launching area for boats. Any size motor is allowed on the lake.

This lake is managed out of the Flagstaff Game and Fish office. For more information on current conditions, call 602/ 789-3701 or visit the Arizona Game and Fish Department website at www.azgfd.com.

Notable
> October 26, 2000, 23-pound, 7.04-ounce northern pike
> June 23, 2001, 23-pound, 1-ounce northern pike
> April 2002, 19-pound northern pike (on an in-line spinner)
> April 2002, 9-pound northern pike
> April 2002, 17.5-pound northern pike
> April 13, 2002, 5-pound, 1.92-ounce rainbow trout
> November 28, 2002, 29-pound, 13.76-ounce northern pike

Northern Pike
Non-native. Back and sides, dusky olive-green with rows of light oval spots. Dorsal, anal and tail fin have round to oblong darkened spots. Dorsal fin located far back on an elongated body. Large canine-like teeth. Cheeks completely scaled, only upper half of the gill cover is scaled.

Luna Lake

Luna Lake, just 4 miles east of Alpine on U.S. Route 180, was impounded in 1893 as a water supply for the city of Luna, New Mexico. At an elevation of 7,890 feet, this lake has a total of 75 surface acres and an average depth of 8 feet. It has more than 3.5 miles of shoreline.

The dam washed out in 1927 but was quickly rebuilt, and in 1951 the Arizona Game and Fish Department added 12 feet to the overall height of the structure.

Luna Lake has an incredible history. Believe it or not, back in 1958 this was one of the sites in Arizona where Kokanee salmon were stocked. Brown trout were added to Luna in 1935, rainbows in 1937 and brook trout in 1943. Unfortunately, in the fall of 2002, the lake suffered a bad fish kill-off, although once water quality improved, the Arizona Game and Fish Department immediately restocked trout.

Anglers can expect to catch rainbow trout, brook trout and an occasional cutthroat. A gill-net survey in 1988 indicated 96 percent of the fish caught here are rainbow trout. Luna Lake also surrendered a huge cutthroat trout: a 6-pound 5-ouncer, in October 1976.

The best months to visit Luna are September, October and November, at least if you want a full stringer.

Access to the lake is paved, and there is a good boat launch. Motor size is limited to 8 horsepower. A nearby store sells groceries, licenses, oil and gas.

Luna Lake Campground has 50 sites, is open May through September, allows trailers of 32 feet and less and is right on the water. Stays of up to 14 days are allowed. For more information on this campground and others nearby contact the Apache-Sitgreaves National Forest, P.O. Box 640, Springerville, AZ 85938 or call 928/333-4301. You can also point your web browser to www.fs.fed.us/r3/asnf.

Luna Lake is also a waterfowl refuge and provides many opportunities for birdwatchers.

For more information on the lake or recreational opportunities in the area write the Arizona Game and Fish Department at 2878 E. White Mountain Blvd., Pinetop, AZ 85935 or call 928/367-4281. For up-to-date fishing reports call 602/789-3701 or visit www.azgfd.com.

Notable
    October 1976, 6-pound, 5-ounce cutthroat trout

Cutthroat Trout
Non-native trout. Body shape similar to rainbow trout. Back and sides are lightly spotted; dorsal, adipose and tail fins are heavily spotted. Red or reddish-orange slash on throat.

Lyman Lake

At 1,400 surface acres and a cool elevation of 5,980 feet, Lyman Lake used to be the ideal answer to northern pike and walleye fishing.

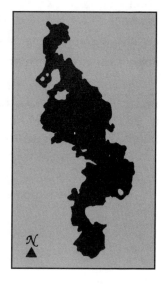

That was before 1989, when the lake was lowered for repairs on the dam's gates and a traditionally serious siltation problem was remedied by the installation of catchments on Coyote Wash above the lake.

Now you'll find some of the area's best trout fishing at Lyman. In fact, five-pounders were being reported regularly to the Arizona Game and Fish Department.

Unfortunately, in October 2002, the Arizona Game and Fish Department issued a mercury warning in regard to consuming fish caught at Lyman Lake. While it may make it more of a "catch-and-release" waterway, therefore surrendering bigger fish with more regularity, it's bound to hurt the once-popular destination's reputation.

Located nearly 17 miles north of Springerville on U.S. Route 191/180, this state park has 38 hookup sites and several dozen more developed camping areas. In all, there are 63 campsites and even hot water showers!

Lyman Lake was Arizona's first state park. The area features a number of archeological sites and petroglyphs, many of which are accessible by boat. A herd of buffalo is also found as you first drive into the park. For details on this and other state parks, visit www.pr.state.az.us or call 602/542-4174.

Lyman Lake, with an average depth of 22 feet and more than 20 miles of shoreline, is one of the prettiest lakes you'll find in Arizona.

*Lyman Lake
State Park has a
well developed boat
launch ramp.*

Species available here include an occasional largemouth bass, sunfish, channel catfish and a few walleye that survived the draining, including the 6-pound walleye that turned up in a survey in May 2002. By far though, most anglers prefer to chase after the drastically improved population of rainbow trout.

Check ahead on conditions though, as the water level is often drawn down, and during the summer of 1999, it was reduced to a fraction of its original size, thanks to the prolonged drought. Call 602/789-3701 or visit www.azgfd.com to check lake conditions prior to leaving.

Petroglyphs like these are abundant in the Lyman Lake area.

Many Farms Lake

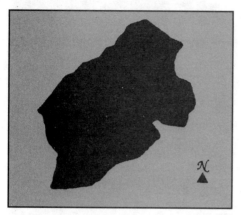

Little, if anything, is ever written about Many Farms Lake, although it covers nearly 1,000 surface acres.

This lake, which is 15 miles north of Chinle (northwest of Canyon de Chelly National Monument) can be found by taking I-40 east from Holbrook. Turn north on U.S. Route 191 toward Ganado. Turn west on State Route 264 and pick up Route 191 north again by turning right (there are plenty of signs). Drive past Chinle, continuing north. Many Farms Lake will be on your right, just past where Route 191 intersects Indian Route 59.

There are no motor restrictions, and Many Farms has a relatively good boat launch. Species of fish available include largemouth bass and catfish. This lake receives very little fishing pressure. It's well worth a try if you're in the area, and if nothing else, at an elevation of 5,400 feet it guarantees a cool getaway during your next vacation.

As of 2003, we're told that Many Farms is extremely low due to the drought. Be sure to call ahead before making the trip.

Remember, you need a current Navajo Recreation fishing permit for this lake. Visit www.navajofishandwildlife.org, call 928/781-3610 or 928/871-6451.

Mexican Hay Lake

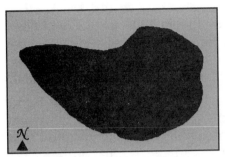

Mexican Hay Lake is located off State Route 261 southwest of Springerville in the White Mountains (the usual route to Crescent Lake). It probably gets its name from the thick line of weeds that encircles the lake. It may not be hay, but in some sections it's thick enough to convince a road-weary fisherman.

Because of the thick weedline, a boat is definitely a plus. But, shore fishermen regularly limit out when the "bite is on."

The best boats to use are cartoppers or inflatables. Electric motors are the most you can use here. There is a small boat launch. For shore fishermen, the highway past the lake offers two pullouts to probe Mexican Hay's wealth of finny residents.

What looks like hay on the shoreline of this lake is really a very dense weedline.

Mexican Hay Lake stands at a chilly altitude of 8,800 feet. Even midsummer, expect enough of a breeze to make coats required. If you've just left 100-degree-plus temperatures, it's definitely a welcome change.

The lake was originally created in 1908 when Fred Colter constructed a dam in Baca Draw to store irrigation water for the Round Valley area. Currently it is owned by the Lyman Water Company; however, it is no longer used for irrigation.

Probably the only drawback to this scenic little lake is the fact that it's pretty shallow, not much more than 6-8 feet deep. At the elevation it occupies in the White Mountains, that translates to regular freezes, and quite often kill-offs (as recorded in the winters of 1985, 1987 and again in the late 1990s). It also has a habit of all but disappearing during prolonged drought.

Regardless what happens during the winter, the Arizona Game and Fish Department makes every effort to start stocking in April of each year. The lake is nutrient rich, and you can expect "catchable"-sized rainbows to grow about an inch a month. By the time the first snows drive many anglers from the lake, the rainbows that were once 8 inches are fat and sassy at 14. On occasion, a mild winter keeps the lake from freezing over, which means early spring anglers can catch a few 3-pounders.

At 35 surface acres (at most it can impound 185 surface acres, and in wet years it expands to 100 surface acres), Mexican Hay Lake is stocked with only rainbow trout, which the Arizona Game and Fish Department first introduced to the lake in 1965.

Check conditions prior to leaving, as during the 1990s, when the lake suffered at least one winter kill, the waterway was not stocked the subsequent summer. Go to www.azgfd.com or call 602/789-3701.

Mormon Lake

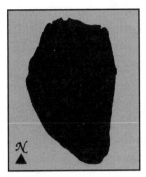

Sometimes Mormon Lake is there, other times it is not. The typically listed as a 70-surface-acre lake all but disappeared during the prolonged drought through the summer of 2000, and periodically you will find all limits taken off at this popular waterway. Check current conditions by calling 602/789-3701 or visit the Arizona Game and Fish Department website at www.azgfd.com.

When the fishing's on at this lake though, it's good. Often really good! Mormon Lake was once home to the state record yellow bullhead, a chunky 4-pound, 8.1-ounce monster caught on July 15, 1989.

Mormon Lake is only 17 miles southeast of Flagstaff on Lake Mary Road. This is also some of Arizona's prime elk territory so stay alert for great sights and sounds.

When full, Mormon Lake can cover 600 surface acres at an average depth of 10 feet. Species available include pike (the main game species here), bullhead and an occasional yellow perch.

There are a number of campsites alongside the water at Mormon Lake. All are managed by the Mormon Lake Ranger District of the Coconino National Forest that can be contacted by calling 928/774-1147 or, visit www.fs.fed.us/r3/coconino.

The lake, one of only two in Arizona that is not manmade (Stoneman is the other), is at an elevation of 7,000 feet, so expect cool to cold temperatures during the fall, winter or early spring. There are nearly 50 "developed" campsites. The boat-launch area is primitive at best, but any motor size is legal.

Notable

July 15, 1989, 4-pound, 8.1-ounce yellow bullhead

Nelson Reservoir

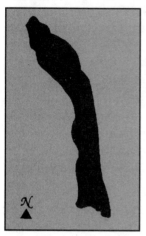

Nelson Reservoir is about 10 miles south of Springerville on U.S. Route 191. It impounds nearly 60 surface acres and averages 15 feet in depth.

Species you can expect to tangle with at Nelson include rainbow trout, brown trout and an occasional brookie. The best times for brookies and brown are traditionally during the late fall.

The lake is at an elevation of 7,410 feet, meaning relatively cool weather even in the summer (or at least more comfortable than the temperatures on the desert floor). There is a boat launch, and motors are limited to electric trolling motors only. In the early 1990s, Nelson Reservoir received a number of additional improvements designed to make handicapped angler access easier. A 300-foot-long concrete ramp for wheelchairs was added, along with special access restrooms and two covered fishing stations capable of sheltering a number of anglers at any one time.

The lake is in the Apache-Sitgreaves National Forest, although there are no developed campsites. There are, however, several picnic areas you can visit from April to November. For more information, contact the Apache-Sitgreaves National Forest office at P.O. Box 640, Springerville, AZ 85938; call 928/333-4301 or visit www.fs.fed.us/r3/asnf.

For up-to-date fishing conditions call 602/789-3701 or visit www.azgfd.com.

Notable

April 1979, 11-pound, 1-ounce rainbow trout

Oak Creek

For an unforgettable day of fishing, be sure to visit Oak Creek Canyon!

Just two hours from Phoenix, Sedona and Oak Creek together offer one of the most scenic fishing destinations in the nation. The short trip along I-17 provides great sightseeing and passes through some of Arizona's most historic regions.

The combination of breathtaking scenery, mild climate and relatively remote location has seen Sedona evolve into Arizona's premier art colony.

To reach Oak Creek, head north from downtown Sedona and follow Alternate Route 89 toward Flagstaff. After you've driven through most of the "urban" areas of town, you'll see Grasshopper Point, a wonderful picnic area worth at least a brief stop. Oak Creek widens here, and a rope is conveniently strung across the water from a huge cottonwood tree. It's a great way to cool off, although these waters can be extremely cold at times.

A few miles up the road, Slide Rock is known for enormous red rock formations and a long natural slide carved by Oak Creek over a period of thousands of years. It's on the west side of the road and comes up rather unexpectedly. You have to pay a daily user fee since it's a state park.

The fishing starts just above Slide Rock, although sometimes someone pulls something surprising out of the creek below. Don't expect a lot of huge fish, but you can anticipate a few stockers (since the Game and Fish Department stocks trout regularly during the summer). On July 21, 1991, a 5-pound brown trout was caught in Upper Oak Creek by an angler who used 4-pound test line and a single kernel of corn.

Species available include rainbow, brown and brook trout along Oak Creek's upper reaches. Below Sedona you can expect largemouth and smallmouth bass and catfish. For more information contact the Flagstaff office of the Arizona Game and Fish Department at 928/774-5045. You can also call 602/789-3701 or visit www.azgfd.com for up-to-date fishing conditions.

There are few developed campsites along Oak Creek Canyon. Only 12 miles north of Sedona are the Cave Spring and Pine Flat camping areas with 140 sites. On holidays and weekends it gets crowded, and these campsites fill up quickly. For more information call the Red Rock Ranger District by calling 928/282-4119 or visit www.fs.fed.us/r3/coconino.

Notable

July 21, 1991, 5-pound brown trout
June 3, 2001, 0-pound, 5.33-ounce rock bass
April 21, 2002, 8.1-ounce rock bass
November 9, 2002, 10-pound, 3.2-ounce rainbow trout

Point of Pines Lake

Point of Pines Lake is not what you'd expect in an area typically associated with a dry climate. The lake is on the San Carlos Apache Indian Reservation atop the Natanes Rim at an elevation of 6,000 feet, and it is one of the most pristine lakes in the entire Southwest.

Reaching this 30-acre lake can be a real challenge, especially if you are foolish, like I was, and go in early April. The road can be a muddy mess

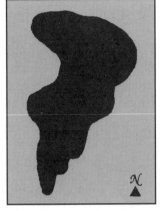

that time of year (and during monsoon season) and a four-wheel-drive vehicle is a must.

The next time I visited Point of Pines, in June, it was much better. Any high-clearance, two-wheel-drive vehicle could have negotiated the trail easily.

The best way get to Point of Pines Lake is to take U.S. Route 70 east from Globe, turn north on Indian Route 8 and bear left

One of the most pristine lakes in Arizona, atop the Natanes Rim.

at the dirt road (north), still on Indian Route 8 toward the dominating rim. Much of this road is dirt, although the short section that crosses Natanes Rim is paved.

There are a number of turnoffs as you ascend the Rim, and in all but the worst weather, you'll be treated to a view that extends for hundreds of miles, not to mention unparalleled sunsets. Once over the Rim, you drop down into the town of Point of Pines, which is really nothing more than a Forest Service location. There is no gas, food or lodging, so be sure to have everything and everybody filled up before you leave.

From the town, just follow the signs. Take your time, since the wild turkey population is pretty healthy, and you'll doubtless see or hear a gobbler or two.

Although Point of Pines is not known for huge fish, it's a pretty safe bet you'll leave with a couple of trophies for the frying pan. Three- and 4-pounders aren't uncommon. In fact, in the 90s the San Carlos Game and Fish Department reported 20-inch brown trout were becoming a regular occurrence. Rainbow trout are the main species, although you never know what to expect from one year to the next.

The San Carlos Apache Game and Fish Department stocks trout in Point of Pines every spring and fall. Couple regular stockings like this with extremely low fishing pressure and Point of Pines offers some incredible fishing.

There are campsites on either side of the lake—a total of 20, which is enough in this remote location. Firewood is easy to find since this is one of the state's least-visited trout fisheries.

You need a San Carlos fishing or recreation permit to visit Point of Pines Lake. For more information contact their Game and Fish Department at Box P.O. 97, San Carlos, AZ 85550 or call 928/475-2343.

Rainbow Lake

Rainbow Lake is in the heart of the White Mountains tourist district, and as such, it is often overfished during the summer. Perhaps the only thing that keeps this reservoir from being "fished out" is the thick weedline that grows along the shore.

Take heart though, the Game and Fish Department regularly trims the weeds with a sort of boat-mounted aquatic mower.

Rainbow Lake covers 80 surface acres. Just off State Route 260 south of Show Low, it is visible from the road, therefore very popular. At 6,700 feet above sea level, expect comfortable temperatures during the summer; however, it periodically experiences a winter freeze. Average depth is only 6 feet.

Species available include rainbow trout, brown trout, largemouth bass, various species of sunfish and channel catfish. By far the most popular catch here is rainbow trout. Expect some pansized fish, but you always stand a chance at something bigger, like the 18-pound, 7.52-ounce channel catfish that was caught and released here on July 31, 2000.

Most years the Arizona Game and Fish Department begins stocking rainbow trout in mid-April. Expect the stocking truck to arrive an average of four times a summer, though bonus stockings are relatively common here.

In the spring of 1992, Rainbow Lake's boat launch was completely redone. Additional improvements to the area include a car-top boat launch, a courtesy dock, restrooms and expanded parking areas.

Motors on the lake are limited to 8 horsepower. For more information contact the Arizona Game and Fish office, by writing 2878 E. White Mountain Blvd., Pinetop, AZ 85935 or by calling 928/367-4281. You can also visit www.azgfd.com.

Camping is allowed nearby in Apache-Sitgreaves National Forest. Contact it by writing the Lakeside Ranger District at 2022 W. White Mountain Blvd., Pinetop-Lakeside, AZ 85935. or call 928/368-5111. You can also visit www.us.fs.fed.us/asnf for more information.

Most of the property around Rainbow Lake is privately owned, however, the Arizona Game and Fish Department does hold a small section of land (and a launch) at the western end of the dam to ensure access for fishermen.

Notable
July 31, 2000, 18-pound, 7.52-ounce channel catfish

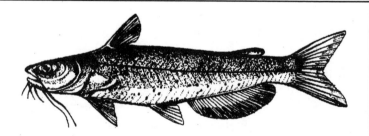

Channel Catfish
Non-native. Scattered black spots on a silver or gray colored back and sides with a white belly. Few spots on large adults. Smooth, scaleless skin and 8 "whiskers." Short base on small adipose fin. Deeply forked tail. Anal fin has 24 to 30 rays and is slightly rounded.

River Reservoir

River Reservoir, is one of the three so-called "Greer Lakes." Bunch Reservoir (see p. 46) and Tunnel Reservoir (see p. 108) are the other two—they are all north of Greer.

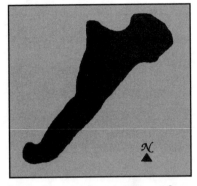

River Reservoir covers 120 surface acres and stands at the bone-chilling elevation of 8,200 feet. High water demands in the area often force the lake to dwindle to about 50 surface acres, or less, by the end of summer.

Species available include rainbow and brown trout. The lake is usually stocked four times a summer, with the first occurring in early June and the last in early August or late July.

To get to the lake, take State Route 260 east from Show Low. Take the Greer Turnoff (State Route 373), and you'll see the lakes off to your left in about 6 miles.

There is a small boat launch area, and boaters are limited to electric trolling motors. Camping is allowed across the road (a long walk from the lakes).

For more information write to the Apache-Sitgreaves National Forest at P.O. Box 640, Springerville, AZ 85938, call 928/333-4301 or visit www.fs.fed.us/r3/asnf.

Lightweight spinning outfits are ideal for River Reservoir.

Scott's Reservoir

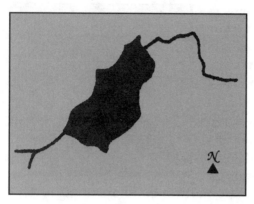

At an elevation of 6,720 feet, Scott's Reservoir impounds 80 surface acres of water in the Apache-Sitgreaves National Forest just north of Lakeside. To reach the lake, take Forest Service Road 45. It's only about two miles off the main highway.

During the fall of 2002 however, the lake was drained for repairs to the dam, so be sure to check ahead.

Species available include rainbow and brown trout, largemouth bass, channel catfish and, of course, bluegill. The first rainbow trout stocking of the year usually comes in early April, and the truck arrives at least four more times during the summer (conditions permitting).

There is a boat launch, but motors are limited to electric trolling motors only. There are no other facilities. This is a good lake for shore fishermen or cartopper boats.

For more information call the Arizona Game and Fish Department in Pinetop-Lakeside, 928/367-4281 or write 2878 E. White Mountain Blvd., Pinetop, AZ 85935. You can also visit www.azgfd.com or call 602/789-3701. For more Apache-Sitgreaves National Forest information contact the Lakeside Ranger District at 2022 W. White Mountain Blvd., Pinetop-Lakeside, AZ 85935 or call 928/368-5111.

Show Low Lake

Show Low Lake, once an under-funded county park, is now an incredible state resource. It's a sterling example of how private industry and the Game and Fish Department can, and do, work together to improve our resources. Improved camping sites, paved parking and a minimum right of way guaranteed along the lake greet today's angler. Add state

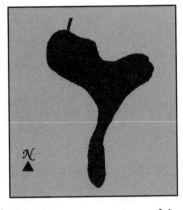

Lake Improvement Funds that were allocated in 1990 (an extra $200,000 was spent on this lake, including improvements to the dock), and this is one of the White Mountains' best.

Show Low Lake was originally created in 1951 when Phelps Dodge, one of Arizona's mining giants, purchased a parcel of land near Show Low. At the time, the company needed an additional source of water for its Morenci operation. A dam was built and the water impounded there soon became known as Show Low Lake. Phelps Dodge also entered into an agreement with the Game and Fish Department to manage the resource "in perpetuity" for the good of Arizona.

Soon trout were being stocked in the 100-acre lake, although it didn't take long for the lake to become overrun with "rough" fish. I can vividly recall several visits to the lake when you could catch sunfish on unbaited hooks as quickly as you could toss them in.

Things have turned around, and dramatically. Today you can expect rainbow and brown trout, largemouth bass, a variety of sunfish, channel catfish and even walleye.

In fact, things are so good now on Show Low Lake that it has been home to the current state inland record walleye several times. The first record from the waterway was a 12-pound fish caught near the dam on April 29, 1989. It was 29.75 inches long and surrendered to a rainbow-colored crankbait. The waterway doesn't show any sign of slowing down though. On July 6, 2000, an 11-pound, 5.6-ounce walleye was caught there, and on November 18, 2002, a 16-pound, 1.76-ounce walleye caught here eclipsed the state record yet again.

Show Low Lake stands at 6,540 feet above sea level, providing comfortable temperatures in the summer and cold weather in the fall, winter and early spring.

To get to the lake, take State Route 260 east out of Show Low. After about 4 miles, you will see signs indicating the way to the lake, which is north of the highway but not visible from the main road. For more information call the Arizona Game and Fish Department at 602/942-3000. Or, for current fishing conditions call 602/789-3701 or visit www.azgfd.com.

Notable

October 15, 2000, 12-pound, 14.4-ounce walleye

June 30, 2001, 12-pound, 11.68-ounce walleye (catch-and-release)

September 7, 2001, 13-pound, 11-ounce walleye (caught on a 4-inch silver Rapala crankbait)

February 2002, 13-pound, 14-ounce walleye (caught by Game and Fish during a survey here and released unharmed)

November 18, 2002, 16-pound, 1.76-ounce walleye

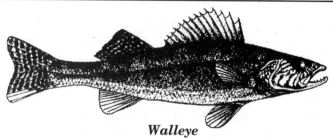

Walleye
Non-native. Back is yellow-olive with a brassy cast. Sides are brassy-yellow with dark mottling. Belly is white. There is a dark spot at rear of spinal dorsal fin. Anal fin and lower lobe of tail fin are white. Eyes are opaque-silver.

Stoneman Lake

At 80 surface acres (on non-drought years) with a depth that averages 9 feet, Stoneman Lake is one of only two Arizona lakes that are not manmade (Mormon Lake is the other). Most think the waterway was created in a volcanic crater; others theorize it occupies a collapsed sinkhole.

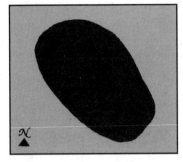

The lake, at an elevation of 6,178 feet, is home to northern pike and yellow perch. In March 1984, what was then the state yellow bass record was set here, twice, when a pair of 1-pound, 10-ouncers were caught only days apart.

There is a boat ramp, although motor sizes are limited to electric trolling motors or less. Camping is not allowed at the lake, which is largely situated on the Coconino National Forest.

The waterway was named in honor of General George Stoneman, who is often remembered for his nearly fatal attempt at hauling supplies down the Gila River. After a meteoric rise in rank during the Civil War, Stoneman was placed in charge of the Military Department of California—a command that included the Arizona Territory.

Take Exit 306 off I-17, about 35 miles south of Flagstaff. The lake is about 10 miles east of the Interstate. The first 6 miles are paved, but only high-clearance vehicles should attempt the final four in poor weather.

For more information contact the Morman Lake Ranger District, 4773 S. Lake Mary Road, Flagstaff, AZ 86001, or call 928/774-1147. You can also visit www.fs.fed.us/r3/coconino.

Stoneman Lake is managed by the Region 2 office of the Arizona Game and Fish Department, which can be reached by writing 3500 S. Lake Mary Road, Flagstaff, AZ 86001 or calling 928/774-5045.

Tunnel Reservoir

Tunnel Reservoir is one of the three Greer Lakes. Bunch (p. 46) and River (p. 103) Reservoirs are the other two. They are all

north of Greer and, coupled with the Little Colorado River, make this area one of the finest angling experiences in the entire state.

Tunnel covers 44 surface acres and offers anglers a chance at some large brown trout and rainbow. It's managed mostly as a "put and take" fishery, where the stocking truck puts them in—and the fishermen take them out.

Generally, catchable-sized rainbow trout are stocked here the last week of April (weather willing) and at least one more time during the summer. Because of the lake's relatively clear shoreline, flyfishing is very productive. During the late fall, flyfishermen regularly land some of the year's biggest fish.

Tunnel stands at a wind-swept elevation of 8,200 feet, and on drought years, or when water demand is heavy, it can shrink to as little as 15 surface acres. Lowered water levels seem to have little affect on the fishing though, since it was low during the 1992 Greer Fishing Derby (which allows fishermen to work any of the three lakes), when the biggest fish caught was a 4.7-pound brown trout.

Some of the best baits to use include a brass colored Z-Ray, Rooster Tails, Super Dupers, green Wooly Worms and Berkley Trout Power Bait.

To get to Tunnel Lake, take State Route 260 east from Show Low, then turn south on State Route 373. The lake is about a mile and a half north of Greer on a paved road, simply follow the signs.

Camping is allowed in nearby Apache-Sitgreaves National Forest. For current information call 602/789-3701; visit www.azgfd.com or www.fs.fed.us/r3/asnf.

Wheatfields Lake

This lake is located in the heart of the Navajo Indian Nation, and if you haven't tried fishing on the reservation, it's time to make a trip. Wheatfields may be a little out of your way, but it's well worth it.

To get to Wheatfields Lake, take I-40 toward the New Mexico border. Just a few miles before you cross into New Mexico, take Indian Route 12 north through Window Rock and Fort Defiance. After about 40 miles, you will come to the impoundment.

Wheatfields is managed strictly as a cold-water fishery. Species you can expect tugging on the line include rainbow and cutthroat trout.

Wheatfields impounds a total of 270 surface acres. There is a small store, Wheatfields Lakeside Store, which is open seasonally. You can usually expect a winter freeze from January to March.

Camping is allowed, but don't forget to purchase a permit. The area is open from April to October, depending on weather conditions. There are restrooms and 25 camping units. For more information on camping or fishing permits, call the Navajo Nation Fish and Wildlife Department at 928/871-6451 or visit www.navajofishandwildlife.org.

Willow Springs Lake

To reach Willow Springs Lake, simply take State Route 260 east from Payson. Once you make the notable and scenic ascent up the Mogollon Rim, the road (Vernon-McNary Road) into Willow Springs will be on your left. It's paved and well signed. The lake is only a few miles north and located at the chilling elevation of 7,520 feet. It was created during the 1960s when the Arizona Game and Fish Department joined forces with the U.S. Forest Service to increase recreation opportunities for Arizona's anglers. In all, the lake impounds 150 surface acres with an average depth of 60 feet.

Species found here include rainbow, brown, brook and cutthroat trout. There are also some largemouth bass. This usually put-and-take water, which is heavily stocked during the summer, has surrendered a rainbow trout that tipped the scales at more than 6 pounds.

Yellow Rooster Tails and salmon eggs have been effective at this lake. Flyfishermen find that dark-colored Wooly Worms usually work best.

Willow Springs has 5 miles of shoreline. There is a boat launching area, and you're allowed up to an 8-horsepower outboard boat motor. The picnic area at the lake is open from April through November. Camping is available nearby in the Apache-Sitgreaves National Forest. For more information visit www.fs.fed.us/r3/asnf or call 928/333-4301. Current fishing conditions are available at www.azgfd.com or call 602/789-3701.

Notable

October 22, 2000, 5-pound, 7.9-ounce rainbow trout
March 28, 2002, 3-pound, 11-ounce brown trout

Woodland Reservoir

In the late 1980s, Woodland Reservoir was improved. The waterway stands at 23 surface acres, and is located in Woodland Park in the center of Pinetop. At an elevation of 6,800 feet, this 10-acre impoundment features rainbow trout, largemouth bass, channel catfish and bluegills. The Arizona Game and Fish Department stocks Woodland with its first trout coming sometime around the end of April, and three more loads come before the water heats up.

To get to Woodland Reservoir, take State Route 260 into Pinetop. At about the heart of town, you will see signs pointing south, toward Woodland Park. It's 1/4 mile southwest of the main highway.

The park has plenty of restrooms, picnic tables, ramadas and barbecues, but these facilities are limited to day use only. Boats with electric motors are allowed on the lake, and a launch is available. Paved parking and roadways make it an ideal stop. For ramada reservations, call Pinetop-Lakeside Parks and Recreation Department; 928/368-6700.

There's plenty of camping in the nearby White Mountain area. For camping information contact the Apache-Sitgreaves National Forest at P.O. Box 640, Springerville, AZ 85938; call 928/333-4301 or visit www.fs.fed.us/r3/asnf.

Water quality was so poor in late 2002 that bag limits were taken off on the waterway. Most of the problem was created by low water levels, so check conditions prior to leaving by calling 602/789-3701 or by visiting www.azgfd.com.

Woods Canyon Lake

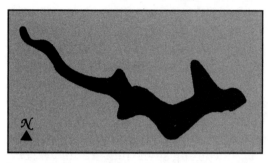

Only a few hours north of Phoenix, Woods Canyon Lake, which stands on the edge of the Mogollon Rim, features a resident population of brown trout, an occasional brookie and is stocked regularly during the summer with rainbows. Just how good the fishing is here is best evidenced by the 10-pound, 11-ounce brown trout caught by an angler here in 1999, when he was working a black Rebel Crickhopper lure.

One of the best ways to limit-out on trout is to use Power Bait. If that doesn't work, consider changing to corn or live worms. Lure fishermen find the traditional color combination of red and gold Z-Ray works best, although a Mepp's spinner or Yellow Jacket is nearly as effective.

The 55-acre impoundment was created in the 1960s when the Arizona Game and Fish Department and the U.S. Forest Service selected different spots along the Rim as potential lake sites. Woods Canyon Lake, which has an average depth of 25 feet, was the first of these to be impounded.

At an elevation of 7,510 feet, this lake also offers Phoenix valley residents a quick and easy getaway from summer heat. It has the best facilities of all the lakes on the Mogollon Rim, which makes camping that much better.

There are two camping areas virtually next to Woods Canyon Lake. Aspen campground overlooks the lake and has a total of 119 sites. Spillway is across the road, within a few walking minutes of the water and has 26 sites.

In the late 1980s another two camping areas were added. Crook and Mogollon are first-come, first-serve. All campgrounds are open from mid-May to mid-October (depending on the weather).

A general store located on the south shore of the lake has boat rentals, licenses, oil and, of course, those often-forgotten camping essentials. The store is open when the campgrounds are open.

To reach Woods Canyon Lake, take State Route 260 east out of Payson. Once you top the Mogollon Rim, take Forest Service Road 300. The lake is only 5 miles from the main highway and the road is paved.

There is a good boat launch here, but motors are limited to electric only.

For more information contact the Apache-Sitgreaves National Forest, by visiting www.fs.fed.us/r3/asnf or calling 928/333-4301. For fishing conditions call 620/789-3701 or visit www.azgfd.com.

Notable
1999, 10-pound, 11-ounce brown trout

Brown Trout
Non-native trout. Olive-brown with yellowish sides. Some orange or red spots on the sides, spots often encircled with light yellow or white. Dark spots on back and sides. Tail fin usually unspotted or vaguely spotted. Adipose fin usually orange or reddish.

White Mountain Apache Reservation

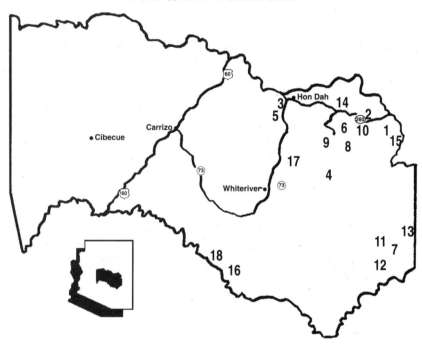

White Mountain Apache Reservation

All persons fishing in and/or operating watercraft on Reservation waters must have a permit. For authorized Reservation permit vendors, see page 261.

Note: Maps are not to scale.

A-1 Lake

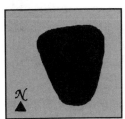

This waterway was named in honor of the great Apache scout, Chief Alchesay, whose native name proved so difficult for U.S. Army officials to pronounce that they simply referred to him as A-1. The label stuck and became his official U.S. Cavalry serial number. I can't think of a more fitting moniker for this waterway—often the first White Mountain Apache Indian Reservation reservoir seen by anglers. It's most befitting of a scout.

At only 24 surface acres, A-1 may not have the stature of the many nearby White Mountain Lakes, but you can expect to catch rainbow, brook and Apache trout here year round. In fact, it's a popular destination for ice fishermen once it freezes, a time when Apache trout are more catchable than the lake's other species.

The lake was created in 1966 and has a maximum depth of 28.7 feet. It has less than a mile of shoreline and only a few campsites. Mid-1990 studies indicated an angler could expect to catch an average of .483 trout per hour at A-1. In June the total catch rate was determined to be slightly higher at .672 fish per hour (.426 Apache trout and .148 rainbow). In July the catch rate dropped to .504 trout per hour and the dog days of August were even worse, at .416.

The lake can suffer a pretty good algae bloom by August, which not only accounts for the green tint it inherits late in the summer, but for the reduced catch rate as well. Anytime visibility is reduced, arm yourself with spinners like a Mepps or Z-Ray, which displace a lot of water, effectively making enough racket to attract fish.

Beginning in May and June, the White Mountain Apache Indian Reservation begins stocking thousands of Apache trout. Although how many go where varies each year. Surveys conducted in 1991 found the most populous resident in A-1 was the Apache trout—roughly 60 percent. A subsequent survey put that number at slightly under 80 percent.

At an elevation of 8,900 feet, A-1 guarantees comfortable temperatures in the summer. Camping is allowed on the south end of this lake, but remember to get your White Mountain Apache permits for camping and fishing and check regulations prior to leaving.

A-1 is easy to find. Simply drive 22 miles east of Pinetop-Lakeside on State Route 260, and turn south at the sign (just west of State Route 273). During the rainy or snowy season, the parking lot may be muddy, but it's usually accessible. Because of this lake's convenient location, it often receives the most pressure of all the Reservation's put-and-take fisheries (almost 5 percent of total use).

For more information, write the White Mountain Apache Game and Fish Department at P.O. Box 220, Whiteriver, AZ 85941. Call 928/338-4385 or visit www.wmatoutdoors.com.

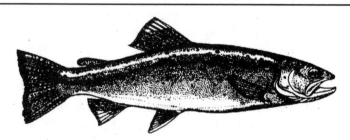

Apache Trout
Native to Arizona. Body color is yellowish-gold; the tip of the head and back are dark olive. Dorsal, anal and pelvic fins are white tipped. Orange to red cutthroat mark usually present under lower jaw. Dark, bold spots on dorsal and tail fin. Body spotting is sparse and may extend below lateral line. Two small black spots on either side of pupil give appearance of black stripe through eye.

Black River

This is one of those rare fisheries that is literally inaccessible unless you have a high-clearance or four-wheel-drive vehicle. Sure, you might negotiate the Apache's back-country route into the Black River in a regular automobile, but if it rains or the road is in poor condition, getting back is another story.

Perhaps the best thing about this particular river is its remote location and guaranteed privacy even during summer holidays. The White Mountain and San Carlos Apache tribes limit the number of people who can purchase permits to fish and camp in this area on any given day, ensuring minimum contact with other anglers.

The Black River is literally the border between the White Mountain Apache Indian Reservation and the San Carlos Apache Indian Reservation. It's important to remember to purchase proper recreation permits from the reservation you'll be driving across to get to the Black River. When you purchase permits, tell tribal officials you're heading into the Black River area, and they will issue you a Black River special use permit. They are different than regular fishing permits, and unless you have one, you will be in violation of the law.

For more information contact the White Mountain Apache Fish and Game Department by writing P.O. Box 220, Whiteriver, AZ 85941. Call 928/338-4385 or visit www.wmatoutdoors.com.

The San Carlos Recreation and Wildlife Department can be contacted at P. O. Box 97, San Carlos, AZ 85550, 928/475-2343.

To reach the Black River from the White Mountains, take State Route 73 from Carrizo toward Fort Apache. Then turn south on Indian Route 9, which, depending on time of year, can look like little more than a small muddy trail.

This road has some breathtaking views though—something every outdoorsman can enjoy. Crossing the White River and descending into its basin from the rim is a real experience.

From the San Carlos Apache Reservation, the quickest way is to take U.S. Route 60 north out of Globe and turn east toward Sycamore Tank (just south of Seneca). The turnoff does not look like much from the highway, but once you're on it, it's a pretty good dirt road. Then turn north at Walker Park Tank turnoff. This road is rough in spots, but again you'll be treated to some of Arizona's most scenic wilderness.

Once there, you'll be at Black River Crossing, the only point for many miles with vehicular access to the waterway. As a result, most of the eddies and pools are largely unexplored by anglers. A bridge at the crossing provides access to either reservation.

For really ambitious anglers there are a number of backpack only or four-wheel-only accesses upstream. For obvious reasons, catch rate in those areas is improved, and the number of humans encountered greatly diminished.

Beyond a doubt, this is Arizona's premier smallmouth bass fishery. No, huge lunkers aren't typically caught here, just full stringers of the bronzebacks—and regularly. The best time to visit is in May and June, before the rainy season turns the water thick and dark brown.

Though the Black River is probably Arizona's best bet for smallmouth action, it wasn't until the U. S. Fish and Wildlife

Service stocked the scrappy fighters in 1960 that the river gained its notoriety. Since the stocking, smallmouth have successfully made their way downstream and established breeding populations in both Roosevelt and Apache lakes.

A campground can be found on the north shore of the river (at the crossing) with plenty of firewood. Campsites are next to the river, and the last time I visited the area, I was so close to the water that its sound kept me awake much of the night.

There are no facilities here. What you pack in, you must pack out. Please, leave this and all of Arizona's outdoors cleaner than you found it.

What you will find at Black River is Arizona like it used to be, including the state's thickest bear concentration. Take the proper precautions and store your food and trash properly to avoid potentially disastrous confrontations, and this is one getaway everyone should enjoy at least once. Stories of bears stealing a day's catch are common.

For best results at Black River Crossing, you'll have to hike a little. Probe those eddies or pools where the river makes a turn, or the water upwells behind the many sizeable boulders.

Upstream, toward the Apache National Forest, trout begin to infest the Black River waters. Try live crayfish or small chartreuse grubs. The water is always fast and often dirty, so you might want to use small spinners on the grubs to grab the fish's attention.

The biggest catches are usually reported near the confluence of the Black and White Rivers, which combine to become the Salt River. Other species available along the Black include catfish and rainbow, brook, brown and native trout. Those areas northeast of the reservations, about 20 miles from Alpine, are best for trout.

Anglers should consult a current set of regulations prior to fishing any of the Black River, as reintroduction of certain species has closed some portions to fishing, and limited others to catch-and-release only.

Bog Tank

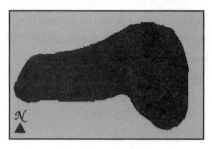

Beyond a doubt, this is one of my favorite fishing holes in Arizona. While my father and I could regularly "limit out" on nearby Hawley, my mother insisted nothing could compare to Bog Tank's action.

So, off we'd go on a thirty-minute drive out of Hawley and across State Route 260 to Bog Tank to let her join the ranks of the "limited." At 12 surface acres and situated in the water-infested White Mountains, Bog Tank, which was originally impounded in 1956, earns its name. It may not be very much to look at, but the fishing is pretty good. At an elevation of 8,100 feet, it's also a cooling experience, even in July.

Bog Tank offers stocker rainbow trout, Apache trout, occasional brookies and browns. Everything from corn to marshmallow-style trout bait seem to work here. I even watched fishermen along the northern shore work a wet fly to catch their limits in minutes one year.

The White Mountain Apache Game and Fish Department statistics prove catch rates on this lake are some of the highest in the area. In the summer of 1991, it determined anyone fishing from shore caught an average of .313 Apache trout per hour and .183 rainbow trout. That meant people were catching .532 fish per hour at Bog Tank, the highest of all the White Mountain Apache Lakes surveyed that year.

The next year, the Game and Fish Department further broke the study into months. In June of 1992, fishermen caught .177 Apache trout per hour and .136 rainbow trout per hour, per angler (total catch rate .443). In July .098 Apache trout showed up on creel per hour and .257 rainbow trout (.366 total). By August, which unlike most other waterways, proved to be the best time to visit Bog Tank, rates increased to .618 Apache trout per hour, per angler, and rainbow trout were caught at .140 per hour. Total expected catch rate per hour at the lake was .758 trout.

Consider too the fact that the White Mountain Apache Game and Fish Department began stocking 2-pound incentive Apache trout just before Memorial Day weekend in the early 1990s. On that holiday, a children's fishing derby is also held annually on this reservoir, so that's one of the few times you can expect crowds.

The dam area seems to produce best, since the trout use the depths to avoid the heat. My mother, somehow, always had good luck right from the parking lot shore.

Small boats and canoes can be launched into the water (check ahead since regulations change). Camping is not allowed, though you will find plenty of other camping areas nearby on the White Mountain Apache Indian Reservation.

To get to Bog Tank, take State Route 260 east out of Pinetop. Pass the Hawley Lake turnoff (State Route 473), and start watching the north side of the road. The dirt access to Bog Tank is just about directly across from Horseshoe Cienega Lake and, at times, is hard to see (periodically the sign disappears). It's only about 200 yards off the highway.

Remember, this little gem is on the White Mountain Apache Indian Reservation and requires its permits. For more information contact the White Mountain Apache Fish and Game Department by writing P.O. Box 220, Whiteriver, AZ 85941. Call 928/338-4385 or visit www.wmatoutdoors.com.

Bootleg Lake

Originally impounded in 1965, Bootleg Lake disappears and reappears from year to year, depending on rainfall.

A number of years ago, some big incentive largemouth bass were stocked in this lake, which impounds part of Carrizo Creek. The lake was deemed a strictly catch-and-release fishery. For a short time, the Game and Fish Department began allowing fishermen to keep five fish under 12 inches in length in order to reduce the number of small fish. Expect a few sunfish as well as an occasional channel catfish.

To fish here, you need a special permit, and you'll need to declare your intention of working this lake when buying it (they limit the number of anglers, and your special permit will be valid only on Bootleg). Studies in the 90s conducted on the 10-acre impoundment indicated 92 percent of the lake's residents were largemouth bass. The other 8 percent were green sunfish. The studies indicate most of the bass caught weighed slightly less than a pound, though older, larger fish were viewed.

To reach Bootleg Lake, take State Route 73 south out of Hon-Dah for 3 miles. Take the first dirt road (milepost 355) running northwest from the highway, and the lake's only two miles away. The lake is open year-round, despite its elevation of 6,800 feet. No camping is allowed.

For more information contact the White Mountain Apache Fish and Game Department by writing P.O. Box 220, Whiteriver, AZ 85941. Call 928/338-4385 or visit www.wmatoutdoors.com.

Christmas Tree Lake

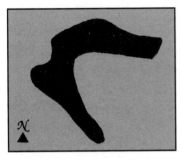

Years ago, when President Lyndon B. Johnson wanted a beautiful Christmas tree for the White House's 1965 display, the "loggers" of Arizona went to work. High atop the rugged White Mountain Apache Indian Reservation, they cut a huge spruce for the White House lawn. The tribal chairman told reporters, "The Tribe was very honored to be chosen for the sponsorship of the tree...This is the first time that any Indian Tribe has been selected to provide a tree which will grace the White House lawn and will be seen by millions of television viewers in December when President Johnson pulls the switch to light the tree."

When a lake was impounded nearby the same year, it was named Christmas Tree Lake in honor of the event. For the avid angler, the real attraction isn't the breathtaking stands of evergreens though; it's the chance of catching one of Arizona's rarest fish, the native Apache trout.

Arizona is the only place in the world where you can catch these speckled beauties. Like their first cousin, the rainbow trout, they promise heart-quickening watertop dances, tackle-testing uncontrollable runs and hours of nonstop fun.

The White Mountain Apache Game and Fish Department has, for years, been managing Christmas Tree Lake as a Blue Ribbon fishery. Artificial lures and flies are all that are allowed on the lake.

Annually, the tribe hosts the state's major outdoor writers in late May to show off this lake—one of its finest. According to the Game and Fish Department, Christmas Tree Lake holds the reservation's biggest population of Apache trout and a decent population of browns.

Since Arizona is the only state where the Apache trout lives, it is also home to every single record in existence. In May 1990, a Scottsdale angler landed the International Game Fish Association All Tackle Record there. It weighed in at 4-pounds, 13-ounces.

In 1991, a new record Apache trout was caught at Christmas Tree Lake. It measured 22.75 inches in length and weighed 5-pounds, 3-ounces.

In May of 1992, Apache trout were stocked in the lake from nearby William's Creek Hatchery. This stocking held something different though, namely, several world-record-sized specimens biologists like to call "incentive" fish.

Christmas Tree Lake is also home to one of Arizona's few limited seasons. Usually it opens in May, and fishing is allowed until September.

On May 25, 1992, opening day, a Chandler angler was sharing the water with the outdoor-writer crowd. At about noon, when the writers had retired to camp for their afternoon siesta, the angler felt something hit the Kastmaster he was working in four feet of water.

Soon he had the lunker in his boat. When he put it on his hand-held scale, it registered 6 pounds.

Thinking nothing of it, but knowing full well it was a trophy worth having mounted, he threw the fish in his cooler. Back in Chandler, he put it in the freezer until he returned from several business trips. Quickly though, he found out from local tackle shops that he probably was holding the new state record Apache trout. By the time he had it weighed, it was 5.88 pounds and measured 24 inches in length.

The Arizona Game and Fish Department certified this catch as the new state record (five months after it had been caught). The angler was extremely lucky he had not cleaned the fish or let it spend any more time in the freezer.

His record stood until June 10, 1993. On that date, an angler working nearby Hurricane Lake brought in a 5.97-pound Apache trout, eclipsing Christmas Tree's previous two records. The fisherman was using a yellow 1/4-ounce Z-Ray with red spots.

To fish Christmas Tree Lake, you must purchase a special permit from the White Mountain Apache Reservation. It deliberately limits the number of anglers on this lake at any one time, ensuring relatively light fishing pressure.

Christmas Tree Lake covers 41 surface acres and stands at an elevation of 8,200 feet.

To get to Christmas Tree Lake, take State Route 473 south toward Hawley Lake. Drive toward the Hawley Lake store and turn right just about at the store. Follow Indian Route 26 to the lake (where Indian Route 27 branches off, bear to the left). The distance from the turnoff at Hawley Lake is about five miles of dirt road. Since this road is regularly used by logging operations, it can be a little rough, especially in the early spring. A high-clearance vehicle shouldn't have too much of a problem at any time of the year, and by midsummer, it's negotiable by passenger cars. There's also a shorter route from near Whiteriver, but I've never taken it.

Be sure to check current regulations before visiting. Permits to fish on this lake can only be purchased at the Hon-Dah Ski & Outdoor Sport. Call 877/226-4868.

For more information contact the White Mountain Apache Fish and Game Department by writing P.O. Box 220, Whiteriver, AZ 85941. Call 928/338-4385 or visit www.wmatoutdoors.com.

Notable
May 1990, 4-pound, 13-ounce Apache trout
1991, 5-pound, 3-ounce Apache trout
May 25, 1992, 5.88-pound Apache trout

Cooley Lake

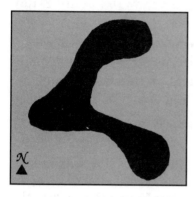

It's only fitting Cooley Lake would be home to the White Mountain Apache Indian Reservation's wildest fisheries experiment. It's named in honor of Corydon E. Cooley, the man who won that famous card game—the same game that gave the city of Show Low its name. Arizona was so wild at the time that Cooley was serving as a scout for General Crook, chasing down the Apaches that now run the lake. Be sure to get the proper permits before visiting.

At 11 surface acres, the lake's not a whole lot to brag about in the lake-infested White Mountains. Of course, add lunker largemouth bass like they did in the 1980s, and it becomes something special. In fact, so special that current regulations force you to get a special White Mountain Recreation permit to fish or camp at this lake (call 928/338-4385 for current information or visit www.wmatoutdoors.com).

The lake stands at an elevation of 7,100 feet, low enough in theory to support a trophy bass fishery. Unfortunately, early 1990s studies indicated the brooder largemouth never did quite take hold. As a result, slot limits were being discussed, as well as lower limits.

There are, however, a lot of smaller bass in the lake, making it an ideal place to take a youngster. If nothing else, the waterway also has a healthy population of channel catfish just waiting for your arrival. Rainbow trout are stocked before ice out, and green sunfish and brown trout are often caught.

To get to the lake, take State Route 260 east from Show Low, through Pinetop-Lakeside to Hon-Dah. From there take State Route 73 south one mile and watch for signs.

Cyclone Lake

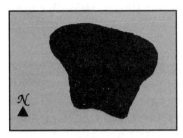

At 37 surface acres and an elevation of 8,100 feet, Cyclone Lake is one of the most scenic destinations on the White Mountain Apache Indian Reservation. Add the fact that it's restricted to group use only, and Cyclone is one of the most unusual fishing getaways in the entire Southwest. With nearly a mile of shoreline, it also offers some incredible fishing.

For a couple hundred dollars, plus a daily-use-fee per person (the price fluctuates, so contact tribal officials for details), companies, groups and organizations can rent this lake for a day. As of this printing, it was still limited to reserved group use only and generally open from late May to early September.

There are no developed facilities or RV hookups. All you'll find here is pristine Arizona wilderness, a cool getaway and incredible fishing.

An ideal site for the perfect fish-and-party weekend!

Species available at Cyclone Lake include rainbow, cut-throat, brook and brown trout. Occasionally the rare Arizona native, Apache trout, shows up in a creel.

Boats can be launched, though the ramp is virtually non-existent and will not support much more than a rowboat. Electric trolling motors are the limit.

Cyclone Lake is situated in the same incredible scenery as Hawley Lake. To find the lake, take State Route 260 east out of Pinetop-Lakeside. Turn south on State Route 473 toward Hawley Lake. Then turn left at the sign (after you've entered the cabin area on the north side of Hawley), and follow the dirt road for about five miles. There's also a much-less traveled route off the main road into Hawley. It's usually a lot rougher.

During the rainy season the main trail can be relatively rough, so take your time and stop to enjoy the alpine streams crossing the road. Keep an eye out for the wild turkeys in the area as well; they're a sight one shouldn't miss.

For more information or for reservations, write the White Mountain Apache Game and Fish Department at P.O. Box 220, Whiteriver, AZ 85941 or call 928/338-4385. You can also visit www.wmatoutdoors.com.

Remember, you cannot even visit this lake without group reservations. So observe the regulations, and if you're interested in reserving the lake, make sure you inquire as to availability at least a year in advance.

Diamond Creek

Varying in elevation from 5,600 feet to 7,500 feet, Diamond Creek courses through huge grassy meadows and stands of tall spruce, aspen and ponderosa pine. Beyond a doubt, it is one of Arizona's most scenic fishable waterways.

To reach Diamond Creek's rainbow, brown and Apache trout populations, take State Route 73 between Whiteriver and Hon-Dah. Turn east on Indian Route 25 (dirt), and in a few miles it will begin to parallel the creek. In all, there are about 11 fishable miles to Diamond Creek, though that will vary from year to year. The drought of 1999-2000 is a good example of how important it is to check ahead, especially in Arizona when visiting less popular waterways like Diamond Creek. That year the stream pretty much dried up in several sections, though the summer of 2000 monsoons certainly helped.

Remember, this stream is also on the White Mountain Apache Indian Reservation, so proper permits are required. Also double check on limits, since they change often. For more information contact the White Mountain Apache Fish and Game Department by writing P.O. Box 220, Whiteriver, AZ 85941. Call 928/338-4385 or visit www.wmatoutdoors.com.

If you follow the waterway far enough, it will branch into the Little Diamond. Usually you'll only find smaller fish there. Note that much of this stream is also on the White Mountain Apache Indian Reservation; make sure to get proper permits.

Drift Fence Lake

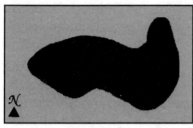

Nearby Hurricane Lake, once home of the world record Apache trout, steals most of the notoriety from Drift Fence Lake. It's a real shame too, since Drift Fence Lake is scenic, with a road curvy and cliffy enough to spawn its own legend, and by the fall it has enough lunker rainbows to attract a near fanatic following.

Perhaps the only problem with the 15-acre impoundment is the simple fact that its depth of only 22 feet at 8,970 feet above sea level can translate to winter freezes and kill-offs.

Take heart though, the White Mountain Apache tribe stocks early in the spring, and by fall the rainbows are big enough to fill any frying pan. There's also a campground at the lake with roughly a dozen sites, so you are guaranteed a tremendous waterside experience if you're staying overnight.

The waterway is also well off the beaten path. There is no direct route to this lake, though consider taking State Route 260 east from Pinetop-Lakeside then take State Route 273 south. Then turn south on Forest Service Road 116 toward Reservation Lake and Hurricane Lake. The turnoff for Drift Fence Lake is just past the turnoff for Hurricane Lake.

Because both the lake and campground are on the White Mountain Apache Indian Reservation, you must have valid recreation/fishing permits. For more information contact the White Mountain Apache Fish and Game Department by writing P.O. Box 220, Whiteriver, AZ 85941. Call 928/338-4385 or visit www.wmatoutdoors.com.

Earl Park Lake

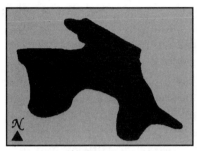

Earl Park Lake is located on the White Mountain Apache Indian Reservation just upstream from Hawley Lake. Permits from the reservation are required for fishing here. At 47 surface acres and an elevation of 8,200 feet, this is one of the most scenic lakes in the White Mountains. Cabins line the water's edge, many still available for rent from the reservation.

The easiest way to get there is to take State Route 260 east from McNary and turn south on State Route 473. Once you reach the junction at Hawley Lake, where the road turns to dirt, bear left and follow the road until it crosses a small stream. Signs direct you toward Earl Park Lake.

Species available include rainbow, brown, cutthroat and brook trout. During the 1980s the water became infested with golden shiners, but you can still limit-out on this small lake. Rules regarding fishing on Earl Park Lake change with regularity. It has been managed as a catch-and-release fishery, Blue Ribbon fishery and lure only—so check regulations.

Remember too, there is a substantial population of bears in the area. Take the necessary precautions, and you don't have much to worry about. On more than one occasion, when accompanied by my oldest son, we ran across a curious bruin. Give them a wide berth and you're fine.

Camping is not allowed on Earl Park Lake, although nearby Hawley Lake does have a good-sized campground. For more information contact the White Mountain Apache Fish and Game Department by writing P.O. Box 220, Whiteriver, AZ 85941. Call 928/338-4385 or visit www.wmatoutdoors.com.

Hawley Lake

Of all Arizona's trout waters, this is my absolute favorite! I'll always fondly remember when I was young and my parents

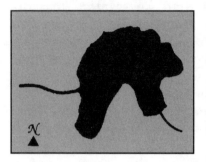

would drag me to its 260 surface acres of water in the early spring, when snow was still underneath the trees. If you visit the lake in April or early May, things can be pretty white, although it was at those frigid times when limits seemed easiest.

Hawley is one of Arizona's highest lakes (8,200 feet), and nighttime temperatures in mid-summer can plunge to downright uncomfortable levels. If you're camping, come prepared. If you're fishing for the day, bring along warm clothes for the dusk bite. Despite the low temperatures, Hawley Lake is one of the few higher elevation lakes in the state where you can usually count on easy early spring/late fall access.

Hawley Lake is located on the White Mountain Apache Indian Reservation and is surrounded by hundreds of cabins—many for rent. For more information contact the White Mountain Apache Fish and Game Department by writing P.O. Box 220, Whiteriver, AZ 85941. Call 928/338-4385 or visit www.wmatoutdoors.com.

To get to Hawley Lake, take State Route 260 east out of McNary and turn south on State Route 473.

Near the lake is a campground, a general store and a small chapel that was once occupied almost every Sunday in summer. Boats are limited to electric trolling motors. If you get your craft on the water, try trolling with cowbells, and in the middle of summer get down deep.

One of the best things about Hawley Lake is its accessible shoreline—nearly 10 miles. The lake is surrounded by

Hawley Lake has an easily accessible shoreline.

thick stands of pines although you can drive to within 100 yards of the water at each corner because of the number of cabin access roads.

Hawley is home to rainbow, cutthroat, brook, brown and Apache trout. For several years its 4-pound, 4.5-ounce brookie, caught in May 1977, stood as the state record, although it was eclipsed in May 1986 by a fish caught on Big Lake. That catch, in turn, was eclipsed by a 4-pound, 15.2-ouncer from Sunrise Lake. Hawley's almost always good for lunkers, whether you're after a record or not. On May 6, 1989, a 7-pound, 15-ounce brown trout was caught by an angler using a brown Wooly Worm.

Try salmon eggs, power-style trout bait or kernels of corn with a marshmallow to add buoyancy. The small finger of water between Earl Park Lake and Hawley Lake has been my favorite for years. If you prefer the action of lures, try slow rolling a red-and-yellow Z-Ray. For some reason, almost no other colors produce the same results for me here, so be sure to bring a generous supply since snags are just about as populous as the fish.

If you prefer trolling, start near the thick weed beds. The best results usually come from using cowbells, and the action is almost always deep.

During the 1970s, my father and I walked the stream between Earl Park Lake and Hawley Lake. We saw a number of huge browns along the shoreline, and my father landed a 7-pounder later that day—probably one of my favorite fishing memories.

Take your time on the drive into Hawley Lake. You can often see wild turkeys crossing the road, and these sightings always add fun to any fishing trip.

If you're adventurous and own a truck, consider taking the back dirt road into Whiteriver. This drive is through one of the state's most pristine areas and the road is usually in pretty good shape. Look for wild strawberries in the summer.

Hawley Lake, impounded in 1959, was built expressly for fishing and water recreation as part of the White Mountain Apache tribe's lake-building program. It was the first of all the lakes built on the reservation under that program.

Every Arizona angler needs to visit Hawley at least once.

Notable
>May 1977, 4-pound, 4.5-ounce brook trout
>May 6, 1989, 7-pound, 15-ounce brown trout
>October 21, 2001, 3-pound, 13-ounce brown trout

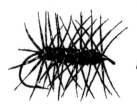

The Woolly Worm is one of the best flies for trout fishing because it can imitate many insects.

Horseshoe Cienega Lake

Horseshoe Cienega Lake was once the site of Arizona's inland waters record brown trout. The catch took place on April 22, 1985, and tipped the scales at 16 pounds, 7.0 ounces. From head to tail, the chunky fish was 29.5 inches long.

It took many years for a bigger brown to surface in Arizona, but on August 5, 1999, a Prescott youth caught a 22-pound, 9.0-ounce brown trout out of Reservation Lake.

At 121 surface acres and 8,100 feet, Horseshoe Cienega Lake is an important fishery on the White Mountain Apache Indian Reservation. At this elevation, it can be pretty cool, so be prepared. Camping is allowed, and there are 68 sites available.

Remember to purchase a permit since the lake is on the Apache Reservation. For more information contact the White Mountain Apache Fish and Game Department by writing P.O. Box 220, Whiteriver, AZ 85941. Call 928/338-4385 or visit www.wmatoutdoors.com.

Species available include rainbow, brook, Apache and, of course, those often huge brown trout.

A general store at the lake rents boats from May to September (weather permitting). If you bring your own watercraft, you need a White Mountain Apache permit to operate on their water, and only electric trolling motors are allowed.

Horseshoe Cienega Lake was originally created in the 1960s, though by the early 1990s it had to be drained and deepened to reduce weed growth. It was reopened in May 1991, after it had been heavily stocked to bring the fishing back up to par. The lake's depth is listed at 30 feet, and it features slightly less than a mile of shoreline.

As usual in the White Mountains, use kernels of corn, salmon eggs or, better yet, any of the paste-style trout baits.

To reach Horseshoe, take State Route 260 east from McNary. It's south of the road a few miles east of the Hawley Lake turnoff and can be seen from Route 260. If all else fails, simply follow the signs on the main highway.

Notable

April 22, 1985, 16-pound, 7-ounce brown trout

Regardless of children's age, Arizona's outdoors are an ideal playground!

Hurricane Lake

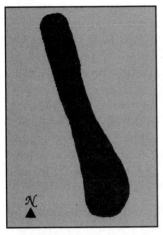

On June 10, 1993, something miraculous happened at Hurricane Lake, high atop the White Mountain Apache Indian Reservation. A young Lakeside resident, fishing with his father, landed a 5-pound, 15.5-ounce Apache trout.

It was not only subsequently certified as the state's largest Apache trout caught that year but was the new state record. It eclipsed the old record caught in May 1992 at Christmas Tree Lake (also on the White Mountain Apache Indian Reservation). At the time, it stood as the largest Apache trout ever caught in the world. Arizona is, after all, the only place this subspecies calls home.

The angler was using a 1/4-ounce yellow Z-Ray with red spots as bait. Like most new records, this one has an interesting story behind it.

Fishing with his father from a small boat, the young man caught the fish at 5 A.M. "It was in the cooler for 27 hours before I had it weighed," he said later. By the time he got the new record on a grocery store's scale, the bottom of the cooler was literally covered with eggs, effectively reducing the weight of the fish.

Arizona Game and Fish Department rules state the fish must be weighed on a certified scale, hence the trip to the nearest grocery store. Ironically, the new world record never even jumped from the water. "I really didn't think she was a big fish," he said. "She never broke water."

Jim Novy, fisheries biologist for the Pinetop-Lakeside region, said another fisherman from New Mexico also called to report a potential record from Hurricane Lake. Subsequently, that lunker Apache trout has been listed with the National Freshwater Fishing Hall of Fame. It had an identical weight, was caught just a few days earlier at Hurricane and surrendered to a fly.

According to Novy, a group of big brooder Apache trout was stocked in Hurricane Lake in early 1993. Several weighed nearly 6 pounds when stocked, and because the lake is unusually deep and nutrient rich, it was hoped any holdovers would be bound to eclipse these records on an annual basis.

Rory Aikens, Information and Education Officer for the Arizona Game and Fish Department, has fond memories of trips to Hurricane Lake. According to him, he and a friend annually drove to the lake in early spring, even before the snow had cleared.

"We had to use chains and four-wheel-drive just to get to the lake," he said. "There was ice around the entire lake when we put the small canoe into the water."

Brown trout that weighed more than 6 pounds would answer the dinner bell though—driving him back to his secret hideaway every spring. With catches like this, Hurricane Lake is one of those rare Arizona angling destinations everyone needs to visit at least once in their lifetime.

At nearly 16 surface acres, the lake was renovated in the early 1980s and re-stocked with Apache trout. Unfortunately, a few of the rainbow trout had managed to remain in the waterway (without anyone's knowledge), and now the lake is home to hybridized Apache-rainbow trout. Efforts are underway to remedy the problem, though as the record clearly shows, big Apache trout are regularly caught here.

There is a small boat launch (if that's what you call it), and anglers should consult a current set of regulations prior to heading out. Artificial lures and barbless hooks are often the requirements, although regulations change regularly. The road into Hurricane isn't exactly the greatest in the world, and early in the spring or late fall, high-clearance vehicles are mandatory. If snow's on the ground, four-wheel-drive may be a necessity.

The most direct route to Hurricane Lake is to take Y55 east from Whiteriver (along the East Fork of the White River). It's a dirt road and rough toward the end, so take your time. After nearly 20 miles, you'll come to Y20. Take it north toward Reservation Lake. Hurricane Lake is off to the left (west) of the road. You can also drive State Route 273 south from Route 260 (between Pinetop-Lakeside and Springerville). Then follow the signs. It's three miles west of Reservation Lake.

Hurricane stands at a bone-chilling altitude of 8,940 feet, so be sure to dress warm. Boaters are limited to electric trolling motors. This lake is also on the White Mountain Apache Indian Reservation and often enrolled in the tribe's Rent-A-Lake program, so be sure to get the proper permits before wetting a line. Also, be sure to check current regulations before visiting.

Permits to fish on this lake can only be purchased at the Hon Dah Ski & Outdoor Sport store at Hon Dah. Call 877/226-4868. For more information contact the White Mountain Apache Fish and Game Department by writing P.O. Box 220, Whiteriver, AZ 85941. Call 928/338-4385 or visit www.wmatoutdoors.com.

Hurricane Lake's 19 surface acres have a real history of setting records. Back in 1989, the then-world-record Apache trout, as listed by the International Game Fish Association record was also set here. It tipped the scales at 2-pounds, 1.5-ounces, a lunker that surrendered to a black and gold Panther Martin spinner.

Notable

1989, 2-pound, 1.5-pound Apache trout
June 10, 1993, 5-pound, 15.5-ounce Apache trout

Pacheta Lake

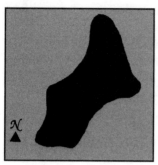

When I first heard the reports I couldn't believe it. A 15-pound, 9-ounce brown trout caught at tiny Pacheta Lake on the White Mountain Apache Indian Reservation in August 1993 came within 14 ounces of eclipsing the old state record. More than a few eyebrows were raised over Pacheta's productivity.

Of course, the reason why I really couldn't believe the report at first was primarily because Pacheta is so far off the beaten path. The lake may only impound a total of 63 surface acres, but there are 2 miles of shoreline to work, and the waterway plummets to a brown trout-pleasing depth of 28 feet in at least one spot.

There is a boat launch at the lake, though boaters are limited to electric trolling motors. To get to the lake, take Y55 east from Whiteriver and turn east at Y80. The lake is on your right, after another mile.

Camping is allowed, which makes lugging that cartop boat a little more palatable. In all, there are 25 unimproved campsites. Be prepared for the cold though, since the lake stands at an elevation of 8,173 feet.

Remember that since this lake and campground are on the White Mountain Apache Indian Reservation, you need valid permits to stay or even visit. This waterway has also been managed as a catch-and-release trophy fishery in the past, so make sure you consult a current set of regulations. For more information contact the White Mountain Apache Fish and Game Department by writing P.O. Box 220, Whiteriver, AZ 85941. Call 928/338-4385 or visit www.wmatoutdoors.com.

Notable

August 1993, 15-pound, 9-ounce brown trout

Reservation Lake

Reservation Lake, which is at a frigid elevation of 9,000 feet above sea level, is a rather out-of-the-way destination on the White Mountain Apache Indian Reservation. Once you get there though, you'll find 280 surface acres of trout-infested waters that include rainbow, brook, brown and Apache.

Of course, it wasn't until a Prescott youth visited Reservation Lake on August 6, 1999, that most of Arizona would even hear about the waterway. After he caught a brown trout that weighed in at 22-pounds, 14.5-ounces and was 36 inches long, every avid angler wanted to visit the lake. The new record catch succumbed to a four-inch silver floating Rapala worked from an inflatable boat at 6 P.M.

The best way to get to Reservation Lake is to take State Route 273 south from State Route 260 toward Big Lake. This road becomes Forest Service Road 113; turn right at Forest Service Road 116. Take 116 south until you reach the lake. Both of these roads are dirt, so be prepared early in the spring or during the rainy season.

Try working the shorelines with small Mepps spinners in red and yellow or any of the marshmallow-style trout baits. When trolling (remember only electric trolling motors are allowed), use cowbells and work deep, especially during the daytime. A silver Rapala probably isn't a bad idea either.

There is a general store that rents boats from May to September. During mild winters, expect lake access to be open from April to November. Camping is allowed, but at this altitude, be sure to come prepared for sudden changes in the weather and cool temperatures. There are 90 campsites.

A creel survey conducted in the '90s showed bank anglers on Reservation Lake could expect to catch .009 brown trout, .042 brook, .018 Apache trout and .067 rainbow trout per hour fishing. Another survey conducted at about the same time determined shore fishermen had the best luck in June for rainbow trout, with a catch rate of .023 per hour. However, total catch rate for any species of trout was highest in August, with .280 fish caught per hour. July was the second-best month with .186 and June third at .062.

During the summer of 1998, the lake surrendered a 6-pound, 8-ounce brown.

For more information contact the White Mountain Apache Fish and Game Department by writing P.O. Box 220, Whiteriver, AZ 85941. Call 928/338-4385 or visit www.wmatoutdoors.com.

Notable

    1998, 6-pound, 8-ounce brown trout
    August 6, 1999, 22-pound, 14.5-ounce brown trout

Memories that last a lifetime!

Shush Be Tou Lake

This is probably one of those lakes you've seen but never fished as you sped through the White Mountain Apache Indian Reservation on your way elsewhere. A few miles east of McNary on State Route 260, Shush Be Tou (Apache for "big bear") is only a quarter-mile north of the road. At 82 surface acres, it's much larger than Shush Be Zahze ("little bear") nearby.

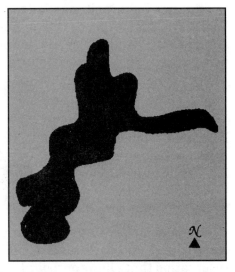

Species available include rainbow, brook, brown and Apache trout. Usually the best fishing is early in the spring and late in the fall, though real lunkers are relatively rare on this small impoundment.

At an elevation of 7,800 feet, the weather is cool even during the summer. High pines are the rule here, and just about the only thing that compromises this alpine experience is the herd of cattle that regularly grazes nearby.

Camping is allowed within walking distance of the water. Remember this is the White Mountain Apache Indian Reservation, and permits are required for both camping and fishing. For more information contact the White Mountain Apache Fish and Game Department by writing P.O. Box 220, Whiteriver, AZ 85941. Call 928/338-4385 or visit www.wmatoutdoors.com.

Sunrise Lake

Sunrise Lake is often called the best fishery resource on the White Mountain Apache Indian Reservation. Big fish in the 5-pound range regularly surrender here, although most anglers just go prepared to accept limiting out. Not a bad prospect!

For more information and permits, contact the White Mountain Apache Fish and Game Department by writing P.O. Box 220, Whiteriver, AZ 85941. Call 928/338-4385 or visit www.wmatoutdoors.com.

Sunrise also has a general store that rents boats with both electric and outboard motors. This is the only lake on the reservation that allows outboards, although they are limited to 10 horsepower. To reach this 900 surface acre lake, take State Route 260 east from McNary and turn south on State Route 273. The lake is just a few minutes away.

Camping is allowed, but again you need a permit. Campsites are at an elevation of 9,200 feet, so be prepared to battle the cold even in midsummer. There are 200 units available, but on holiday weekends they fill quickly.

Species available include rainbow, brook and Apache trout. Those elusive grayling also call Sunrise home, so you never know what's lurking below. Fishing here can be nothing short of spectacular. In early March 2000, one angler used a Kastmaster spoon to catch a five-fish limit of rainbow trout—the entire limit weighed a total of 22 pounds.

If you're fishing from a boat, troll the middle of the lake with cowbells. During the summer, fishermen who trail their cowbells with live nightcrawlers or green and brown flies can land at least one 3-pounder in a day. Anglers who work from the shore will find deep areas near the dam some of the most productive.

White River

Like many of Arizona's fishable rivers, the White River has a number of separate branches, each with different access points. The various areas also display slightly different characteristics as well, making this one of the White Mountains' most diverse and popular fishing areas.

The so-called "North Fork" of the White River has a total length of 50 miles and varies in elevation from 5,000 feet to 6,800 feet. Trout species available include Apache (though not a huge population), rainbow, brook, brown and cutthroat. By the time you reach Diamond Creek, expect a few catfish in your creel.

One of the easiest accesses to the White River is to take State Route 260 east from Pinetop-Lakeside and turn south on State Route 473. Here the river is relatively large, though not anything like the size it attains well downstream. As you make the turn toward Hawley Lake, you will cross the White River after a few hundred yards. There is plenty of parking there, the route is paved and the water is shallow enough to ford in many spots.

Another popular access is to take Upper Log Road. Again, take State Route 260 east from Pinetop-Lakeside, then just after McNary, turn south toward the logging ponds and west on Upper Log Road. The White River is just south of the road. You can also access it directly from State Route 73, toward the town of Whiteriver. Both routes are dirt. There are nearly two dozen campsites scattered along the river in this stretch. Roberts Ranch Road will also take you to the White River, though this access is also dirt.

The North Fork of the White River continues all the way into the city of Whiteriver and is exceptionally close to the road. You can probe the waterway for its finny residents through most of this area, though you must have a current White Mountain Apache fishing permit (so be sure to purchase one before going).

Lower Log Road will also take you into the North Fork of the White River. It is found on the east side of State Route 73, about 4 miles south of Hon Dah. There is no sign, so you need to turn toward Williams Creek National Hatchery, then after a mile of dirt beyond that point, follow the signs. Campsites are available downstream from the crossing, and the road is covered with cinders, making it accessible for nearly every vehicle.

The North Fork of the White "officially" ends at Fort Apache, where it joins the East Fork. Then the White works its way south and west to meet the Black. Where the Black and White rivers join, the Salt River begins. There is a naturally spawning population of trout in the White River, and from May to September the Apache Game and Fish Department stocks regularly from nearby Alchesay Hatchery.

The East Fork of the White River varies in elevation from 5,000 to 6,500 feet. To reach this section of the waterway, drive State Route 73 into Fort Apache. Turn east into the city until the road turns into Indian Route 8. The road crosses the river, and parallels it until you reach a closed area (many of the areas upstream are closed to non-Apaches to provide an enhanced environment for the Apache trout to spawn). It is paved as it follows the river.

Most of this river is stocked with native Apache trout. Occasionally you will also catch a brown or two. You never really know how big the fish are going to be here. In the early spring of 1992, the waterway surrendered a 10-pound rainbow and a 7-pound brown trout. The previous year, a 13.5-pound brown was also caught out of the White River.

Downstream from where the North and East forks of the White River meet, expect to catch more catfish and smallmouth bass. The closer you get to the Salt, the higher the percentage of these species you should expect.

Fishing this area requires a White Mountain Apache Indian Reservation permit. For more information contact the White Mountain Apache Fish and Game Department by writing P.O. Box 220, Whiteriver, AZ 85941. Call 928/338-4385 or visit www.wmatoutdoors.com.

Notable

1991, 13.5-pound brown trout
1992, 10-pound rainbow trout

Region Three

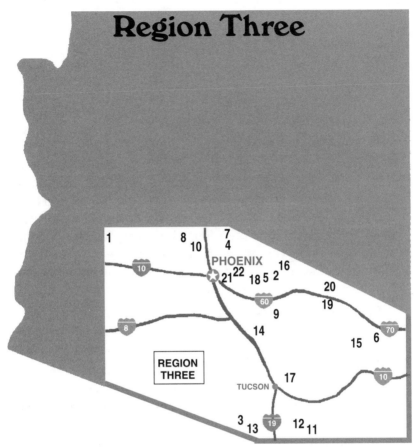

Region Three—Lakes & Rivers

Note: Maps are not to scale.

Alamo Lake

When the U.S. Army Corps of Engineers completed work on a 970-foot earthen dam on the Bill Williams River in 1968—where the Big Sandy and Santa Maria Rivers meet—it was primarily designed as a flood-control device. It didn't take long, however, for the Arizona Game and Fish Department to recognize the growing impoundment's sport fishing potential, and in less than a year it had already been stocked with largemouth bass.

Today, Alamo Lake's primary mission remains flood control, a fact highlighted by its ability to rise 11 feet overnight. Filled to capacity, it is capable of holding 1,043,000 acre-feet of potentially deadly water.

In 1969, the property for Alamo Lake State Park was acquired from a state land lease, and today the sprawling 8,400-acre complex, 30 miles east of the Colorado River, includes more than 250 campsites and the lake itself, which averages 3,200 surface acres. The park's generous facilities (which include RV hookups and even a shower), coupled with incredible fishing and almost-routine encounters with panhandling wild burros, make it one of the state's best-kept wintertime secrets.

The main reason Alamo is best visited in the winter is because its elevation—only 1,100 feet above sea level—makes it downright inhospitable in the summer. Daytime highs can hover near or above 110 by July. In December the high averages are somewhere around 65 degrees, and in January things "heat up" to 70.

As if temperature alone isn't enough to define Alamo Lake as a winter destination, consider the fact that it can also dwindle to 500 surface acres, or less, during the summer. Regardless of when you're going though, call ahead. Low water levels can also be a hazard in the winter. In February 2000, temporary docks had to be brought in to facilitate boat launching.

There is no restriction on boat motor size on Alamo Lake, and a pair of paved boat launches make it easy to get fishing, pleasure and ski boats on the water. As always, it's best to exercise caution at flood-control reservoirs like Alamo, due to often wildly fluctuating water levels. In fact, there are times when Alamo's average surface acreage routinely swells by 1,000 surface acres.

Alamo Lake's real attraction, however, is some of Arizona's premier largemouth bass and crappie action. The lake's reputation for surrendering lots of broad-shouldered largemouth bass is a hard-earned prize, thanks to aggressive management that historically has included a strictly enforced slot limit first enacted in the late 1980s. Its crappie reputation, however, is more of an accident, or nightmare, depending upon your point of view.

One look at the lake and you'll understand why it's named Alamo, which is Spanish for cottonwood. Partially or completely submerged trees are everywhere, providing nearly ideal cover for big largemouth bass to ambush unsuspecting meals.

In fact, this is one of the few lakes in Arizona where working timber from shore is not only possible, but often as effective as getting out in a boat. Some of the lake's more notable catches include a 7.78-pound largemouth bass caught on February 1, 2002, and a 4.86-pounder on March 17, 2002. Change your tactics to the cooler depths near the dam during the summer, and chartreuse spinnerbaits are always a good bet.

While Alamo is the site of one of Arizona's real success stories, it's also the site of what biologists at first considered a tragedy. Crappie were never stocked in the lake, nor were they seriously considered by state officials for residency. Somehow they've taken hold though—in a serious way. By the late 1990s and early in 2000, crappie were detected by the thousands, staging for the spawn in Alamo. They attracted anglers from throughout the Southwest to what has become a spring spectacle rivaled only on Roosevelt or Pleasant lakes. Just how good it has become is exemplified by the 2-pound, 5-ounce black crappie caught here on February 4, 2001.

The nearest lodging is slightly more than 30 miles away, so anglers interested in getting on the water early, or staying late, will find Alamo's varied camping a real advantage. For more information, current fees or conditions, Alamo State Park can be reached by calling 928/669-2088. You can also visit the Arizona State Parks website at www.pr.state.az.us or write the Alamo State Park, P.O. Box 38, Wenden, AZ 85357.

Don't despair if you forget anything. Alamo Lake Store has all those last-minute oversights, gas and even boat rentals. For more information visit www.azod.com/webs/lakealamostore or call 928/925-0133.

Alamo Lake also has a population of bullheads, a fish many people mistakenly throw back as stunted catfish. Channel and flathead catfish can also be caught. Flatheads are most prevalent in the 2- to 3-pound range, although an occasional 10-pounder surfaces.

You can also expect to catch carp, bluegill, tilapia, green sunfish and redear sunfish. If you bring your children along, give them some dough bait made of rolled-up slices of bread with a little garlic or Velveeta cheese, and they'll soon be busy taking carp off their hooks.

Add another uninvited resident, striped bass, and it's little wonder so many claim Alamo as their favorite Arizona fishing hole. A 23-pound, 8.32-ounce striped bass caught here on May 3, 1997, stood as the state's inland waters record.

To get to Alamo Lake, take I-10 west toward Blythe, turn north at the Vicksburg turnoff, turn right on U.S. Route 60 to Wenden and follow the signs. For more on fishing conditions call the Arizona Game and Fish Department at 602/789-3701 or visit www.azgfd.com.

Notable

    May 3, 1997, 23-pound, 8.32-ounce striped bass
    February 4, 2001, 2-pound, 5-ounce black crappie
    February 1, 2002, 7.78-pound largemouth bass
    February 2002, 2.79-pound black crappie

Apache Lake

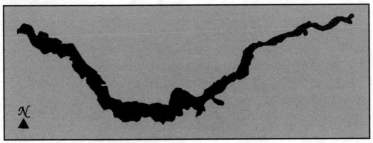

Despite its proximity to Phoenix—only 63 miles northeast–Apache Lake is the least visited of Arizona's Salt River chain of lakes. The notorious reputation of Fish Creek Hill, on Apache Trail between the lake and Apache Junction, may be mainly to blame. It's certainly not the fishing.

Arguably one of Arizona's most scenic hideaways, Apache Lake is worth a visit for the views alone. Add world-class fishing that includes a chance at walleye, and it's little wonder Apache Lake is garnering an enviable reputation nationwide.

At nearly 17 miles long, with 41.5 miles of shore and the capacity to impound 2,600 surface acres when full, Apache Lake has taught anglers more than a few new tricks in its 80-year history. It may well be the most diverse waterway in the entire Southwest, combining traditional fare—like largemouth and smallmouth bass—with an incredible cold-water fishery.

A February 2001 fish survey by the Arizona Game and Fish Department, near shore in less than 30 feet of water, yielded more than 140 walleye in less than two hours. Almost all of the walleye were 17 to 19 inches in length.

Big walleye aren't anything new to Apache. A 1991 winter fish survey—by both electro-shocking and netting—produced a walleye sampling nearly eight times heavier than in previous years. Of the 24 walleye in the survey, two weighed more than 9 pounds, eight weighed more than 8 pounds, ten weighed from 6 to 6.5 pounds, two were 5 to 5.5 pounds and the pair of

World-class fishing garners a nationwide reputation for Apache Lake.

"lightweights" tipped the scales at 4.5 pounds. These walleye were found in 25 to 35 feet of water, on major points. It didn't take long for the Arizona Game and Fish Department to decide that stocking walleye was a good idea. The June 2000 stocking of nearly 80,000 sac fry walleye is considered average today.

The same 1991 survey confirmed another cold-water species was thriving in Apache. Trout stocked a few years earlier were growing fast, averaging 19.5 inches in length and tipping the scales at 2 pounds. The survey also reported a number of 4- and 5-pound trout. Biologists started to rethink Apache Lake's management, especially when, in July 1991, rainbow trout fry were discovered in Alder Creek Canyon.

While not exactly earth-shattering news, it was an important discovery because Arizona typically lacks enough streams to produce trout at the rate they are caught. Nearly every trout in the state has been hatchery reared. Biologists estimated the naturally occurring spawn in Apache was a "once in a decade" occurrence. Yet it spoke volumes about the future of this lightly pressured fishery, its untapped potential and, perhaps more importantly, the success of the 1989 stocking of 113,396 Kamloop- and McConaughy-strain rainbow trout.

By 2000 though, conditions forced Arizona Game and Fish to discontinue managing Apache Lake as a trout fishery. While the effort is the kind of thing legends are built upon—especially with the kind of lunkers the lake regularly produced—rainbow trout have not been stocked in Apache Lake for a number of years prior to this book's printing.

According to creel surveys by the Game and Fish Department, bluegill and sunfish are the most caught of this lake's finny residents, with largemouth bass a close second. April and May were the best months to catch walleye. With an average depth of 240 feet, Apache Lake annually yields some huge catfish. You never know what's lurking in the depths either. On June 19, 2002, a 40-pound, 5-ounce black buffalo was caught. Of course, big black buffalo aren't really news here. In 1998, a 31-pound, 1.8-ouncer was caught here and on August 9, 1991, a 22.5-pounder.

There are enough "flats" in this lake to support spawning populations of crappie and yellow bass, which are schooling fish—if you catch one, cast into the same area and hang on. A 1-pound, 13.6-ounce yellow bass was caught here by an angler in March 2000, narrowly missing what was then the state record.

And don't forget carp. Arizona's annual Carp Camp, which was held on Apache in May 2000, yielded some huge stringers. The biggest lunker caught was 15.5 pounds, and all totaled, the "average" fish landed weighed more than 5 pounds.

But it's largemouth and smallmouth bass that bring anglers back. The lake is literally lined with the cliffy rubble that lends cover to the aggressive predators. In March 1990, a 10.71-pound largemouth bass was caught here, and the lake surrendered an 11.73-pounder on June 2, 1991. Despite a thriving population of walleye, things have only gotten better. More recent notable largemouths include a 7.63-pounder caught on February 26, 2000, an 8.64-pounder on March 25, 2000, and on July 28, 2001, a 9.88-pounder was caught. In 2002 alone, a 7.01-pound largemouth was caught on February 9; a 7.59-pounder was boated in June; and 8.21-, 8.05- and 8.19-pounders were caught in August.

Good-sized smallmouth bass are regularly caught on Apache Lake, and on July 6, 2002, a 5-pounder surrendered to a blue-and-white crankbait.

Apache Lake, at an elevation of 1,900 feet, can be near the 100-degree mark in the summer. Camping is allowed on the lake, including several sites near the resort. For more information contact Apache Lake Resort by writing P.O. Box 15627 Apache Lake, Tortilla Flat, AZ 85920 or call 928/467-2511. You can also visit www.apachelake.com.

Daily water flows here and everywhere else on Salt River Project waterways can be monitored at www.srpnet.com/water/daily. For more information on Apache Lake write the Tonto Basin Ranger District, HCO2 P.O. Box 4800, Roosevelt, AZ 85545, call 928/467-3200 or visit www.fs.fed.us/r3/tonto. For more on fishing information, contact the Arizona Game and Fish Department. Call 480/981-9400 or visit www.azgfd.com.

There is no limit to boat motor size on Apache Lake, but you rarely see many skiers or pleasure boaters. The paved boat launch near the resort is kept in extremely good shape, as is the one at Burnt Corral.

To get to Apache Lake, take the Apache Trail (State Route 88) north from Apache Junction. Be forewarned though, you'll be traversing that notorious unpaved section of Fish Creek Hill. A much easier route is to go east on U.S. Route 60. Just before Globe, turn north on State Route 88 which takes you to Roosevelt Lake's dam. From there, follow State Route 88 west (it becomes a dirt road at this point) to the lake. It's roughly 36 miles from Globe, or 29 from Apache Junction.

Notable
March 1990, 10.71-pound largemouth bass
June 2, 1991, 11.73-pound largemouth bass
1998, 31-pound, 1.8-ounce black buffalo
March 2000, 1-pound, 13.6-ounce yellow bass
May 2000, 15.5-pound carp
January 13, 2001, 4-pound, 0.48-ounce smallmouth bass
July 28, 2001, 9.88-pound largemouth bass
December 10, 2001, 18-pound, 2.88-ounce channel catfish
June 19, 2002, 40-pound, 5-ounce black buffalo
July 6, 2002, 5-pound smallmouth bass

Arivaca Lake

For a unique combination of fishing and history, Arivaca Lake is one of those destinations you have to visit at least once. Located an hour south of Tucson, Arivaca Lake can be reached by taking I-19 south and turning west at the Arivaca turnoff. Don't be in any great hurry though. The road is full of curves and passes through some of southern Arizona's richest history.

From the city of Arivaca, turn left at the junction, then follow the signs. Ignore the legends of bars of hidden silver somewhere in the few remaining crumbling adobe houses in town, unless of course, you enjoy these kinds of stories. Follow the paved road for about 7 more miles and turn left at the sign. The last mile or so is dirt, but typically easily negotiable by recreational vehicles.

Originally purchased by the Arizona Game and Fish Department in 1959, Arivaca Lake's 90 surface acres—when full—barely resemble the 12-acre impoundment originally created by area ranchers. At an elevation of 3,750 feet, it's hot enough during the summer to be quite uncomfortable, although it's a great place during cooler months.

It didn't take long for Arivaca Lake's largemouth bass reputation to grow after the original stocking of some 3,000 fingerlings in 1970. Within a few years, Tucson's outdoor pages were filled with stories of 11- and 12-pounders from the waterway, and news of an incredible spring topwater bite would attract flyfishermen from California, New Mexico and Nevada.

It may be small, but its largemouth bass action is legendary, or at least it was until the summer of 1999. That's when the heat, sun and the unusually fertile waters (which have always been noted for growing large fish quickly) combined to generate an algae bloom that literally sucked all of the oxygen from the water. As a result, what was arguably southern Arizona's premier largemouth bass fishery saw most of its finny residents suffocate overnight.

Surveys by the Arizona Game and Fish Department a month later showed only a very few small fish—in the 2-inch range or smaller—had survived. Even by the summer of 2000, fish larger than 12 inches in length were still not being sampled. Predictions that 2-pounders would be caught by that fall proved premature, particularly after a series of smaller fish kills that continued through the summer.

By October 2002, thanks to aggressive management, a newly enacted catch-and-release rule and Arivaca's fertile water, things had turned around. Largemouth bass that tipped the scales as high as 4.5 pounds were again being caught.

Of course, the lake still had a long way to go before being considered back to normal. It has a history of yielding 8- and 9-pounders, and 10-pounders surfaced every spring until the 1999 disaster struck. In September 1992, a 10-pound largemouth bass was caught at Arivaca by a fisherman working a Sluggo (a floating worm) just above the weedline. A 28-inch, 11-pound, 8-ouncer was caught here in 1984. Even during the winter, bass fishing stayed good, as evidenced by the 8.5-pounder caught on January 1, 1993.

The lake's woes really began back in the mid 1990s when the Arizona Department of Environmental Quality discovered mercury was somehow seeping into the water, and ultimately into the fish. As a result, a health advisory was issued warning anglers not to consume any fish caught at Arivaca Lake.

There are no developed campsites at Arivaca Lake, no

drinking water, no electric hookups for RVs and no daily fees. The only facility here is a pit toilet. Since this is one of southern Arizona's truly under-utilized lakes, there is usually plenty of room to camp, and an upper parking lot ensures parking on all but the busiest holiday weekends. Arrive early and you may be able to get a spot right next to the water.

A thick weedline will all but encircle the lake by summer's end (another byproduct of that fertile water), making shoreline fishing tough or impossible in many spots. When the weeds get heaviest it's the best time to visit with a boat. The largemouth tend to congregate along the outer edge of the weeds, and early in the morning and late in the evening the topwater action is often best described as incredible.

Many anglers swear the best way to land a lunker largemouth is to "walk a rat" across the top of these thick weeds. Basically, walking a rat is a method of tossing a rat imitation on top of a thick weedline, then slowly working it back toward your boat or the shoreline. Usually the lunker will swell up from the protective structure to hit your offering.

In April 1983, a Tucson angler set what was then the inland waters state record by catching a 31-pound 10-ounce channel catfish at Arivaca. Though that record fell in 1987, catfishing remained phenomenal until the kill-off. Over the years Arivaca has held the state record for redear sunfish three times.

Arivaca Lake has a boat launch, although boat propulsion is restricted to electric motors or oars. Considering how small the lake is, that doesn't present much of a problem.

This lake is managed by the Tucson office of the Arizona Game and Fish Department. For up-to-date reports call 520/628-5376 or visit www.azgfd.com.

Notable
April 1983, 31-pound, 10-ounce channel catfish
1984, 11-pound, 8-ounce largemouth bass
September 1992, 10-pound largemouth bass
January 1, 1993, 8.5-pound largemouth bass

Here's my favorite piece of local lore:

The Legend of Cerro Colorado's Silver Mine

Arivaca Lake is near the crumbling ruins of the town of Cerro Colorado. During the 1860s, one of the Cerro Colorado mines was the largest silver producer in southern Arizona.

Then came the unexplained cave-in.

Mine supervisors routinely separated workers into Hispanic and Native American groups to help relieve racial tension and overcome language barriers. Unfortunately, when the walls of the silver mine came tumbling down, more than a dozen Native Americans were trapped and killed. Their bodies were never recovered, and the unmarked wreck of a mine stands as a gruesome monument to those who died—their bodies still interred.

The surviving Native Americans, who suspected their Hispanic counterparts had a hand in the fatal cave-in, vowed revenge and slowly drifted back into the desert.

Morale deteriorated steadily and hit an all-time low when the mine foreman was called away and his younger, allegedly meaner, brother was left in charge. Soon after, most of the work force had deserted to relative safety south of the border.

One fateful afternoon, one of the few remaining Hispanic shift supervisors was caught red-handed smuggling silver out of the mining camp. He was made an example for the other workers, who were all lined up and forced to watch as he was executed. Within the next few weeks the remaining Hispanic workers, fearing for their safety, fled across the border. The only people left in the once-busy town of Cerro Colorado were the merciless foreman and two German supervisors.

All three men were mysteriously murdered and buried near the town, and it is said that $30,000 in silver remains hidden somewhere in the gently rolling countryside nearby. Some say the killers were banditos who had heard of the missing silver, while others insist it was the group of vengeful ex-miners with a long memory. Either way, the results were the same.

To find Cerro Colorado, take the paved road from I-19 toward the town of Arivaca. Slow down at mile marker 9 and turn right on the dirt road behind the Circle 46 Ranch mailbox. Within a quarter mile, the surprisingly well-preserved grave of the foreman, Poston, is easy to see on the left. You can see the ruins of Cerro Colorado by walking up the hill behind the grave.

Bartlett Lake

Bartlett Lake, fed by the Verde River, may be smaller than most of central Arizona's reservoirs, but its fishy waters put it on par with the others. It averages from 1,130 to 2,000 surface acres and has roughly 33 miles of shoreline.

Historically the only drawback to Bartlett was the fact that access was via an 11-mile dirt road. In the 1990s the U.S. Forest Service began paving the last 6 miles. Combined with a 500-boat marina, an improved boat ramp and a distance of only 48 miles from Phoenix, the lake's renewed prominence was ensured.

Species of fish available in Bartlett include largemouth bass, crappie, sunfish, channel catfish, carp, an occasional smallmouth bass and once in a while a northern pike. In addition, flathead catfish were introduced to the lake in the 1970s, and they now flourish in its waters (average depth is 100 feet), especially in deep areas along the north shore of the lake where 30-pounders are regularly caught. Crappie too can grow pretty large here, and in February 2001 a 2.5-pound specimen was caught at the lake, and a 1-pound, 6-ounce black crappie caught on July 18, 2000, was the state's Big Fish of the Year for that species.

Larger fish are relatively common, with an April 2000 catch a good example: The 68-pound, 8-ounce flathead catfish caught on Bartlett was 52-inches long and had a girth of 34-inches. Yes, flatheads have taken hold in Bartlett in an amazing way.

Some of the best areas for largemouth bass are along the east shoreline where they often hold tight to the salt cedars. While huge bass are moderately scarce here, catches like the

September 2000, 5.83- and 5.66-pounders; July 2002's 6.03-pounder; and October 12, 2002's 5.34-pounder are common. Another good technique for largemouth is to try any of the coves early in the morning for topwater action in the fall or spring. You can also use a threadfin shad imitation, a forage species added to the lake by the Arizona Game and Fish Department.

During the late 1980s and early 1990s, Anglers United, a non-profit conservation organization dedicated to improving fishing in Arizona, collected smallmouth bass from the Black River and transported them by helicopter to Bartlett Lake's ideal-for-breeding rocky structure. The effort worked, and today the lake has a decent population of smallies that are a pretty good bet during the winter.

To get to Bartlett Lake, take the paved road east out of Cave Creek and follow the signs. The lake's elevation of 1,600 feet means hot weather in the summer. Camping is available in a number of locations and is managed by the Tonto National Forest. For more information contact its headquarters, 2324 E. McDowell Road, Phoenix, AZ 85006, 602/225-5200. Or visit www.fs.fed.us/r3/tonto. The area is open year-round.

For a number of years talk circulated that Bartlett would yield the state's next record catfish. The lake has both channel cats and flatheads. From March to May, the catfish here make an annual spawning run up the Verde River, conveniently concentrating themselves for anglers. You can locate them in the deeper pockets, where they lay their eggs.

For the bigger catfish, use live bait such as small carp, bluegills or sunfish. Many anglers who use this system claim bigger flatheads prefer bluegills (check current regulations).

A live bluegill rig starts with a 9-0 hook attached to one of two 24-inch leaders. Place a two-ounce sliding sinker on the leader with the hook. It will allow the fish to swim up, down and of course sideways to attract foraging catfish. On the other leader, at a distance you consider proper for the depth you're working, place a large bobber to indicate strikes. The fish will stay alive forever if you hook the bluegill just under the dorsal fin on its back without hurting it.

How well does it work? On October 18, 1991, at 3 A.M., anglers using this live bluegill rig landed a pair of flatheads on Bartlett that tipped the scales at 62 and 45 pounds. And the big catfish are still there. On September 20, 2002, a 57-pound flathead was also caught at Bartlett. Of course, Bartlett surrendered what was Arizona's inland record carp, a 37-pound monster on August 8, 1987—so there is at least one good reason to brave the heat.

Remember, Bartlett's threadfin shad are a major food source for game fish. Any time you see a group of threadfin shad breaking the water, you can assume there's a "big" fish lunching on them. Throw a crankbait right in the middle of the watery explosion and hang on!

For more information contact the Mesa office of the Arizona Game and Fish Department: 480/981-9400. For a current fishing report visit www.azgfd.com or call 602/789-3701.

Notable
August 8, 1987, 37-pound carp
October 18, 1991, 62-pound flathead catfish
April 2000, 68-pound, 8-ounce flathead catfish
July 18, 2000, 1-pound, 6-ounce black crappie
February 2001, 2.5-pound black crappie
February 2002, 2.96-pound black crappie
September 20, 2002, 57-pound flathead catfish

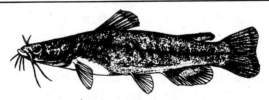

Flathead Catfish
Non-native. Back and sides mottled, dark-brown to yellow-brown; belly is yellowish-white. Head is broad and flat with small eyes. Large mouth, lower jaw projecting beyond the upper jaw. Adipose fin is large; tail fin is flat or slightly notched.

Canyon Lake

For years people theorized Canyon Lake could be the home of Arizona's heaviest largemouth bass—a suspicion reinforced a few years ago after an "angler" officially weighed a 15-pound monster from there. It didn't take long for authorities to become suspicious of the construction worker who, as it turned out, had used a quarter-inch stick of dynamite to boat the lunker. As a result, his name is not in the record books, and his wallet is a little thinner after paying a $1,000 fine.

A few speculated this fish was either a pure Florida-strain largemouth bass or the result of interbreeding. The Arizona Game and Fish Department had planted 500 Florida-strain largemouth here during the 1970s and another 2,000 fingerlings in 1972. However, fisheries biologists insisted the fish, now hanging in the Mesa Game and Fish Office, was not a Florida-strain bass or even a hybrid.

All discussion of that particular fish came to a screeching halt on December 3, 1991, when 19-year-old Matt Shura from Gilbert caught a 15.86-pound largemouth bass at Canyon Lake, eclipsing the old state record by a full pound.

Shura caught the fish in only three feet of water, despite a winter storm. He used a 3/8-ounce white-with-silver-flake spinnerbait so close to the marina that he worried the lunker would become entangled in the dock's wire.

Shura's catch was eclipsed, again at Canyon Lake, on April 22, 1997, when Randall E. White caught a 16-pound, 7.68-ounce largemouth bass. Other big largemouth bass that have been caught here include a 13-pound, 10-ouncer caught in 13 feet of water on a black-and-chartreuse worm. A 14-pound, 9.6-ouncer, caught March 26, 2000, was Big Fish of the Year. In February 2001, a 12-pounder was caught on a Basstrix and another 11-pound largemouth surrendered to a jig. More recently, an 11.23-pound largemouth was caught on June 22, 2002, a 10-pound, 4.16-ouncer on August 15, 2002, and a 12-pounder surrendered to a shad-colored crankbait on October 14, 2002.

Big largemouth surfacing with regularity is nothing new on Canyon though. A 13.86-pounder was caught in July 1990. It surrendered to a 4-inch red-and-purple worm in less than 2 feet of water. This fish was caught near some cliffs and was nosed into a small ledge.

More recently, what would have been a new record from Canyon wound up being added to the Arizona Game and Fish Department's relatively new catch-and-release records. Calculated by the fish's measurements, this unusual program allows an angler to photograph and measure a fish, releasing it unharmed. This particular largemouth bass was caught February 21, 2002, and tipped official scales at a record-shattering 17.46 pounds. Because the lunker was transported live for official weighing, it was disqualified. However, using the catch-and-release calculations, which it did qualify for, it has been listed as a 22-pound, 4.8-ouncer.

Night fishermen always find the lake productive. In August 1992, a pair of 12-pound bucketmouths were caught during the night, on rockpiles submerged in 25 feet of water, by fishermen using brown-and-purple jigs. Consider the fact that a 14-pound, 8-ounce largemouth was caught and released at Canyon Lake in July 1999—and it leaves little question as to just how big the fish are at Canyon.

In fall and winter the largemouth usually go deep, although you'd never know it by where the former state record was caught. Start by probing the depths around 20 feet; at times the largemouth will even hold in 40 feet of water.

At one time the state inland waters record for yellow bass was also set at Canyon Lake. On June 3, 1985, a 1-pound, 11-

ounce specimen was caught here. On May 19, 1995, that record was broken by a 1-pound, 15.8-ouncer caught on Upper Lake Mary. A 35-pound, 6.72-ounce black buffalo was caught here on May 24, 1995, which was the inland waters record for Arizona at the time.

Canyon Lake was created when the Salt River Project built Mormon Flats Dam in 1925. Today, the lake totals 926 surface acres and has an average depth of 130 feet. Obviously, the water flooded a rather steep canyon, as the average depth indicates. There are 28 miles of shoreline.

Species available at Canyon include rainbow trout (stocked from November to March), largemouth bass, smallmouth bass, yellow bass, crappie, sunfish, channel catfish and—believe it or not—walleye. Because Canyon Lake is deep enough to stay cool year-round, you never know how big that fish on the end of your line is going to be until you land it.

According to the Game and Fish Department, walleye in Canyon Lake range from the main basin all the way down to the lower channel (they were originally stocked in the mid-60s). In July 1991, in something of a rare occurrence, the walleye began feeding regularly in the shallows and beaches. According to Game and Fish, most of the walleye were 20 inches long and tipped the scales at between 1.75 and 2.0 pounds. At the time they were being landed with heavy-action lures or spinnerbaits at dusk.

Game and Fish creel surveys indicate bluegills are the most harvested fish at Canyon at 42 percent. Largemouth bass follow at 33 percent. Bluegills are most easily caught in the summer and fall, with rainbow trout accounting for most of the fish taken in winter and early spring. In February 1993, a 6.9-pound rainbow trout was caught here. Kamloop trout originally slated for Apache Lake were dumped into Canyon Lake during that same month.

The best time to visit Canyon (elevation 1,660 feet) is during the spring or fall. There are plenty of camping areas near the lake. For more information you can contact the Tonto National Forest, 2324 E. McDowell Road, Phoenix, AZ 85006,

602/225-5200. You can also visit www.fs.fed.us/r3/tonto. For up-to-date fishing conditions, call 602/789-3701 or go to www.azgfd.com.

To reach Canyon Lake, take Apache Trail (State Route 88) north from Apache Junction for about 13 miles.

Notable

June 3, 1985, 1-pound, 11-ounce yellow bass
July 1990, 13.86-pound largemouth bass
February 1993, 6.9-pound rainbow trout
May 24, 1995, 35-pound, 6.72-ounce black buffalo
April 22, 1997, 16-pound, 7.68-ounce largemouth bass
March 26, 2000, 14-pound, 9.6-ounce largemouth bass
June 14, 2001, 16-pound, 1.12-ounce largemouth bass
December 29, 2001, 16-pound, 0.16-ounce largemouth bass
(catch-and-release)
February 21, 2002, 22-pound, 4.8-ounce largemouth bass
(catch-and-release)
April 2002, 10-pound rainbow trout (on a small Castaic trout bait)
May 2002, 10-pound largemouth (along a canyon wall, with a jig in 15 feet of water)
August 15, 2002, 10-pound, 4.16-ounce largemouth bass
October 14, 2002, 12-pound largemouth bass
December 2002, 14-pound, 0-ounce largemouth bass (catch-and-release)

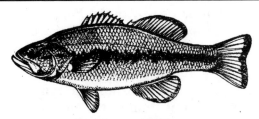

Largemouth Bass
Non-native. Large mouth with upper jaw of adults extending beyond rear margin of eye. Dark olive-green on back, green sides shading to white belly. Dark horizontal band on each side. Deep notch in dorsal fin. Soft dorsal fin with 12 to 13 rays.

Dankworth Pond

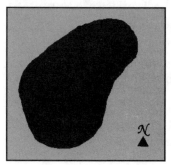

Dankworth Pond is part of the Dankworth/Roper Lake State Park unit and is located only 8 miles south of Safford off of U.S. Route 191. Dankworth Pond may only impound abut 10 surface acres, but it's an important fishery for the region's anglers.

Originally the area was owned by a Mr. Dankworth, who used six smaller ponds in the area to raise fish. Once the state took over, the smaller ponds were allowed to go dry, and management of the larger pond (10-acre Dankworth) began.

Unfortunately, by May 1992, more than half of Dankworth was covered in cattails. As a result, fishing for the resident largemouth bass, crappie, sunfish and channel catfish had become nearly impossible.

To remedy the situation, the Arizona Game and Fish Department drained the lake into many of the old ponds. The effort at killing off the cattail population was relatively effective, and while the lake was dry, artificial structure was added to enhance habitat.

Camping is allowed nearby in the Roper State Park unit, and the facilities are excellent. For more information on camping or facilities, visit www.pr.state.az.us or call the park at 928/428-6760.

During the winter or early spring, you'll discover why many southern Arizonans count Dankworth among the state's best winter experiences. An elevation of only 3,100 feet can make summer visits uncomfortable, though you can expect December temperatures to average slightly above 61 degrees.

For current fishing conditions call the Arizona Game and Fish Department at 602/789-3701 or visit www.azgfd.com.

Horseshoe Lake

Located just north of Phoenix, Horseshoe Lake impounds the Verde River upstream of Bartlett. It usually holds 790 surface acres of water, although its service as a flood-control device can see it swell to 2,700 surface acres. Its elevation is only 2,200 feet above sea level, so it can fall victim to pretty warm summertime temperatures, and on occasion it dwindles to a mere pool—or less. In fact, a November 2002 Game and Fish report listed the lake as "empty."

When it has water, this lake is managed as a warmwater fishery, and you can expect to catch largemouth bass, smallmouth bass, crappie, channel and flathead catfish and several kinds of sunfish. A 3-pound, 2-ounce black crappie caught at Horseshoe was the largest black crappie caught in the state (or at least reported), during 1999, so you never know what's going to answer the dinner bell.

You should always check conditions prior to leaving. Call the Arizona Game and Fish Department at 602/789-3701 for up-to-date information before you leave or visit www.azgfd.com. Camping is permitted in certain areas, though not much is developed. For more information contact the Tonto National Forest by calling 602/225-5200 or visit www.fs.fed.us/r3/tonto.

To reach Horseshoe Lake, take I-17 north out of Phoenix and turn east on Carefree Highway (Exit 223). Turn north about six miles beyond the Camp Creek turnoff. The directions to the lake are well-signed, and for obvious reasons, during most of the summer season you can usually follow the traffic.

Horsethief Basin

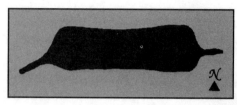

In the early 1930s, Phoenix, like the rest of the nation, was caught firmly in the grips of the Great Depression. People in the "Valley" area needed a nearby spot to rest, relax and forget their troubles.

The city of Phoenix tried to help remedy the problem by working to create a park nearly 70 miles away. This wasn't an ordinary park though. It featured cabins, an independent water system and campgrounds. The Horsethief Basin recreation area was created by the Civilian Conservation Corps, a federally managed program during the depression designed to put people back to work.

The entire park was created near the then-aging town of Crown King. Located in Prescott National Forest, north of Phoenix, it was close to the pines and offered views incredible enough to guarantee visitors even today.

In the 1960s, the recreation area was turned over to Prescott National Forest. The most eloquent statement on yesteryear's craftsmanship is the fact that everything is still functional, even the water system. There's even a tennis court.

Horsethief Basin Lake was also created during the '30s project. Today it covers a total of 3 surface acres at an average depth of 10 feet. Unfortunately, there's so much algae and other organic growth in the water that oxygen levels below ten feet are literally unlivable for most fish. Every so often, the lake's total oxygen level can reach a level low enough to suffer a kill-off. Vegetation covers nearly 80 percent of the shoreline, and consists mostly of cattails.

According to the Arizona Game and Fish Department, largemouth bass were first stocked here in 1960. Channel catfish arrived in 1965 and 1966. In 1975, surveys found black crappie and bluegill in the lake as well.

In the late 1970s, the lake was drained and dredged, and the Game and Fish Department stocked largemouth bass, channel catfish and sunfish. In 1987, even though a few people were pushing for rainbow trout to be stocked in the lake, the Game and Fish Department decided against it. According to Game and Fish, the oxygen levels were too low at the lake's lowest levels and water temperature was typically too high.

It may be a relatively small impoundment, but some big fish have come from its waters, including a 5-pound largemouth in the spring of 1992. The lake is often stocked every other year, although it, like many of the state's lesser lakes, may well fall victim to environmental concerns.

In November 1992, a stocking of 6-inch channel catfish took place. An aerator system was also being planned in conjunction with the Forest Service, which would effectively make those lower reaches of the lake livable for fish species.

To get to Horsethief Basin, take I-17 north out of Phoenix, and take the Bumble Bee/Crown King turnoff. Take Forest Service Road 259 to Crown King, then Forest Service Road 259A south to Forest Service Road 52. Go southeast about 6 miles to the lake. All of the Forest Service roads are dirt. The total trip is just over 40 miles from the north edge of Phoenix.

This lake's elevation (6,000 feet) guarantees cooler weather in the summer and it can get down to some pretty chilly temperatures the rest of the year.

For more information contact Prescott National Forest by writing, 344 South Cortez Street, Prescott, AZ 86303 or call 928/443-8000. You can also visit www.fs.fed.us/r3/prescott.

Note: At time of publication, this lake was not open to the public; call for details.

Kearny Park Lake

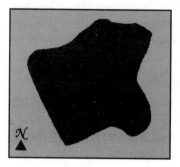

Strategically located on State Route 177 between Winkelman and Superior, the city of Kearny receives little attention. Of course, that's the way area anglers like it—Kearny Park Lake as their own little-known secret.

At 13 surface acres, Kearny Park Lake was created after the disastrous flooding of October 1983. After a major portion of the existing park was swept away, officials decided they would create a lake, stock it with fish and charge people to probe the depths with rod and reel.

Unfortunately, monies available to create such a reservoir also carry stipulations that the area must be a public fishery. Today, the area is managed by the Kearny Parks Department, and it's the city's only park. There is a day-use-only picnic area, a boat launch and a camping facility with 12 campsites.

The small impoundment doesn't even qualify for the Urban Fishing Program, thanks to a little-known rule regarding city populations. Under that program, a population of 25,000 is required to live nearby, clearly above the combined 20,000 that call Mammoth, Superior, Winkelman and Kearny home.

In other words, Kearny Park Lake is open to anglers who have a current Arizona fishing license. It is stocked from November to March with catchable-sized rainbow trout. Other species available include largemouth bass, catfish and, of course, sunfish. Boats are allowed on the lake, although motors are limited to electric trolling motors.

Be sure to check water quality prior to leaving; due to water-quality issues, Kearny Park Lake missed several stockings during the winter of 2002-2003. For up-to-date information call 602/789-3701 or visit www.azgfd.com.

Lake Pleasant

Lake Pleasant was created in 1927 when Waddell Dam impounded a portion of the Agua Fria River northwest of Phoenix. The lake is named after Carl Pleasant, the engineer who designed the dam. Its proximity to Phoenix makes Pleasant one of Arizona's most popular water recreation sites.

From Phoenix, take I-17 north out of the Valley and turn west on State Route 74, also known as the Carefree Highway.

Historically, Pleasant was only capable of holding 3,000 surface acres of water, but after the dam's modification in the 90s, it routinely swelled to 10,200. The minimum guaranteed pool on Pleasant is now 1,400 surface acres, and it is possible the lake's level will vary by as much as 120 vertical feet during the course of a year.

When Central Arizona Project water began to be added to the lake, it inundated most of the old facilities. The Bureau of Reclamation has added three multi-lane boat ramps, 450 picnic sites, 225 campsites, 4 view sites (the Waddell Dam overlook is already one of the most scenic in the entire state), 14 group-use sites, a full-service station and concession facilities with a price tag of more than $18.5 million.

Undoubtedly, Pleasant is not only one of the state's most user-friendly lake facilities, it's arguably Arizona's best warmwater fishery. In fact, a survey conducted in 2001 indicated it was now home to the most angling pressure in the entire state of Arizona.

Surveys conducted by the Arizona Game and Fish Department in 1993 indicated stripers had not yet entered Pleasant. However, as a prophylactic measure (many bass fishermen feel the presence of stripers will hurt the lake's largemouth bass), the department suspended striper limits on Pleasant. It wasn't long until stripers started showing up on stringers, including a chunky 7.25-pounder caught in August 2000 that surrendered to a live shad in 25 feet of water and a 15-pound, 2-ouncer on October 13 of the same year.

By April 2002, anglers were catching striped bass with eggs in them, indicating they were going into the spawn. However, Arizona Game and Fish announced that upon inspection of the fish, the eggs were being "reabsorbed," rather than dropped. Gill nets were set out to sample for possible fingerlings, and the impact, if any, striped bass will have on Pleasant's largemouth bass is yet to be determined.

Species of fish identified in a 2001 Lake Pleasant survey include common carp, red shiner, threadfin shad, channel catfish, flathead catfish, green sunfish, bluegill, redear sunfish, hybrid sunfish, largemouth bass, white bass, striped bass, golden shiner, white crappie, black crappie and tilapia. Add the state record pacu, a 5-pound monster caught here on September 8, 1999, and few waterways can compare to Pleasant's diversity.

Lake Pleasant is also home to Arizona's only real white bass population, and thus holds the state inland waters record. The record-setting fish, caught in April 1972, came from the upper end of the lake and weighed in at 4 pounds, 11.7 ounces.

White bass were first introduced to Lake Pleasant in the 1960s when the Game and Fish Department decided to give anglers a more diversified resource. A white bass looks much like a small striper, which really made things confusing once the first striper was caught. Add the fact that stripers and whites can interbreed, resulting in "hybrids," and you may need a biology degree to figure out exactly what you caught.

When the summer heat begins, try trolling deep for this particular fish. At night and early in the morning, the schooling fish can often be seen "boiling" on threadfin shad. Look for explosions and commotion on the surface of the water and you'll be into a group of white bass. Move quickly though, since the action is usually short-lived.

Once you locate a school, use small spinners, shad-imitating crankbaits or spoons. Smart anglers who get into those thick schools will find the action literally non-stop. Remember, white bass are much like crappie, and although they stay pretty much together in huge groups, they do roam the lake freely. A high-quality depth finder can help, and when all else fails use a small jig at various depths as you drift across the water. Fishing is great for whites, and on April 15, 2000, a 2-pound, 9.12-ouncer caught at Pleasant was Big Fish of the Year.

The largemouth bass fishing on Lake Pleasant turned incredible once the waterway increased in size. Largemouth bass in the 10-13 pound range have been caught here for years. Lures that have worked for recent giants include a chartreuse Bomber, a crayfish, a black Berkley Power Worm and a Yamamoto curly-tailed grub.

If that's not enough to send you packing to Pleasant, consider the phone call the Arizona Game and Fish Department received in August 1992. It seems the Sheriff's substation had just weighed a 16.2-pound largemouth, caught at Pleasant, which would have easily eclipsed the state record. Because the Sheriff's scale was not certified, they sent the angler packing for the nearest state-certified scale. Unfortunately, that fisherman, and fish, were never heard from again. Then Public Information Officer for the Arizona Game and Fish Department, Rory Aikens, theorized the lunker lost too much weight on the way to an official scale.

Things haven't slowed down either. In March 2000, an 11.30-pound largemouth was caught here. As if that wasn't enough, the same day an 11.80-pound largemouth surrendered to a live waterdog for bait. Later that month, on March 25, a pair of 10-pounders were boated.

In April of the same year a 9.46-pound largemouth bass was caught here and in May a 12-pound, 4-ouncer was caught when it tried to snack on a live shad in 25 feet of water. Big fish are caught in the summer, too. Later that year, in late July, a 13-pounder and a pair of tens were caught during a bass tournament here. Add the 10.07-pounder caught on May 4, 2002, and it's pretty easy to see why Pleasant is quickly growing into the state's favorite angling destination.

For largemouth, start near Castle Creek. Be sure to watch for "balls of shad" trying to escape predators—a pretty good indication a hungry largemouth is somewhere nearby.

Surveys conducted during 2001 by the Arizona Game and Fish Department indicated that more than 251,000 anglers spent a total of 1,460,011 hours fishing at Lake Pleasant. The study estimated that 637,274 fish were caught at the lake, or 0.38 fish per hour, per fisherman. In all, 382,434 largemouth bass were caught, although only 38,450, or 10 percent of total catch, were kept. Slightly more than 4,500 striped bass were caught. More than 90 percent of the anglers at the lake are adult, and the three most populous species of fish at the lake by the biologist's survey, were largemouth bass, white bass and threadfin shad.

In 1980, Lake Pleasant was stocked with 142 fingerling Florida-strain largemouth bass. None have been certified as caught, and most biologists agree the stocking was either too small or else the fish cross-bred with the resident population.

It can get pretty hot at Lake Pleasant in the summer (elevation 1,700 feet), but during the winter, early spring and late fall it's very comfortable. Boats and motors of any size are allowed on the water, and on an average summer weekend the lake is full of jet skiers, sailboaters and all kinds of other watersport enthusiasts and their gear.

With construction completed on Waddell Dam, Pleasant's maximum depth will be nearly 250 feet (though you need to take into account the lake's wildly fluctuating level due to seasonally high water demands on CAP water). It is also Arizona's second largest inland reservoir, with only Roosevelt Lake larger.

Lake Pleasant also holds the state inland waters record for white crappie. The 3-pound, 5.28-ounce monster was caught on February 22, 1982. In November 1991 another white bass that weighed more than 3 pounds was caught on Lake Pleasant.

Expect Ten Lane boat ramp to attract the vast majority of boaters, with Castle Creek and the Marina well behind. Oddly, Castle Creek accounts for about half of the lake's boat-based angling, but less than 10 percent of the overall boat launches.

A netting survey, conducted in November 2002, caught a total of 2,800 fish at the lake. The effort to determine what impact striped bass were having found most fish caught were threadfin shad (2,000), with white bass (538) a distant second. Only 39 stripers were caught—the largest a 7-pounder.

Notable

> April 1972, 4-pound, 11.7-ounce white bass
> February 22, 1982, 3-pound, 5.28-ounce white crappie
> August 1991, 10-pound largemouth bass
> September 8, 1999, 5-pound, 0.2-ounce pacu
> April 15, 2000, 2-pound, 9.12-ounce white bass
> March 2000, 11.30-pound largemouth bass
> March 2000, 11.80-pound largemouth bass
> March 30, 2001, 2-pound, 0.32-ounce white bass
> April 2, 2001, 27-pound, 11.04-ounce carp
> April 13, 2002, 9-pound largemouth bass
> May 2002, 12-pound, 4-ounce largemouth bass

Lower Salt River

The Lower Salt River, below Saguaro Lake's Stewart Mountain Dam, has the distinction of being the only cold-water trout fishery in the nation located in a desert, according to the Arizona Game and Fish Department. Add the fact that the waterway, once considered little more than a tuber's paradise, is so close to metropolitan Phoenix, and it's little wonder its reputation is growing quickly.

"This is truly a remarkable fishery," said Arizona Game and Fish Department Information Officer Rory Aikens. "I run across people who fish for trout before going to work in the morning or after getting off work in the evening."

The Lower Salt River is located along Bush Highway between Usery Pass on the south and State Route 87 (Beeline Highway) on the north. Take U.S. Route 60 east from Mesa and exit on Bush Highway. Travel north for 6 or 7 miles to Granite Reef Dam.

The Lower Salt River is stocked every winter with catchable-sized rainbow trout. Expect Phon D. Sutton and Granite Reef areas to be stocked in the winter and Blue Point and Water Users areas to get trout in the summer.

For current fishing conditions contact the Arizona Game and Fish Department by calling 602/789-3701 or visit www.azgfd.com.

Parker Canyon Lake

Just two hours southeast of Tucson, Parker Canyon Lake offers some of the most varied fishing in the region. It is also home to one of Arizona's biggest controversies. There is an ongoing debate whether to poison or temporarily drain the lake to remedy illegally introduced northern pike—a species allegedly chronically killing stocked trout. Public hearings were held in September 2000, in both Tucson and Sierra Vista, though no decision was rendered at the time.

Patagonia Lake may be more popular, but anyone striving to lose the crowd and fish alone should know about Parker Canyon Lake, only a few miles farther southeast.

If you're suffering withdrawal from high-mountain scenery, you'll find relief in Parker Lake's "transition zone" elevation of 5,400 feet. Its autumn and spring nights are rather chilly, but its sunny, lethargic afternoons are the real attraction.

Parker Canyon Lake was created in 1966 by the Coronado National Forest and the Arizona Game and Fish Department. Despite criticism, the government agencies smoothed the entire bottom of the lake to resemble a huge bowl, and as it turned out, the critics were right. For the first few years the fish didn't do too well from lack of suitable habitat. But the weeds and aquatic vegetation have finally taken hold, and the fishing is usually pretty good.

The U.S. Forest Service estimates more than 200,000 people visit the area annually. This is one of southern Arizona's best overnight camping spots. For camping information call the Coronado National Forest: 520/670-4552 or visit www.fs.fed.us/r3/coronado.

A small general store rents rowboats and sells everything under the sun except gas. The paved boat launch makes this a perfect place for water recreation buffs, though fluctuating water levels during 1999 and 2000 made launching a risky affair. Motors are limited to 8 horsepower, but that shouldn't make much difference since the lake stands at only 125 surface acres even when it is rain-swollen.

This is definitely one of the most important fisheries in the area. Catfish, largemouth bass and sunfish are available, and rainbow trout are stocked regularly, making it a good place to dangle your rod. Trout are stocked through most of the winter, and they prefer the same corn they're fed in the hatchery.

Catfish love stink baits, and the no-muss, no-fuss commercial types are perfect. The old standby, of course, is chicken liver soaked overnight in onion and garlic powder. Although this always seems to work, a 32-pound, 4-ounce state record channel catfish was caught here when the angler cut up a bluegill and used it for bait (off the prominent point that juts out from the north end of the lake).

One of the most interesting "fish" stories I've ever heard also came out of Parker Canyon Lake. It seems someone from the Midwest caught what would have been a new state record channel catfish, but, filleted it instead of having it weighed. According to the then owner of the store, the angler came into the marina in July 1989 and remarked he had just caught a catfish that weighed between 40 and 60 pounds.

Everyone was skeptical at first, but when the angler dug the head and skeleton out of the garbage, they quickly became believers. Later, Game and Fish Wildlife Manager John Millican weighed the "carcass" in at 14 pounds, estimating the fish should have weighed between 40 and 45 pounds, almost 8 full pounds above what was then the current record. So there are some huge catfish in this lake—even if they are considerably lighter than most midwestern records!

Parker Canyon Lake was named for the Parker family that originally homesteaded and ranched the area. George Parker, family patriarch, always complained about the Game and Fish

Department's plans to poison off the largemouth bass that someone illegally planted. Up until he died, he insisted largemouth and trout could coexist in the lake. As it turns out, he was right. The high weedbeds encircling the lake promise to hold those "illegal" largemouth bass—many an angler's favorite. Try working the southernmost end of these thick weeds at dusk, and during the winter jig the deep drop-offs found there.

On September 9, 2002, the new state record black bullhead was caught here. It tipped the scales at 2-pounds, 6.1-ounces. The lake also surrendered the state's inland green sunfish record, which was caught here on July 27, 1996. The lunker tipped the scales at 1-pound, 9-ounces.

In the late 1980s, the U.S. Forest Service installed a fully accessible fishing dock for the handicapped, wheelchair ramps and trails; dredged the area directly in front of the general store (to allow for better shore fishing); and landscaped and reinforced the shoreline near the dock.

To get to Parker Canyon Lake, take State Route 83 south from I-10 just east of Tucson. Drive through Sonoita, staying on Route 83, and follow the signs. It's about 23 miles south of Sonoita (slightly over 10 miles of dirt road).

To catch northern pike, work the weeds, deep in the summer and shallow in the winter. During the summer most anglers claimed they were "lucky" if they caught two of the toothy predators in an 8-hour period, though reading most news reports would lead you to believe otherwise. A survey conducted by the Arizona Game and Fish Department in April 2000 landed one 14-pound pike and another 10-pounder.

For more on current fishing conditions call 602/789-3701 or visit www.azgfd.com.

Notable
April 24, 1987, 32-pound, 4-ounce channel catfish
July 27, 1996, 1-pound, 9-ounce green sunfish
September 9, 2002, 2-pound, 6.1-ounce black bullhead

*Parker Canyon Lake, one of southern Arizona's best
fishing and camping destinations, has a great fishing dock.*

*High weedbeds encircling Parker Canyon Lake promise largemouth
bass—many an angler's favorite.*

Patagonia Lake

Now here's a fishing story!

Slowing to enter yet another cove, the trolling motor wheezed in complaint. Sneaking up on a school of crappie is tough enough without the constant whine of an ancient engine. Inching toward shore, only our wake creased the water's glasslike surface. We finally spotted them, just 5 feet from dry land.

Inches below our hull, dozens cautiously eyed the shallows. Almost symmetrically spaced, none seemed in a hurry to fan nests or lay eggs this early evening. Periodically a confused sunfish would join their ranks, though they were much less content to watch an unmoving shoreline. A sudden, unexpected watery explosion from behind signalled my fishing partner's first "papermouth" on the line. What seemed a mostly airborne battle lasted 10 minutes, until he boated the 2-pounder. Not a bad catch on 4-pound test.

Only then did we begin the serious work of plucking the rest of the school from the water. For at least an hour before sunset, we were actually able to choose the fish we wanted, jig in front of it, and add another to our swelling stringer. For the first time in my life, I watched them open their mouths and swallow the bait—which doesn't necessarily make setting the hook any easier.

That unforgettable scene a few years ago started what can only be described as a love affair with crappie. Even the smallest "slabbie" is a scrappy fighter, and the light tackle best for catching them transforms each into a worthy opponent, regardless of skill level.

Once a crappie is on line, stand back and be prepared for anything. Their aerial acrobatics rival that of rainbow trout—

Patagonia Lake's crappie fishing can be great!

lunging, leaping and twisting in mid-air, somehow hoping to elude your frying pan. Since they're easy to fillet, with some of the sweetest and firmest meat of all Arizona's fish, I prefer mine in the skillet (try rolling the fillets in Italian bread crumbs and Parmesan cheese prior to frying).

For the meager investment of 2 hours, Tucson anglers can be camped alongside this kind of exciting action at Patagonia Lake. Patagonia Lake State Park is easily reached by taking I-10 east from Tucson. Turn south toward Sonoita on State Route 83, then west on State Route 82.

When the lake is filled to capacity, it stands at more than 260 surface acres and has a depth of roughly 90 feet. Expect nearly 8 miles of shoreline, though much of it is inaccessible unless you have a boat. There are no restrictions on boat motor size, although there are severe limitations on where and when you can water ski. For details on this and other state parks, visit www.pr.state.az.us or call 602/542-4174.

A "no wake" area near the campsites provides a clean,

sandy beach for swimmers and peace and solitude for overnight visitors. Perhaps the most attractive features for RV campers are the lakeside sites. Not only do they have a view of the water, but a few areas are on a small isolated hillside that resembles an island. There is a dump station for RV campers, fresh water is available, as are relatively modern toilets. A small general store offers groceries, and row and paddle boats can be rented.

A few years ago, the boat ramp was vastly improved along with the campsites (now there are 300 campsites). Although Lake Patagonia still routinely fills on summer weekends, the extra number of camping areas lessens overcrowding.

Besides being a favorite for boaters in the southern half of the state, Patagonia Lake is also a fisherman's paradise. In the winter it receives regular stockings of rainbow trout. For the latest report contact the Tucson Game and Fish Office at 520/ 628-5376 or visit www.azgfd.com.

Besides the rainbow trout you can also expect to catch catfish, largemouth bass, crappie, sunfish and bluegill. Patagonia Lake stands at an elevation of 4,050 feet above sea level, so despite relatively warm summers, you can expect it to be a few degrees cooler than Tucson.

In Patagonia Lake you never know exactly what's tugging at the end of your line. One time, a night fisherman using a seven-inch pumpkin-colored Berkley Power Worm caught a 12-pound, 6-ounce largemouth bass. On another occasion, an angler brought in a 41-pound flathead catfish, proving that there are a lot of big fish in Patagonia Lake.

During the fall, Patagonia Lake will often do what's called "turning"—the water exposed to the colder weather on top will condense, become heavier than the "warm" water on the bottom, and the lake will become turbulent as the water swaps positions. When this happens, you can usually tell as the lake will be severely stained, and it will almost look like someone has stirred a huge soup caldron. Look for lots of moss and weeds floating, and at that time expect the bass to retreat to a depth of 20 or 30 feet and develop a sudden case of lockjaw.

Patagonia Lake was once home for the state record green sunfish. The 1-pound, 8.0-ouncer was caught on May 1, 1989, though that record was subsequently rewritten by a 1-pound, 9-ounce catch at nearby Parker Canyon Lake.

Patagonia is, however, currently the state record holder for hybrid sunfish. The 2-pound, 2.22-ounce monster was caught on June 5, 1998, and was heavier than the current National Fresh Water Fishing Hall of Fame record.

Ironically, Patagonia Lake did not start out as a state recreation area. It began when a group of businessmen decided they would create a private, for-profit lake of their own. They constructed the lake in 1968 by building a 90-foot dam on Sonoita Creek. They didn't limit their plans to simply collecting money from fishermen and boating enthusiasts—high-priced private cabins around the water's edge were also scheduled for construction. Profits never did materialize and in 1975, the area was acquired by the State Parks Board.

Notable

May 1, 1989, 1-pound, 8-ounce green sunfish
1992, 41-pound flathead catfish
August 1992, 12-pound, 6-ounce largemouth bass
June 5, 1998, 2-pound, 2.22-ounce hybrid sunfish

Green Sunfish

Non-native. Large mouth with blue-green striations on the cheeks. Opercle flap is black with reddish or orange border. Body olive-green in color, dark vertical bars on sides. Pectoral fin short and rounded. Caudal fin and lower fin margins are white or yellowish with dusky spots at rear of dorsal and anal fins.

Pena Blanca Lake

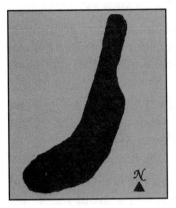

One of southern Arizona's most scenic destinations, Pena Blanca Lake, has suffered more than its fair share of grief. The Coronado National Forest didn't renew the previous concession's permit in the late 1990s, so you can no longer rent boats or savor that special German fare once found there. Add a mercury warning, where all warmwater species of fish are unsafe for human consumption, and the only silver lining is the fact that Pena Blanca Lake is no longer routinely overfished.

Pena Blanca Lake, a 45-surface-acre impoundment just 18 miles north and west of Nogales, is still home for some of southern Arizona's finest crappie fishing—at least for those anglers who know how to properly prospect for the speckled beauties (again, anglers should practice catch-and-release due to elevated mercury readings).

A few years ago, I watched in amazement as a visitor from the Midwest regularly boated between 40 and 60 of the fish during a three-day stretch. He used a tiny tube jig in green, periodically changing to yellow or gold, depending on the finicky fish's mood.

Trout are also voracious when they hit the small lake's water. Because they spend so little time in the lake, the Arizona Game and Fish Department emphasizes that it is safe to consume the trout.

For many years during my adolescence, my parents and I would make a minimum of four trips annually to Pena Blanca to catch the stocker rainbows. Corn always seemed best, especially when floated off the bottom with a marshmallow.

My children and I have found Power Bait the most irresistible offering to the salmonoids. It floats on its own, and includes a fish attracting scent that ensures more strikes (and usually more fish in the frying pan, depending on your skill level).

Largemouth bass also call Pena Blanca home. With all of the lakes I've visited across the nation, it's still hard to believe one of the biggest largemouths I've caught came from this small impoundment.

I'm not the only bass fisherman who has good luck on Pena Blanca. In August 1992, an angler landed a 6-pound largemouth there using a black Berkley Power Worm.

In 1990 and early 1991, a survey conducted by the Arizona Game and Fish Department determined the lake was suffering a serious overfishing problem. The number of trout taken out of the lake annually was nearly identical to the number stocked, and as a result, finding even a single holdover on a stringer was a rare occurrence.

According to the results, it was possible the entire bass population in the 45 surface acres was caught at least once a year. In fact, the results indicated there was enough fishing pressure to harvest the lake's entire largemouth population 20 times annually.

The survey discovered Pena Blanca Lake is fished most from March to May and least from September to December. On the "average" day, before the mercury warnings, you could expect to find 8.1 people fishing from shore and another 9 in boats. Most anglers spent only four hours per fishing day here.

Fish most often kept at Pena Blanca Lake, in descending order, were; rainbow trout; bluegill and redear sunfish; black crappie; channel catfish; largemouth bass; and yellow bullhead. The fish most often caught, in descending order, were; bluegill and redear sunfish; trout; black crappie; largemouth bass; channel catfish; and yellow bullheads.

The survey showed fishermen at Pena Blanca kept 81 percent of the trout they caught, 74 percent of the crappie, 54 percent of the channel catfish and an incredibly low 27 percent of the largemouth bass. Of all the fish caught at Pena Blanca, only 57 percent were taken home.

The source of this lake's mercury contamination was later discovered to be an old mining operation upstream. Mercury was often used in the amalgamation process, and residue had migrated into the lake. Though the site of the contamination has been cleaned up, the lake's level remains high.

Pena Blanca also has a dubious problem with chronic siltation. In 1955 the lake was measured to be 52 surface acres, and today it has shrunk to 45.

In 1992, in an effort to improve the lake's habitat, the Arizona Game and Fish Department installed 75 bluegill bungalows and 75 fish trees. That artificial habitat was designed to increase the amount of cover and shade for the lake's bass, bluegill and sunfish. The bluegill bungalows are six-inch plastic pipes and fish trees are six-to-nine foot high plastic trees with leaves that extend from the "trunk." Other lakes

A handicapped fishing dock and paved trail makes Pena Blanca a great destination for the physically challenged.

across Arizona have had tremendous results with such structures, and biologists hoped another population explosion would occur here.

Pena Blanca Lake was created when the Arizona Game and Fish Department built a dam impounding Pena Blanca Creek northwest of Nogales in 1954. The lake was filled by the next year and largemouth bass, crappie, channel catfish and bluegills stocked then have been reproducing naturally.

Periodically some of these natives reach lunker proportions. In fact, in September one year, an 11.5-pound largemouth bass was caught here. The lake stands at an elevation of 4,000 feet, which means fishing is relatively warm even in the winter, though pretty hot in the summer.

A new boat launch makes putting your boat into Pena Blanca easier than ever. Motors however, are limited to electric trolling. A handicapped fishing dock and paved trail makes this a great destination for the physically challenged. On one of our anniversaries, my wife and I helped organize a fishing outing with the hospice unit of Tucson's VA hospital, and that fishing dock worked perfectly. In fact, we had trouble convincing the handicapped vets it was time to leave—it was probably the most emotional wedding anniversary my wife and I ever had. You see, both our fathers were veterans.

To get to Pena Blanca Lake, take I-19 south from Tucson. Drive nearly all the way into Nogales, and turn west on State Route 289. It's about 20 miles of pavement before you reach the lake. For current fishing conditions call 520/628-5376.

Notable

September 1992, 11.5-pound largemouth bass

Picacho Reservoir

Picacho Reservoir suffered a complete fish kill during the summer of 2000, and late in 2002 the Arizona Game and Fish Department was listing it as "dry." Take heart though, surveys after a partial kill-off in 1999 indicated bass routinely migrating downstream provide new broodstock, regardless of conditions.

Check conditions by calling 602/789-3701 or by visiting www.azgfd.com.

Conveniently located in the heart of Arizona, Picacho Reservoir can offer some of the best bass fishing in the entire state. While record-breaking heat may drive many anglers from its water, those who brave the soaring temperatures regularly return with stories of broken rods, incredible hits and catches of up to twenty fish a day, including some in the 5-pound class.

Arizona fishermen rarely talk about Picacho Reservoir. Instead they deliberately "forget" all about its productive depths. They hope the unmarked route will remain unmarked. An hour north of Tucson and only 12 miles from Casa Grande, this lake could well be area anglers' best-kept secret.

When it is filled to capacity Picacho Reservoir holds 50 surface acres. Its back channels and streams, used primarily for irrigation, account for another 30 miles of fishable water. Picacho's average depth is only 10 feet, when it does have water, that is. However, it has historically been home for some of the biggest largemouth in the state, along with crappie, sunfish, channel catfish and huge carp—a fact that has made bow-fishing increasingly popular here.

There are no facilities on Picacho and launching the smallest of boats is impossible when the water is low. The boat ramps are primitive. Car-toppers with electric trolling motor do well.

*This Picacho
largemouth put
up quite a scrap!*

The entire lake is a group of submerged trees, and it takes quite a bit of meandering to find your way out into the main water. Once you're there, though, you'll find thick stands of tules on one end of the reservoir and a number of rocky structures on the other.

To reach Picacho Reservoir take I-10 north from Tucson. Turn north on State Route 87 and follow it about 8 miles. Turn right (east) on Selma. Follow the dirt road until you cross the railroad tracks. Turn right again and drive for another mile or two along the irrigation canal. Picacho will be to your left.

At an elevation of 1,500 feet, temperatures around the lake are hot in the summer. In 1990, when Arizona was caught in the grips of a serious drought, Picacho all but disappeared. Some estimated nearly the entire fish population died, although the wet winter of 1991 and the flooding of January and February of 1993 refilled the reservoir. Surveys conducted by the Game and Fish Department just prior to the 1993 flooding indicated enough largemouth bass had spilled out of San Carlos Lake, miles upstream, that stocking was unnecessary. In fact, the fertile water washed down from the flooding prompted it to issue a bulletin that Picacho was going to go through a "new lake" phenomenon.

Riggs Flat Lake

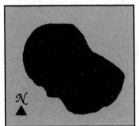

Riggs Flat Lake, high atop Mt. Graham southwest of Safford, is one of the area's most important trout fisheries. It also boasts incredible scenery and the endangered Mt. Graham red squirrels that environmentalists and scientists continue to argue over.

Don't expect to see many of the squirrels near the lake though. They prefer solitude.

Riggs Flat Lake's elevation of 9,000 feet means it can be a cool getaway during the dead of summer and is virtually inaccessible during winter.

The lake impounds a total of 10 surface acres, with an average depth of 45 feet. Though deep enough for the stocked trout to survive through the winter, rarely are lunkers caught here. Species available include an occasional brown and brook trout. Rainbows are stocked from late April to mid-September.

You can pretty much expect the gates to the lake to close around late October. On the average summer, expect the stocking truck to arrive about seven times.

To get to the lake from Phoenix, take U.S. 60 and then U.S. 70 east to Safford. In Safford, take U.S. Route 191 south for 9 miles to the entrance of the Coronado National Forest. Turn right and you will be on State Route 366. The road is paved for the first 21 miles up the mountain and then you will be on a graded dirt road for 12.9 miles. The lake is quite a few cliffy miles up the mountainous road, so take your time, and savor the views.

There is no real boat launch site to speak of, but that's not much of a problem because motors are restricted to electric trolling motors.

For more information call the Coronado National Forest Safford Ranger District at 928/428-4150 or visit www.azgfd.com.

Roosevelt Lake

It didn't take Arizonans long to realize the recreational potential of Roosevelt's 9,750 surface acres, even though the lake was originally designed for flood control, irrigation and power. Construction completed in the late 1990s made it even bigger, enhancing the attraction. When today's Roosevelt Lake is at capacity it extends 23 miles from the Salt River to the Tonto River and features 88 miles of shoreline.

Theodore Roosevelt dedicated the dam in 1911, which at the time was the world's largest masonry structure. After 80 years, it received a facelift, and as construction was completed, the face of Roosevelt Dam was transformed from rough, textured masonry to smooth concrete.

The dam was strengthened and heightened 77 feet, providing a total of 1.6 million acre-feet storage capacity, up significantly over its previous 1.3 million acre-feet. Roosevelt Lake is shared by water skiers, houseboaters, campers and fishermen, and at times it is the single-most-popular recreational facility in Arizona.

Water levels constantly fluctuate because of droughts, periodic maintenance requirements and runoff from nearby mountains. Depths can vary so dramatically that Roosevelt Lake Marina installed the state's largest floating dock.

The constantly changing water volume may be frustrating for boaters, but it's a blessing for fishermen. When the water level drops in early summer, previously unknown habitat and fishing "holes" are revealed to observant anglers. While the water is down, new vegetation has a chance to grow. When the

Roosevelt Lake Marina. After a hearty breakfast . . .

Head out for the day . . .

And enjoy central Arizona's premier angling experience!

water comes back, valuable nutrients and cover have been added to the lake, resulting in an increase in both the size of the fish and the fish population.

This odd balancing act has resulted in one of the best fisheries available to the Arizona angler. Roosevelt Lake is known for vicious crappie spawns, and it is also one of the most pleasant places in the nation to spend early spring. Temperatures in March and April shoot into the seventies and eighties, making the area the perfect cabin fever remedy.

Crappie are one of the easiest, most exciting fish to catch. The panfish usually puts up an aggressive fight and provides a few moments of heart-stopping aerial combat. Even if you don't land a lunker, an early April visit almost always guarantees a frying pan filled with their white, meaty fillets.

For the uninitiated angler, encountering a school of spawning crappie is an unforgettable experience. During the darkness, literally hundreds of them infest the shallows, either fanning nests or filling them with eggs. Shore fishermen and boaters alike can pick the fish they're going to catch, and long jigging rods are perfect for the fast-paced action.

Live minnows worked slowly along the shoreline are extremely productive, as are yellow mini-jigs. Traditionally the biggest panfish catches have come from the eastern end near Schoolhouse Point (where the spawn usually begins). The tiny coves on the marina side of Windy Hill are also good.

According to the Arizona Game and Fish Department, Roosevelt Lake is so fertile that crappie can grow to 3-4 inches in the first year, 11 inches by year two, 15 by year three and 16 by the fourth year of life.

Roosevelt Lake was also the home of Arizona's inland largemouth bass record for some time. On April 16, 1988, a 14-pound, 8-ounce largemouth was caught here, eclipsing the previous state record largemouth, a 14-pound, 2-ouncer, which was caught on Roosevelt in 1956.

The new record was set by a Tucson angler near the sheriff's substation, a half-mile east of the dam. He used a chartreuse-

and-black 1/16-ounce Canyon mini-jig. Although largemouth usually like to orient themselves to some sort of structure, the fish was caught almost 150 feet from the shoreline. The 28.33-inch-long fish had a girth of 21.13 inches.

On March 18, 1988, a 7-pound, 0.96-ounce smallmouth was taken on Roosevelt, erasing the old state record of 6-pounds, 14-ounces, also caught on these fertile waters. The lunker surrendered to a live minnow being trolled from Windy Hill back to the main boat launch. The angler was on his way back to take the boat out of the water when the lunker hit.

Big smallies continue to surface, and on April 15, 2000, a 4-pound, 4.16-ouncer was caught, and on July 16, 2000, a 5-pound, 1.23-ouncer was boated and released. Things don't slow down in the winter either, as evidenced by the January 9, 2002, catch of a 5-pound, 10.88-ounce smallmouth on Roosevelt.

Roosevelt has historically had a slot limit, though such regulations continue to evolve across the state. Avoid the confusion and consult a current set of fishing regulations prior to leaving by calling 602/942-3000 or by visiting www.azgfd.com.

Before the original slot limit at Roosevelt, which was instituted in the early 1990s, bass fishermen were harvesting fully 50 percent of what they caught. After the new regulation was imposed, they were only keeping 10 percent. So this lake has been transformed into one of Arizona's premier largemouth bass fisheries thanks to scientifically based management.

How good has Roosevelt historically been for bass? In 1980, the Arizona Game and Fish Department estimated that female bass old enough to reproduce numbered around 70,000 in the lake. Since each can yield 25,000 eggs, that converts to a projected 1.75 billion hatchlings. About 50 percent of those hatchlings survive to fingerling size (4 inches), which means that in 1988 there were an estimated 875 million largemouth bass fingerlings in Roosevelt.

Roosevelt Lake received 1,110 Florida-strain bass fingerlings in 1980 (4 inches), although apparently none of those were ever caught. Most feel they simply cross-bred with other bass in the lake, effectively disappearing.

One of the best spots to look for largemouth is in Salome (affectionately called "Sally Mae") Cove on the north side of the lake and east of the main boat launch. It's the largest cove on the lake and holds an incredible number of fish.

Lots of big largemouth are caught on Roosevelt annually, including the 10.11-pounder caught on December 4, 1999, or the early June 2000 catch of a 9.31-pounder. On June 27 of the same year, a 10.14-pound largemouth was caught, and in 2001, 9.46- (March), 9.94- (September 22) and 10.15-pounders (October 17) were caught. The next year, big catches included an 8.74-pounder on March 3 and an 8.08-pounder on June 8.

The place to start searching for smallmouth is usually on the Tonto end of the Lake, especially near the dam. Though it has been a while since the smallmouth record has been broken, big fish continue to surface.

Other species available include an occasional rainbow trout, sunfish and both species of catfish. Try split-shotting a waterdog on the Salt River end of the lake when the water is low, or use traditional stink baits on the flats when water is high for big fish.

Of course you never really know what's going to take your bait on Roosevelt Lake. In August 1991, 16.5-pound and 16.0-pound channel catfish were caught on live bluegills where the Salt River enters the lake. As if that's not enough, earlier in the month a single angler caught three catfish near Schoolhouse Point that tipped the scales at 22, 44 and 50 pounds, again using live bluegills.

The most incredible story came in July though, when two friends brought in five flatheads that combined to weigh 139 pounds. All five were caught from Schoolhouse Point and came in on live bluegills and sunfish. The two men used a 9-0 hook, 2-ounce sliding sinker and a huge bobber on the live bluegill rig mentioned in this book's Tips and Tricks chapter.

Creel surveys among catfishermen found that 96 percent of the "cats" caught were channel cats and 4 percent were flatheads. According to the survey, the harvest ratio in the upper Salt River was .5 fish per hour and the most productive bait was liver.

Additional Game and Fish surveys found bluegills are the most abundant species harvested at Roosevelt, although the total weight of largemouth bass taken is greater than the bluegill numbers. The latest survey, however, found black crappie to be the most abundant, again followed in weight by largemouth bass.

The Game and Fish Department surveys showed the best time to catch sunfish/bluegill is May. Largemouth bass are caught most often during the spring and fall, with catfish predominating stringers during July. Crappie are good through most of the spring and again in November.

You can access the lake by going north on State Route 88, just before Globe. There are hundreds of campsites on Roosevelt Lake. For more information write the Tonto National Forest at 2324 E. McDowell Road, Phoenix, AZ 85006, or call 602/225-5200. You can also visit www.fs.fed.us/r3/tonto.

You can also rent boats at Roosevelt Lake Marina (928/467-2245). Any size motor and boat is legal on the lake. There are plenty of boat ramps, and during the weekend, expect to see houseboats, skiers, sailboats and canoes on the water.

For current fishing conditions visit www.azgfd.com or call 602/789-3701.

Notable
> 1956, 14-pound, 2-ounce largemouth bass
> April 16, 1988, 14-pound, 8-ounce largemouth bass
> March 18, 1988, 7-pound, 0.96-ounce smallmouth bass
> March 14, 1995, 36-pound, 6-ounce bigmouth buffalo
> May 10, 1998, 71-pound flathead catfish
> April 2000, 2.9-pound black crappie
> June 27, 2000, 10.14-pound largemouth bass
> July 16, 2000, 5-pound, 1.23-ounce smallmouth bass
> October 17, 2001, 10.15-pound largemouth bass
> January 9, 2002, 5-pound, 10.88-ounce, smallmouth bass
> April 2002, 10.5-pound largemouth bass

Rose Canyon Lake

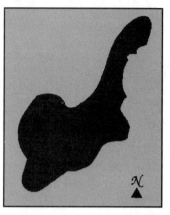

For most of the summer, Rose Canyon Lake, high atop the Santa Catalina Mountains north of Tucson, receives biweekly summertime stockings of rainbow trout from the Arizona Game and Fish Department. Because of its proximity to a major city and the cooler climate associated with its relatively high altitude (7,000 feet), however, most of the fish are gone by the next day.

Further complicating matters is the fact that during the hot summer of 1999 water quality degraded to the point that stockings had to be cancelled. This continued through the beginning of summer 2000, though the Forest Service began a $200,000 project to remove sediment from the lake. Engineers estimate that as much as 375 cubic yards of sediment accumulates in the lake annually, threatening the health of the fishery. During an unusually heavy rain on July 16, 1999, as much as 10,000 cubic yards of sediment wound up in the lake.

The lake was drained in the winter of 2001. The effort was designed to remove sediment and eradicate green sunfish. By the winter of 2002, the lake was up to half capacity, and stockings had already begun. In early 2003, a new fishing dock for the physically challenged was dedicated.

To reach Rose Canyon Lake, take the Catalina Highway toward Mt. Lemmon for nearly 18 miles to the turnoff sign. The road winds for another mile or so to the parking lot. From the parking lot, it's still a 300-yard hike to the water's edge.

Camping is restricted to designated areas away from the water but are usually within walking distance. Parking is limited to pavement only and a daily recreation fee is charged.

Areas on the left of the drive are generally for picnics only. A huge picnic area is located just above the lake. There is no dump station and no electric hookups—just that wonderful mountain ambiance. For more camping information call 520/670-4552 or visit www.fs.fed.us/r3/coronado.

This lake is small—only 7 surface acres—but it is an important resource. Traditionally, anglers have the best luck in the deeper waters off the dam. To get to the dam, follow the path on the right side of the lake. The dam is hidden from view, and unless you know better it's easy to walk the wrong way.

The most popular of all snacks for the rainbow trout in residence is corn, just like they cooked at the hatchery, and of course that hypnotic Berkley Trout Power Bait. I've also brought in a fish or two with a yellow-and-red Z-Ray. Whatever you use, make sure it rides high in the water where oxygen is plentiful (once the heat sets in, the lower portion of the lake loses a lot of its oxygen-holding capacity).

Expect Rose Canyon Lake to receive its first stocking of rainbow trout sometime in early April and the last in mid-September. On the average, it receives seven stockings, but again—call the Arizona Game and Fish Department at 520/628-5376, the Santa Catalina Ranger District at 520/749-8700 or visit the Arizona Game and Fish website: www.azgfd.com.

Note: In mid-2003 the lake was closed due to fire restrictions.

A beautiful summer retreat!

Saguaro Lake

Saguaro Lake is the proverbial "good news/bad news" for anglers. The bad news is it's near Phoenix and is host to water skiers, jet skiers and virtually every imaginable watercraft short of an aircraft carrier. The good news is that most anglers go somewhere else to fish because of the crowds, so the fishing pressure is somewhat reduced.

To reach Saguaro Lake, take State Route 87 (Beeline) northeast out of Mesa and turn on Bush Highway. You can also· take Bush Highway north from U.S. Route 60.

Saguaro Lake was created in 1930 when Stewart Mountain Dam impounded a section of the Salt River. At 1,300 surface acres, the lake has 22.2 miles of shoreline, is nearly 10 miles long and has an average depth of 90 feet. The lake is 2,200 feet above sea level.

In October 1989, an ambitious program called the Fish Habitat Improvement Project was undertaken on Saguaro Lake by the cooperative efforts of the U.S. Forest Service, the Arizona Game and Fish Department and Anglers United. While the lake was lowered for maintenance, crappie condos, bass bungalows and cathouses were strategically placed around the lake bottom. Like many of Arizona's lakes, Saguaro was showing its age and with that came a severe loss of critical habitat.

Eleven surface acres of the lake were enhanced, shoreline trails were improved, angler access was enhanced, breakwaters were constructed and floating fishing docks were put in place. Just how effective is the habitat? When fisheries biologists from the Game and Fish Department put on their SCUBA gear in June 1991 to check the structures, they found a number of fish, including some of the state's largest, were using the artificial structures. Fishermen were catching baskets of bluegill, which were also entering the spawn; there were largemouth, smallmouth, and yellow bass in or around the structures; and catfish had taken up residence in the cathouses.

Another survey of the artificial structure, conducted by the Arizona Game and Fish Department in January of 1992, showed that of 11 sites, 97 percent of the fish in the immediate area were relating to the structure. As if by design, a few months later (on April 1, 1992), a 13-pound, 6-ounce, largemouth bass was caught out of the structure by a fisherman using a Fat Rap #9. A summer 1992 creel survey showed Saguaro has an angler success rate of nearly 64 percent (though most of the fish caught were bluegill).

In all, 1,200 volunteers donated nearly 17,000 hours to this unusual project. In 1991, the project was one of 119 winners nationwide in the Fifth Annual Take Pride in America National Awards Program.

Fishing has only continued to improve on Saguaro. A 12.9-pound largemouth was caught here early April 2000, on a topwater bait. On December 30 of the same year, a 7-pound largemouth was caught, and the next year an 8.23-pounder was caught in August.

What was then a new state record tilapia was caught here on April 7, 2000. It tipped the scales at 6 pounds easily eclipsing the old record, which was also set on Saguaro in 1996. Subsequently a 7-pound, 1-ounce tilapia was caught here on October 14, 2000. On March 31, 2002, a 7-pound, 8.18-ouncer was caught on Saguaro. If you're after tilapia, this is the place to go.

A rainbow trout is occasionally caught in Saguaro, although the species of choice is by far the largemouth bass.

You might begin your search for largemouth near Shiprock. At times a lot of fish can be found on the side that borders the main river channel. In fact, on February 3, 1993, a fisherman caught a largemouth that weighed just under 14 pounds there using a chartreuse spinnerbait. Bass seem to orient to structure with nearby deep water.

The only other state record held on Saguaro is a 39-pound, 8.0-ounce bigmouth buffalo, a peculiar species of fish that almost never takes any sort of bait or lure. It was taken by a bowfisherman on March 28, 1990. Species available include smallmouth bass, yellow bass, crappie, sunfish, channel catfish, walleye and an occasional yellow perch.

For more information on facilities, which continue to improve, write the Tonto National Forest, 2324 E. McDowell Road, Phoenix, AZ 85006 or call 602/225-5200. For current fishing conditions call 602/789-3701 or visit www.azgfd.com.

Notable

April 1, 1992, 13-pound, 6-ounce largemouth bass
February 16, 2000, 4-pound, 16-ounce walleye
April 2000, 12.9-pound largemouth bass
April 7, 2000, 6-pound tilapia
October 14, 2000, 7-pound, 1-ounce tilapia
December 15, 2000, 10-pound, 7.2-ounce carp (Big Fish of the Year)
January 6, 2001, 8.5-pound channel catfish (near Boat Ramp #1)
April 16, 2001, 7-pound, 2.56-ounce tilapia
February 2002, 11.5-pound largemouth bass (Lucky Craft jerkbait)
March 31, 2002, 7-pound, 8.8-ounce tilapia
April 2002, 7-pound, 8-ounce largemouth bass (on a crankbait)
April 13, 2002, 8.5-pound largemouth bass
May 14, 2002, 21-pound, 5.12-ounce carp
May 18, 2002, 6-pound largemouth bass
May 29, 2002, 27-pound, 4.16-ounce carp
June 2, 2002, 2-pound, 0.48 ounce black crappie
June 30, 2002, 1-pound, 3.52-ounce yellow bass
September 2002, 7-pound, 12-ounce largemouth bass (on a Hula Popper)
November 2002, 12-pound largemouth bass (on a stickbait in shallow water)

San Carlos Lake

When Calvin Coolidge and Will Rogers attended the dedication of Coolidge Dam on March 4, 1930, they had no idea what a controversy the structure would generate in the 1990s. Perhaps Rogers put it best when he looked down at the grassy meadow that would soon be flooded and become San Carlos Lake and said, "If it was my lake, I'd mow it."

During the next sixty years, the water level often dropped to a point low enough to cause a fish kill-off (the last draw-down and total kill-off was in 1974) and allow mowing.

As Will Rogers once said about San Carlos Lake,
"If it was my lake, I'd mow it."

When San Carlos Lake is filled, it is one of Arizona's largest inland bodies of water. But in 1989 when Arizona was in the grips of a serious drought, agricultural water users downstream put such a demand on the reservoir that total volume dropped to only 36,000 acre-feet and the specter of yet another total kill-off was raised. Some experts prophesied the lake would completely disappear by August 1990.

Luckily, in May 1990, President George Bush Sr., signed legislation mandating a minimum pool of 30,000 acre-feet on the lake. Unfortunately that agreement expired on December 31, 1990.

Today, San Carlos Lake stands much as it has throughout its lifetime—on the edge of disaster. There is no permanent agreement protecting one of south central Arizona's most precious fishery resources. Talk began circulating again in the summer of 2000, before the monsoons granted yet another reprieve, that the waterway could go belly up.

San Carlos Lake is on the San Carlos Apache Indian Reservation. Before you can visit the scenic area, you must purchase a recreation or fishing permit from the tribe. Permits are available at a number of places, including convenience stores and virtually every fishing tackle shop in the Globe/Miami area. You can also get them at the lake store or from the San Carlos Recreation and Wildlife Department, Box 97, San Carlos, AZ 85550, 928/475-2343.

Visit www.sancarlosrecreationandwildlife.com for more information.

There are no developed campsites on San Carlos Lake, although thousands of primitive areas surround the lake. Expect an occasional ramada and pit toilets, but trees for shade are at a premium. In summer the relatively low elevation makes for almost unbearable temperatures. Bring all your drinking and cooking water. Near Soda Canyon, on the road toward the dam, is a general store that sells permits and essential items.

There are several good boat launches around the lake, and there is no limit on motor or boat size. Remember though, you must also purchase a boat permit to operate your watercraft on the reservation, whether it is licensed in Arizona or not. New Government Corral has plenty of parking, but the launch is dirt and can sometimes be completely out of the water or non-negotiable, depending on the water level and weather. Soda Canyon's launch is nearly always good, even though camping/parking is not quite as generous.

San Carlos Lake's chief drawback is also one of its chief advantages. Each time the water lowers for any length of time, the salt cedar bushes re-grow along the shoreline. As the water raises and floods the new timber, structure and nutrients are added to the lake, and for the next few years fish populations literally explode.

As a result, largemouth bass seem to thrive in its water. Even when the lake is down to minimum pool, they stack up in the deep water near the dam, and it is nearly impossible not to jig or worm a limit. As if to emphasize that point, San Carlos yielded a 9-pound largemouth on June 21, 1991. It was caught with a Bagley crankbait in shallow water near Soda Canyon. In September 1991, a 10.09-pounder was caught here.

During the early spring, work the northern coves that warm up early when the water is still cool. Chartreuse-and-white spinnerbaits are always a good bet when the fish are shallow, and rubber worms are a good backup pattern. If you're totally confused or are fishing the lake for the first time, consider a trip to an area affectionately called the "Lava Beds." More than one bass tournament has been won there. Another good spot is where the old railroad line runs into the water.

River inlets are also good areas for bass, particularly when the water is high enough to allow entry by boat. The Gila and San Carlos rivers are the two major confluences that dump into the lake.

Crappie are found in San Carlos Lake, and many fishermen claim the spring spawn rivals or exceeds the voracious bite of Roosevelt Lake. The state inland record black crappie was caught here in 1959. It tipped the scales at 4-pounds, 10-ounces.

Catfish are another favorite. The state inland flathead catfish record was set at San Carlos Lake back in 1951. The flathead weighed an incredible 65 pounds, though that record has subsequently been eclipsed by a monster caught at Roosevelt Lake in 1998. At times the cats prefer to lunch on waterdogs, though you cannot count on the lake's general store stocking them, so come prepared.

Also lurking in the sometimes-deep water are channel catfish (some as large as 22 pounds), bluegill, green sunfish, carp and bullheads. The main forage species for game fish are red shiners and threadfin shad, so watch for those occasional boils that often indicate big fish on the prowl.

Coolidge Dam was deemed "the most dangerous dam" in the United States during the 1980s and subsequently underwent serious renovation. Safety repairs completed shortly thereafter cost $50 million, while the original structure cost only $5.5 million.

To reach San Carlos Lake, take U.S. Route 70 east from Globe (about 20 miles) and turn south at Indian Route 3 (it's well-signed and hard to miss).

Notable
    1951, 65-pound flathead catfish
    1959, 4-pound, 10-ounce black crappie
    September 1991, 10.09-pound largemouth bass
    April 10, 2001, 53-pound, 14.88-ounce flathead catfish
    April 13, 2002, 11.52-pound largemouth bass
    April 20, 2002, 9.63-pound largemouth bass
    April 28, 2002, 9.72-pound largemouth bass

San Carlos' crappie are always a nice catch!

Talkalai Lake

This is one of the most over-looked lakes in east central Arizona. Located on the San Carlos Apache Indian Reservation, and covering 600 surface acres, Talkalai is an important resource for southern Arizona anglers. Believe me, it's also one of the most scenic warmwater fisheries you'll ever see.

Talkalai Lake is named for Chief Talkalai, a full-blooded Apache who not only served as an Indian scout for General Miles, General Howard and General Crook, but was Chief of Police on the San Carlos Indian Reservation for twenty-one years. He was instrumental in the capture of Geronimo.

In the late 1970s, the dam that impounds Talkalai Lake failed. By October 10, 1979, it had been rebuilt and the lake was once again opened to the public. At that time largemouth bass, crappie and channel catfish were stocked in a cooperative effort by the San Carlos Apache tribe and the U.S. Fish and Wildlife Service. In 1991, a 29-pound channel catfish was caught here.

Reaching Talkalai is an adventure in itself. No signs point the way (most of the time), and even after you find the lake once, the next trip can still be just as exciting. To get there, take U.S. Route 60 east out of Globe, then U.S. Route 70 southeast to Peridot. In Peridot proceed north on the paved road one block east of the Game and Fish headquarters toward San Carlos. After a little more than a mile, start looking for a road that fords the San Carlos River.

You can cross at the river and head north, although I would not recommend it in anything less than a four-wheel-drive vehicle. Instead, once you spot the crossing continue north and watch for the next good dirt road that heads toward the river. A small sign is sometimes posted at the junction, but don't count on it.

Take the good road and stay on the main trail. The lake should be about another mile, but allow extra time for exploration.

Once at the lake, you will find the rarest of all commodities in Arizona—big trees at the water's edge. The cattails and tules are so thick in spots that they actually impede water access from the many campsites. Of course, that also means more privacy.

Camping is allowed, and although there's no developed boat launch, a small craft can easily be put on the water. Nothing larger than an electric trolling motor is allowed.

Firewood may be scarce, but this is some of the finest camping in the state. The last time I was there I stayed right at the water's edge and was awakened in the morning by the yipping of several coyotes only a few hundred feet away.

Ambitious fishermen can take one of the many crossings over the San Carlos River, which runs year-round here, and find an even more secluded cove to camp in on the other side. Be forewarned: I have gotten stuck here in a four-wheel-drive vehicle.

Stick to the west side of the lake/river and even a subcompact car can negotiate the dirt road.

During the spring and fall, crappie runs on Talkalai can be amazing. The thick structure in the middle of the lake always holds a number of bass, and more often than not, you will land a lunker catfish or two during the night.

This is part of the San Carlos Apache Indian Reservation, and non-tribal fishermen need to purchase a permit. For more information contact the San Carlos Recreation and Wildlife Department, Box 97, San Carlos, AZ 85550, 928/475-2343. Visit www.sancarlosrecreationandwildlife.com.

Notable

June 1991, 29-pound channel catfish

Tempe Town Lake

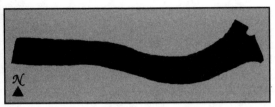

As of this printing, you need a regular Arizona Game and Fish Department fishing license (plus trout stamp in the winter) to fish the new Tempe Town Lake. Yes, it's in an urban setting, but this waterway is something unusual. Urban licenses won't work, at least for now.

For more than 10 years politicians argued, but in the summer of 1999, more than 977 million gallons of water—flowing through Papago Park—was impounded in a new, 2-mile-long lake called Tempe Town Lake. In all, the waterway covers 224 surface acres at a depth of 19 feet.

The lake can be accessed from the Rio Salado Parkway, and there are plenty of parking sites, including near the Red River Music Hall. For more on access, or questions on park regulations, call 480/350-8625.

What sets the lake apart is the fact that it's created by inflatable rubber dams at either end, which means if a flood is about to occur along the Salt River, the structures can be deflated in as little as 30 minutes.

The lake was stocked with 15,000 rainbow trout—2.5 tons—in the fall of 2002. Anglers surveyed at the waterway caught most of their trout on Power Bait (39 percent), spinners (30 percent) and night crawlers (13 percent). Interestingly, 50 percent of the trout caught were released.

The waterway also has crappie, largemouth and yellow bass, sunfish and a number of other species available for anglers. For current fishing conditions call 602/789-3701 or visit www.azgfd.com.

Arizona's Urban Lakes

Overview

Imagine a program that allows inner-city youth to walk to a nearby lake and fish for rainbow trout, channel catfish, hybrid sunfish, grass carp and an occasional lunker large-mouth—usually without a license. Add reasonably priced adult licenses that don't require trout stamps, with the ability of an out-of-state visitor to purchase an urban fishing license at the same price as residents, and you have the formula for success.

Youngsters, who might otherwise think they have little opportunity to enjoy the great outdoors, suddenly have a wonderful chance to engage in a productive activity rather than getting into trouble with the law. Grandparents and parents alike, regardless where they live, if they're on a fixed income or how long they're visiting, can spend quality time with their family, inexpensively passing on an appreciation for nature.

Regardless of social status, economic plight or physical challenge, Arizona's Urban Fishing Program allows families to

Urban Lakes Table of Contents

*Recently added. For more information, call the Arizona Fish and Game Dept., 602-942-3000 or visit their website: azgfd.com.

pass on this wonderful heritage we call fishing. I consider it the most important program developed by the Arizona Game and Fish Department in its entire history. In the 1990s, I coordinated the Tucson Inner City Kids Fishing Derby for five years in an effort to spread the word.

The participating city simply enrolls a lake for the program, paying a small portion of the fish stocking fee. The bulk of the money and law-enforcement manpower is provided by the Arizona Game and Fish Department. In fact, for every dollar a municipality spends, $5.70 worth of fish are stocked, services are rendered (including law enforcement, public outreach and educational efforts) and clinics are held. In 2002, 13,000 Tucsonans participated in the program—20 percent of which were youngsters and 13 percent seniors. In Tucson alone, urban anglers generated 150,000 angler recreation days, spending an average of $8 each day they fished, accounting for more than 9,000 urban fishing licenses.

Unfortunately, not everyone has witnessed firsthand the benefits of this incredible program.

While every effort has been made to include all of the lakes that participate in Arizona's Urban Fishing Program—18 waterways as of May 2003—a few listed in this chapter may have been removed because of water quality concerns or the winds of political change. Others may have been added or regulations changed. Consult a current set of Arizona Game and Fish Urban Fishing Regulations for more information or go to www.azgfd.com.

Waterways enrolled in the Urban Fishing Program are stocked with rainbow trout every other week from November to March. Expect to see catfish spilling out of the stocking truck every two weeks from April to October. In each stocking there are a number of larger incentive fish, with the average catfish stocked tipping the scales at 1.6 pounds. In addition to regularly scheduled fish plantings, an incentive trout stocking has become an annual event in January, including 2- to 4- pound rainbows. "The philosophy of the Urban Program is that if people can't get out to the fish, we will bring the fish to the people," said Eric Swanson, Arizona Game and Fish Urban Fisheries manager.

The exact number of fish stocked is calculated according to the waterway's surface acreage. Fast-growing hybrid sunfish are also routinely added, as was the case in mid-2002 when all urban lakes received three good stockings of these broad-shouldered fighters.

Expect daily fish limits to be different from rural regions of the state. And remember, each municipality's park rules apply. That means the park will close at the same time all other parks in that city do; open- or glass-container laws will be enforced; and boats and motors may not be allowed on the lakes.

Alvord Lake

Alvord Lake, located in south-west Phoenix at 35th Avenue and Baseline Road (in Cesar Chavez Park), covers 25 surface acres and is home to channel catfish, flat-head catfish, rainbow trout, blue-gill, tilapia, carp and largemouth bass. Alvord's maximum depth is 18 feet; its average is 14 feet.

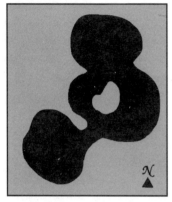

The lake may seem small, but as the October 7, 2002 catch of a 26-pound, 12-ounce flathead catfish shows, you never know what's lurking in Alvord's depths. In fact, Arizona Game and Fish officials claim they have never stocked flathead catfish, leading to speculation that the lunker made its way into the lake through one of the SRP canals that feed the lake. The fish surrendered to a bluegill used for bait.

Big fish weren't always the case at Alvord. A study conducted in November 1987 determined growth rates of large-mouth bass and bluegill were lower than biologists expected. Hoping to remedy the problem, the Arizona Game and Fish Department submerged 500 Christmas trees in six different locations in the lake in 1989, effectively adding ambush structure for the predatory fish.

An electro-fishing survey conducted in November of the same year indicated bluegill were the most abundant species at 43.6 percent of the lake's population. Redear sunfish followed closely at 40.2 percent. Threadfin shad accounted for 8.5 percent; largemouth bass, 5.1 percent; channel catfish, 1.7 percent; and green sunfish, 0.9 percent. The study also showed a number of heavier largemouth bass, which were noticeably missing from the original survey a few years before—proving the experiment an overwhelming success.

During the winter, when trout are stocked biweekly, a separate study determined angler catch rates at Alvord average 0.21 trout per hour. The same study determined when catfish are stocked, fishermen can expect to catch 0.15 catfish per hour. The best day to visit when chasing trout is the third day after the fish are stocked (the catch rate jumps to nearly 0.7 trout per hour, per angler) and catfish catch rates peak the same day the fish arrive at 0.7 catfish per hour.

For more information on the lake contact the Arizona Game and Fish Department at 602/789-3701 or visit www.azgfd.com. For park regulations call 602/262-6111.

Notable

October 7, 2002, 26-pound, 12-ounce flathead catfish

Alvord Lake is home to some huge catfish!

Canal Pond

At only three surface acres, with a maximum depth of seven feet (on a good day), one might not expect much from Tempe's Canal Pond.

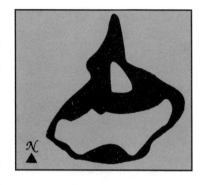

Looks can be deceiving.

In December 1992, a Phoenix man decided to spend his lunch hour at the lake with his cane pole. After a little while, someone walked up and asked if that was his pole skiing across the water. After retrieving it, he found a seven-pound catfish on the other end. He claimed to "not remember" what he was using for bait.

In June 1993, a 14-pound catfish was caught at Canal Pond (along with another 7-pounder). The same month, a 13-pound carp and an 8-pound bass were caught at the lake. On December 1, 1996, a state record Sonora sucker was caught here. It tipped the scales at 5 pounds, 6.4 ounces.

Canal Pond is located in Tempe's Canal Park. It's found at the intersection of McKellips Road and College Avenue, about a half mile west of Scottsdale Road.

Species available include channel catfish, rainbow trout, redear sunfish, hybrid sunfish, largemouth bass, bluegill, white amur and carp.

For up-to-date information on this lake call the Arizona Game and Fish Department at 602/789-3701 or visit www.azgfd.com. To learn more about park regulations call 480/350-5200.

Notable
June 1993, 14-pound channel catfish
June 1993, 13-pound carp
June 1993, 8.0-pound largemouth bass
December 1, 1996, 5-pound, 6.4-ounce Sonora sucker

Chaparral Park Lake

Chaparral Park Lake, in Scottsdale, is a quality fishery for crappie, channel catfish, rainbow trout, flathead catfish, redear sunfish, hybrid sunfish, bluegill, largemouth bass and carp. It has also been home to some interesting catches. For example, a few years ago a 12-pound catfish surrendered to a minnow rigged with a marshmallow as a "floater." It took the fisherman more than thirty minutes to land the lunker. And an 8-pound, 1-ounce catfish surrendered here to a stinkbait—so the catfishing at Chaparral has historically been downright good.

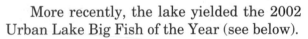

More recently, the lake yielded the 2002 Urban Lake Big Fish of the Year (see below).

Chaparral Park Lake covers 10 surface acres and has a maximum depth of 15 feet (average depth is 10 feet). According to a Game and Fish study, the best time to catch a lot of trout at Chaparral was the day after the stocking truck arrived, although the number of trout caught per hour (0.4 trout) was unchanged between day one and three after stocking.

The average number of trout caught, per angler, during the trout stocking season at Chaparral is 0.29 fish per hour. The number of catfish caught, per angler, during the catfish stocking season is identical. When catfish arrive, the best day to fish is the day after stocking. Catch rate, per angler, peaks on the same day at nearly 0.7 fish per hour.

The lake is at Hayden and Chaparral roads. For more information call the Game and Fish office at 602/789-3701. You can also visit www.azgdf.com. To learn more about park regulations call 480/312-2353.

Notable

December 20, 1992, 12-pound channel catfish
November 13, 2002, 1-pound, 15.52-ounce black crappie

Cortez Lake

Northwest Phoenix's Cortez Lake at the northeast corner of 35th Avenue and Dunlap Avenue may measure only three surface acres, but its fishing is much better than its size indicates. With a maximum depth of 14 feet, and averaging 10-foot depths, it's hard 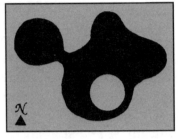 to believe rainbow trout of any size survive from stocking to stocking. Yet that's exactly what one Phoenix angler found in January 1992. Not only did he get a limit that day, but the last fish he put on the stringer was a 2-pounder that was 17 inches long.

Catfish seem to like the lake as well. On May 18, 2001, a 5-pound, 6-ounce channel cat was caught here. In August 1992, a fisherman caught an 8-pound channel catfish here using a "secret" spiced hamburger recipe for bait (raw hamburger with flour and garlic).

Species available include rainbow trout, channel catfish, largemouth bass, hybrid sunfish, bluegill, redear sunfish and carp. The largemouth bass fishing occasionally turns hot on this lake, as was the case in June 1993 when one angler caught four bass in only an hour, each weighing more than 2 pounds.

In late 2000, the lake was drained, and a $300,000 renovation project began that included deepening the lake by 4 feet; adding a new aeration system to ensure an ample oxygen supply for finny residents; and adding $10,000 of artificial habitat.

For more information call the Arizona Game and Fish Department at 602/789-3701 or visit www.azgfd.com. For information on park regulations call 602/262-6575.

Notable

August 1992, 8-pound channel catfish

May 18, 2001, 5-pound, 6-ounce channel catfish

Desert Breeze Lake

Located in west Chandler's Desert Breeze Park, this waterway is southwest of Ray Road and McClintock Drive on Desert Breeze Boulevard. Desert Breeze Lake impounds a total of 4 surface acres at a maximum depth of 12 feet. Average depth is 8 feet.

Species available include largemouth bass, bluegill, redear sunfish, hybrid sunfish, carp, channel catfish and rainbow trout. Boating times are limited at this lake, so consult current urban regulations prior to leaving.

For more information call the Arizona Game and Fish Department at 602/789-3701 or visit www.azgfd.com. For more information, call the City of Chandler Parks and Recreation at 480/782-2727.

Desert West Lake

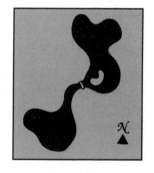

Desert West Lake is in Desert West Park in southwest Phoenix at 63rd Avenue between Virginia Avenue and Encanto Boulevard. The lake covers 5 surface acres with a maximum depth of 15 feet. Depths average around 11 feet. Here you'll find channel catfish, bluegill, rainbow trout, hybrid sunfish, redear sunfish, white amur, largemouth bass and carp.

For information on this lake call the Arizona Game and Fish Department at 602/789-3701 or visit www.azgfd.com. For more park regulations call 602/495-3700.

Notable

February 26, 2000, 8-pound, 12.5-ounce largemouth bass

Encanto Lake

Encanto Lake is in the heart of central Phoenix's Encanto Park, between 7th and 15th avenues and north of Encanto Boulevard. At 7.5 surface acres, this lake has a maximum depth of 10 feet. Several side channels that encircle much of the area can also be fished. Most of them are no deeper than 4 feet.

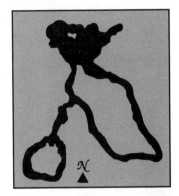

Residents in this lake include channel catfish, rainbow trout, largemouth bass, bluegill, hybrid sunfish, carp and redear sunfish. Like most urban fisheries, you never really know what you're going to catch.

Encanto is home to some huge carp, which are ideal for youngsters. In April 2002, a 30-pounder was caught, and only a month before an 18-pound carp surrendered to dough balls. Urban Big Fish of the Year for 2000 was a December 1 catch of a 19-pound, 13.3-ounce carp at Encanto.

If you're looking for some rod-ripping action, white amur, which were first introduced to help reduce the lake's weedline, are routinely caught at Encanto. On April 8, 1998, what was then a state record white amur was caught here. It tipped the scales at 40-pounds, 3.68-ounces. A 47-pound white amur, caught on Encanto in July 2002, subsequently eclipsed that record. There have been many more between, including the 44-pound, 3-ouncer caught on July 23, 2000; the 39-pounder caught on February 28 of the same year; and the 30-pound, 0.6-ouncer caught on March 11, 2002.

White amur are an extremely valuable species, and therefore anglers are typically required to release any they catch immediately. Consult a current set of urban fishing regulations for up-to-date information.

Catfish in Encanto are a strange breed—at least the big ones. In August 1993, an angler using in-line spinners slow-rolled the bait to catch three of the whiskerfish over 5 pounds each. Big catfish at this waterway are no surprise, however, as evidenced by the March 22, 2002, 6-pound, 12.8-ounce channel catfish the lake surrendered.

You never know what's going to answer the dinner bell. For example, on April 4, 1992, a woman fishing the golf course side of the lake caught a huge 2.24-pound bluegill. The lunker tried to lunch on a Canadian crawler. In October 1993, another fisherman at the lake caught a 6.5-pound largemouth bass. He was using a silver-bladed spinnerbait with a white and chartreuse skirt.

For more information call the Game and Fish Department at 602/789-3701. Call the Encanto Parks Department for more information at 602/261-8994.

Notable

April 4, 1992, 2.24-pound bluegill
October 1993, 6.5-pound largemouth bass
April 8, 1998, 40-pound, 3.68-ounce white amur
February 28, 2000, 39-pound white amur
July 23, 2000, 44-pound, 3-ounce white amur
December 1, 2002, 19-pound, 13.3-ounce carp
March 11, 2002, 30-pound, 0.6-ounce carp
March 22, 2002, 6-pound, 12.8-ounce channel catfish
April 2002, 18-pound carp
July 12, 2002, 47-pound, 1.6-ounce white amur

Green Valley Lakes

Lower (Main) Lake   **Middle Lake**   **Upper Lake**

The three Green Valley Lakes are located in Payson in Green Valley Park. The park is on Main Street, one mile west of State Route 87. It is one of the newest entries in the Urban Fishing Program. The lower lake covers 10 surface acres, the middle lake 1 acre and the upper lake is 2 surface acres. The upper lake reaches a maximum depth of 21 feet.

Every three weeks, from October to May, trout are stocked here. Unlike most other urban waterways, catfish are not stocked. Anglers can expect to catch hybrid sunfish, bluegill, green sunfish, channel catfish and largemouth bass.

Despite their urban location, these lakes offer anglers a cool retreat in the middle of summer. Their relatively short history means reliable reports of big catches are still a rarity, although the waterway did surrender a 7-pound, 3.84-ounce largemouth bass on November 15, 2001.

For up-to-date information on these lakes call the Arizona Game and Fish Department at 602/789-3701 or visit www.azgfd.com. For regulations regarding Green Valley Park call 928/474-5242, Ext. 7.

Notable
November 15, 2001, 7-pound, 3.84-ounce largemouth bass

Kennedy Lake

Kennedy Lake, located on Tucson's southwest side, is reached by taking Ajo Way west from I-19. Turn north on La Cholla Boulevard (the first street light past Mission Road), then follow the signs. Kennedy covers 10 surface acres and has an average depth of 8 feet. It may sound small, but it is definitely one of the state's most popular urban fisheries.

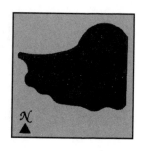

When I organized and conducted the Inner City Kids Fishing Derby at Kennedy Lake in the 1990s, only a few of the children who attended went home empty-handed. There wasn't an overabundance of lunkers, just plenty of stockers.

Respectable catches are nothing new to Kennedy. In January 1993, a 3.5-pound rainbow trout surrendered to an angler using Berkley Power Bait (at 8 P.M.). Add a 5-pound largemouth bass in the late 1980s; a 16.75-pound channel catfish on September 2, 1992 (the fish later got off the stringer and swam off); and a 9.7-pound carp in May 1993.

While action at Kennedy hasn't slowed, big catches at other urban waterways keep it out of the headlines. With rainbow trout, hybrid sunfish, largemouth bass, redear sunfish, carp and channel catfish, this inner-city waterway is more than worth a visit, and an ideal evening getaway. For more information on fishing Kennedy, contact the Tucson office of the Game and Fish Department by calling 520/628-5376. For details on park regulations call 520/791-5909.

Notable

> September 2, 1992, 16.75-pound channel catfish (chicken livers)
> September 2, 1992, 10-pound channel catfish (same angler as above)
> January 1993, 3.5-pound rainbow trout (Berkley Power Bait)
> May 1993, 8-pound channel catfish
> May 1993, 9.7-pound carp

Kiwanis Lake

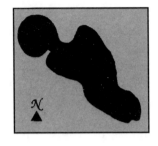

Kiwanis Lake is located in Tempe and is hard to miss at the intersection of Baseline Road and Mill Avenue in Kiwanis Park. It covers a total of 13 surface acres and has a maximum depth of 8 feet.

Don't let its small stature fool you! You never know what might be tugging at the other end of the line at Kiwanis. Consider the 6-pound, 7.52-ounce largemouth bass that was caught and released here on January 6, 2001; the 3-pound, 7.84-ounce tilapia (also released); or the December 22, 1992, 2.7-pound rainbow trout that the angler inadvertently foul hooked while retrieving a jig'n'pig.

But then, if you want to hear a real fish story, consider the June 1993 flyfisherman who latched into an 18-pound carp while using six-pound test.

As always, consult a current set of regulations for boating and fishing information, or give Game and Fish a call at 602/789-3701. You can also visit www.azgfd.com. For details on park regulations call 480/350-5200.

Notable

> December 22, 1992, 2.7-pound rainbow trout (foul hooked on a jig'n'pig)
>
> June 1993, 18-pound carp
>
> January 6, 2001, 6-pound, 7.52-ounce largemouth bass (catch-and-release)
>
> September 15, 2001, 3-pound, 7.84-ounce tilapia (catch-and-release)

Lakeside Lake

Lakeside Lake is located on the east side of Tucson in Chuck Ford-Lakeside Park. To reach the waterway, take Golf Links Road east past Davis-Monthan Air Force Base, turn south on Pantano, then east on Stella. There is a boat launch, but nothing larger than an electric trolling motor is allowed.

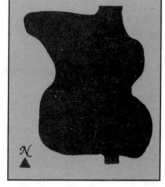

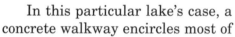

In this particular lake's case, a concrete walkway encircles most of the lake for easy wheelchair access. The east side of the lake even has a small "pier" that overlooks the water on those occasions when the lake is full.

Though Lakeside Lake may not look much different than other urban fisheries, it has a colorful history. When the original dam failed, a new, higher dam was created. A boat launch was originally located on the lake's east side.

The very first person to put a boat onto the water found the ramp a little more than simply steep and slippery. In fact, all that marked where the wrecker could find his truck, boat and trailer was the antenna sticking out of the water. It wasn't long until a new boat launch was installed on the northwest corner of the lake. It's paved, not very steep and reduces the chances that your vehicle meets the same watery grave.

I once watched a catfisherman for an hour one night as he struggled with what he thought was a huge lunker that refused to surrender any line. When I walked around to the other side of the lake, another angler was caught in exactly the same predicament. An hour later, the two fishermen walked around to one another and untangled their lines.

Obviously, urban fishing can be entertaining, whether the fish are cooperative, or not.

In the spring of 1992, tragedy struck. The lake's reclaimed water resulted in the waterway suffering with a pH level of 10.6—at the time the highest ever seen on an urban fishery. When the stocking truck arrived, they had not yet detected the problem, and as a result many of the trout died. Stocking was immediately suspended and in May 1992 the lake was treated with an algae retardant to lower pH levels and the biweekly summertime stockings of catfish were resumed. Unfortunately, complete fish kills-offs took place in 1999 and 2000.

When full, the lake covers 14 surface acres at a maximum depth of 35 feet. Average depth is 15 feet. Reclaimed water was first introduced to the lake in 1990. The city's "permanent" solution to the high pH problem—aerators—were installed in the winter of 1992-93. They didn't work and when the pH of the nutrient-loaded water again "spiked" in the spring and summer of 1993, a huge fish kill ensued. I won't even detail the experimental addition of sulfuric acid at about the same time.

The good news is that a state-of-the-art aeration system was installed at Lakeside in the summer of 2002 and the lake is in better condition than it has been for the past 10 years.

Lakeside Lake offers bluegills, catfish, hybrid sunfish, and redear sunfish. The waterway averages roughly 32,000 angler visits annually, and in at least one survey it was determined to have more youngsters fishing there than at any other lake in the entire state. With gently sloping shores, a resident population of ducks to feed, and plenty of park facilities nearby, it's easy to understand why.

For up-to-date information call the Arizona Game and Fish Department at 602/798-3701 or visit www.azgfd.com. For more on park rules call 520/791-5930.

Notable

January 25, 2001, 6-pound, 11-ounce rainbow trout (caught on a Super Duper. This fish was later disqualified for Big Fish of the Year because the angler snagged the lunker while it was languishing in shallow water.)

The Papago Ponds

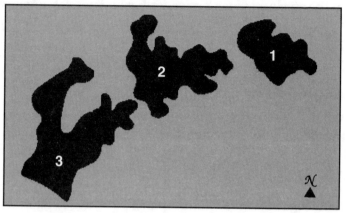

An elite group of fishermen invaded the Phoenix Zoo's ponds on September 25, 1992. Their job was a simple one— catch a few of the huge bass in the Zoo's five different ponds.

Game and Fish was standing by. Soon these fish were in the stocking truck and happily on their way to nearby Papago Park where they were released the next day into three different ponds, providing months of fun for metro-Phoenix's urban anglers. Papago Park is located next to the entrance of the Phoenix Zoo, north of Van Buren Street and east of the Galvin Parkway. Follow the signs once you're in the area.

The 11-pound, 10.4-ounce largemouth bass caught at one of the Papago Ponds in 2000 is evidence of how well the experiment worked. The fish surrendered to a two-inch Kalin pearl-colored lunker grub.

Of course, largemouth bass aren't the only thing the Papago Ponds offer. In February 1992, an angler using a plastic worm latched into a 36-pound, 8-ounce flathead catfish that took him 45 minutes to land.

The annual largemouth bass transplant from inside the protected Zoo's waterway has made the Papago Ponds into something special. In fact, it's being managed as an urban Blue Ribbon fishery for bass.

The entire Papago Park complex was created in 1932 by the Works Project Administration. Originally, there were eight lakes on the premises. When the City of Phoenix took over management of the area in 1961, five of the small impoundments were incorporated into the Phoenix Zoo grounds. They are not open to public angling, though the remaining three are.

Of those open to the public, Pond #1 covers a single surface acre and has a maximum depth of 8 feet; Pond #2 covers 2 surface acres and has a maximum depth of 7 feet; Pond #3 covers 3 surface acres at a maximum depth of 11 feet.

Even before the first organized volunteer transplant took place, creel surveys conducted in August 1992 showed the ponds were yielding some large bass. Things improved almost instantly. In December 1992, a 6.8-pound largemouth was caught on a crawdad colored Rat-L-Trap in the shallows at sunrise. In March 1993, an angler's single day of fishing with a rubber worm saw him catch and release 4-, 6- and a 7-pound, 12-ounce bass.

In June 1993 another angler caught a 6-pounder using a chartreuse spinnerbait, and in October 1993 another fisherman caught a pair of 5-pounders using a Zara Puppy. The reports out of Papago are always good, including in the dead of winter. And things have only gotten better and bigger, as evidenced by a March 3, 2000, 11-pound, 10.4-ounce largemouth bass—which was released.

The waterway has special Blue Ribbon regulations that are strictly enforced. For information call the City of Phoenix Parks and Recreation—Papago Park Rangers at 602/261-8318, the Arizona Game and Fish Urban Lakes Program at 602/789-3263 or call 602/789-3701. You can also visit www.azgfd.com.

Notable

February 1992, 36-pound, 8-ounce flathead catfish
December 1992, 6.8-pound largemouth bass
March 3, 2000, 11-pound, 10.4-ounce largemouth

Red Mountain Lake

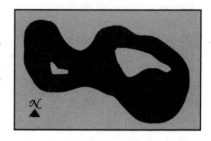

This lake is located in Red Mountain Park in east Mesa, at the southeast corner of Brown Road and Sun Valley Boulevard (3/4 mile east of Power Road).

At 8 surface acres, Red Mountain Lake is gaining a reputation for sizeable catches, including the 7-pound, 9.6-ounce largemouth bass caught here on November 22, 2002. It has a maximum depth of 17 feet and averages 12.

Anglers will find rainbow trout, channel catfish, bluegill, largemouth bass, hybrid sunfish, carp and white amur.

For more information call the Game and Fish Department at 602/789-3701 or visit www.azgfd.com. For information on the park and its regulations call 480/644-5319.

Notable

November 22, 2002, 7-pound, 9.6-ounce largemouth bass

Riverview Lake

Located in Riverview Park at 8th Street and Dobson Road in Mesa, Riverview Lake impounds 3 surface acres at an average depth of 10 feet. Maximum depth is listed at 16 feet—deep enough for those summertime channel catfish. Fish you can expect to catch include channel catfish,  rainbow trout, redear sunfish, hybrid sunfish, bluegill, tilapia, largemouth bass and carp.

For more information call the Game and Fish Department at 602/789-3701 or visit www.azgfd.com. For information on the park and its regulations call 480/644-4271.

Sahuarita Lake

Sahuarita Lake was added to Arizona's urban fisheries program on February 9, 2002.

To get there, take I-19 south from downtown Tucson for 18 miles then take the Sahuarita Road exit (Exit 75) and go 1 mile east to La Villita Road. Take La Villita Road 1.2 miles north to the north shore of the lake.

Rancho Sahuarita Lake Park, a 10-surface-acre impoundment has a maximum depth of 12 feet (7 foot average).

Fish available include largemouth bass, hybrid sunfish, redear sunfish, bluegill and seasonal stockings of channel catfish and rainbow trout.

For more information on this lake call the Arizona Game and Fish Department at 602/789-3701 or visit www.azgfd.com. For park regulations call 520/625-2731

Quite a variety of sunfish are available at urban lakes, making the lakes ideal for youngsters.

Silverbell Lake

Silverbell Lake is located in north-west Tucson in Christopher Columbus Park. The park is east of Silverbell Road between Camino del Cerro and Grant Road.

Silverbell Lake covers 13 surface acres at a maximum depth of 6 feet. Its depth averages 4 feet.

The lake was added to the urban fisheries program when the dam of Lakeside Lake, on the east side of Tucson, failed in 1984, and excess fish were dumped into Silverbell Lake. The Game and Fish Department claims fish were never stocked in the lake prior to that time.

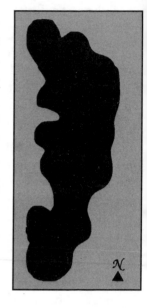

The fastest way to get to the lake is to take Grant Road west from I-10. Turn north on Silverbell, and keep an eye to the east of the road for the park. It's hard to miss (4600 North Silverbell).

Silverbell offers everything from channel catfish to rainbow trout, redear sunfish, bluegill, hybrid sunfish, largemouth bass, crappie and even carp.

Although water-quality tests a few years ago by the Arizona Game and Fish Department showed the lake was extremely nutrient rich and had plenty of forage for bass and larger bluegills, they didn't find the numbers and sizes of fish they expected. As a result, habitat and water improvement projects began.

Christmas trees were submerged along an area of the southwestern end of the lake, as well as forty special, gravel-filled spawning beds.

The results have been spectacular. In fact, in January of 2003 this lake surrendered the new urban record rainbow trout, a 4-pound, .32-ounce whopper, measuring in at 22 inches long!

For up-to-date information on this lake call the Arizona Game and Fish Department at 520/628-5376 or visit www.azgfd.com. You can also call 520/791-5890 for information on park regulations.

An assortment of crankbaits

 # Surprise Lake

Surprise Lake, located in the city of Surprise between Bell Road and Greenway Road, east of Bullard Avenue, covers 5 surface acres. Its average depth is 8 feet, and maximum depth is 12 feet. It is the most recent of the lakes to be added to the urban fishing program, joining their ranks on January 1, 2003.

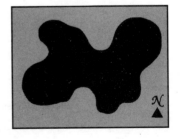

Anglers can expect to catch bluegill, redear sunfish, hybrid sunfish, channel catfish, rainbow trout and largemouth bass.

For more information on this lake call the Arizona Game and Fish Department at 602/789-3701 or visit www.azgfd.com. For park regulations call 623/583-0002.

Water Ranch Lake

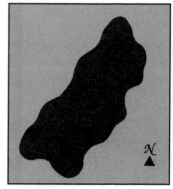

Located in Gilbert, at the intersection of Guadalupe and Greenfield roads, Water Ranch Lake impounds 5 surface acres at a maximum depth of 15 feet. Depth averages 11 feet. Fish you can expect to catch include hybrid sunfish, crappie, largemouth bass, channel catfish, rainbow trout, bluegill, redear sunfish, tilapia and carp.

For more information call the Arizona Game and Fish Department at 602/789-3701 or visit www.azgfd.com. For information on the park or its regulations, call 480/503-6200.

Notable

October 7, 2002, 2-pound, 0.96-ounce tilapia

This largemouth would please any angler!

South of the Border

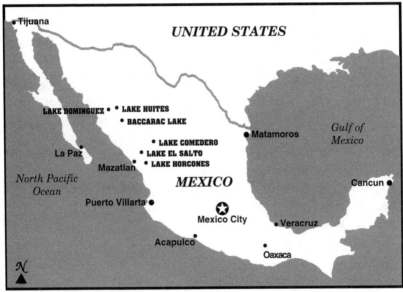

Map not to scale

Mexico is home to some of the best largemouth bass fishing in the world. Anglers have discovered everything from huge waterways—where running across even a single angler in an eight hour period is rare—to much smaller lakes just south of Douglas or outside Mazatlan.

Unfortunately, part of the south-of-the-border fishing mystique has historically been based upon stories of *banditos,* treacherous roads and official demands for *mordida* (bribes). While I can't address some of the more notorious stories, I can tell you that in the number of excursions I've taken into Mexico, my problems have been minimal.

I've boarded a plane in Phoenix, only to discover I had three times the cameras and four times the fishing rods Mexico legally allows tourists to bring into the country. It's the kind of problem easily avoided by simply studying regulations prior to departure, although Mexican customs agents were extremely understanding.

When the water pump in our car went out near Hermosillo, it was fixed in less than an hour at a lower rate than you'd expect in Tucson. Vehicle insurance procured before the trip, north of the border, has always been reasonable, and even those few "unsavory" characters I've encountered along the way have turned out to be little more than memorable sidebars to uneventful trips.

As always, be careful when you venture south of the border. Take your time, and first and foremost, remember you are a visitor in another country. More than likely you'll have a great time, like thousands before, but be sure to consult a current set of U.S. and Mexico regulations prior to leaving. Rules governing fishing in Mexico change with alarming regularity, and heightened Homeland Security efforts guarantee that international border-crossing regulations, regardless of direction, will continue to evolve.

Procure and fill out a visa before you hit the border. Airlines often provide you with the proper forms, and if you're flying in to engage a local guide service (often the easier route), ask your travel agent or outfitter.

All warnings aside, you owe it to yourself to visit Mexico, at least once, to fish some of the bassiest water on the entire planet. Though far from complete, what follows is a few of the most popular destinations for Arizona anglers.

Spinnerbaits are great in Mexican waters.

Baccarac Lake

Sometime toward the end of the '70s, the Mexican government impounded a section of river near Bacubirito. The 25-mile-long, 5-mile-wide impoundment today is known as Baccarac Lake, and it covers nearly 30,000 surface acres.

Baccarac Lake's primary purpose is to provide water for the area's huge agricultural industry. It also generates electricity, although the number of sprawling farms in this section of the state of Sinaloa makes its critical water-supply role obvious.

Some claim it was 1980, just after the lake filled, when 5,000 Florida-strain largemouth bass were transplanted from Texas and other Mexican lakes into Baccarac. Others argue it was 1978, and the government who did the planting, rather than a local physician who worked for the Southern Pacific Railroad. Either way, this nutrient-rich lake quickly acquired a reputation for growing big bass, fast.

Add the fact that commercial fishing is typically not allowed on the lake, and it's little wonder a delegation of Americans who visited the lake in the mid-1980s declared it would soon become world famous among bass fishermen. Although the prediction proved premature, it wasn't long after the lake opened to recreational anglers in 1983 that some huge fish were caught, including a 16.5-pounder in 1992, and the lake record 19.10-pound largemouth bass in January 1993.

Unusually fertile water also lends itself to thick weed growth, a problem the Mexican government attempted to remedy by treating the waterway with copper sulfate in 2000. The effort proved a disaster and resulted in a huge fish kill.

Take heart though, the lake's strategic location in a lush mountainous region, some 600 miles south of the border, means recovery is already underway. Nestled in a jungled foothill of the Sierra Madres, this is the kind of history-laden destination worth a trip in itself. Arrive at the right time, and the rain-swollen lake makes a scenic 80-mile run upstream possible.

Lake El Salto

Lake El Salto, which impounds 23,000 surface acres, lies only 20 miles from the Mexican coast some 50 miles north of Mazatlan. Formed when the government impounded the Elota

River, it rests roughly 500 feet above sea level, has a maximum depth of 150 feet and is most often claimed to be Mexico's most popular bass fishing destination.

The Florida-strain largemouth bass originally stocked in 1986 thrive in this relatively new lake—which has tons of cover—by ambushing the tilapia, crayfish and shad that also call these tropical waters home. The lower end of the lake features two cities that were completely submerged when the lake filled, with cemeteries famous for yielding big fish and incredibly thick cover. It's probably the best site to start working the lake there. El Salto has yielded an 18.5-pounder and in 2000 an 18-pound, 1-ounce, largemouth bass.

Like most of the Mexican Lakes, El Salto is new enough to be experiencing a "new lake" phenomenon. That is, the flooded timber and structure has only begun to decay, which translates to the kind of nutrient-rich water that allows the fish to grow at astonishing rates. Add tropical temperatures, and it's easy to see why Mexico's bass lakes continue to grow in legend.

Lake Comedero

Lake Comedero, 3 1/2 hours by road northeast of Mazatlan, was formed when a dam impounding the Rio San Lorenzo was completed in 1982. As is the case with most of the south-of-the-border waterways, it was originally designed to generate power and provide a stable water supply for nearby farms.

In the late 1980s, the 33,000-surface-acre waterway, which can reach depths of up to 300 feet, began receiving stockings of Florida-strain largemouth bass. It wasn't long until yet another Sierra Madre legend began to grow, one where 100 fish a day are possible and the lake record is an 18-pound largemouth.

Lake Comedero has traditionally been the site of some of Mexico's most aggressive freshwater management. It once had a unique slot limit, where every largemouth that tipped the scales at more than three pounds had to be returned to the lake—although anglers were allowed to keep one trophy fish per trip. It has also been a catch-and-release waterway, so be sure and consult a current set of regulations prior to departure.

The road to Lake Comedero from Mazatlan, although only 100 miles, can be extremely rough. Launching a boat with anything except four-wheel-drive vehicles is also often hazardous, so this is one destination where it's advisable to engage the services of a reputable guide or outfitter.

Lake Dominguez

Lake Dominguez, some 480 miles south of the border near Los Mochis, is 15 miles long and 10 miles across at its widest. It has a huge population of largemouth bass, although gill nets left by commercial fishermen can make working the water a real challenge.

Long casts, huge plastic worms and heavy weights are the key to big fish on Dominguez. Make sure to bring plenty of plastic worms, as the fish tear up whatever you're tossing in after a few casts. Getting to Lake Dominguez is as simple as following Mexican Route 15 south from Nogales or flying in to Los Mochis. There are several campsites, although their availability changes frequently—so call and reserve your site well ahead. Better yet, use one of the many guide services available.

I've personally witnessed fish in excess of 10 pounds caught here, although reports are sketchy and conflicting regarding any sort of unofficial "lake record." The waterway has plenty of cover, and despite the chronically fertile water guaranteed in the foothills of the Sierra Madre, angling pressure is always extremely light.

And more bass. . . .

Lake Huites

Located only three hours from the commercial airport at Los Mochis, Lake Huites is 30 miles long and impounds some 30,000 surface acres. Dam construction was completed in 1993. Originally intended to supply water for nearby irrigation and generate power, it was opened to American anglers in the spring of 1997.

Initially stocked with some 80,000 Florida-strain largemouth bass, this waterway has traditionally been managed as a catch-and-release-only fishery (check current regulations). At an elevation of 4,500 feet above sea level, expect comfortable temperatures and hot fishing. The lake has already surrendered a 13.6-pounder, on October 7, 2002, and a 12-pounder on March 12 of the same year. Most often the fishing season runs from October to the end of June.

Los Horcones Lake

Our guide's prehistoric Volkswagen bus wound through the pre-dawn, dusty back roads of Mazatlan. One final turn east and the rows of high-rise hotels and seafood restaurants were left behind, gradually replaced by tiny tenements that began crowding the road. We passed through several small villages, finally reaching the nearest freshwater lake to Mazatlan, Los Horcones, just as the sun heralded a new day.

Where the Pacific Ocean and Sea of Cortez meet, lies Mazatlan. With blue, black and striped marlin, sailfish, shark, broadbill swordfish, yellowfin tuna and dorado, its "blue line" is arguably one of the most productive billfishing destinations in the entire world.

But there's more, much more, in fact.

With lakes like Baccarac, Mateos and Hidalgo becoming increasingly familiar to north-of-the-border bass anglers, others like Los Horcones and El Salto hold the promise of legend as well. Add Florida-strain largemouth bass, and many are already regularly producing trophy-class bucketmouths.

At 600 surface acres, Los Horcones is extremely small by Mexican-lake standards, although it regularly produces some of the biggest tilapia I've ever seen. It also holds a sizeable population of bass. The real draw, however, is its strategic location, within minutes of one of the West Coast's most popular vacation destinations.

I had long heard about Mexico's voracious largemouth, although this was the first lake I had visited south of the border. When finally we launched the rustic boat, a gentle steam was rising from its tropical waters as we meandered out into the main lake.

My guide for the morning was an American who has called Mazatlan home for nearly 20 years. Finding a good guide for the lake is often as easy as asking the desk clerk at your hotel, which is exactly how we connected.

When you book one of the local guides, talk to them at length. Make sure they indeed will be picking you up instead of expecting you to find the lake, and get a feel for how good they are. Hold onto your money until after the trip, or try and pay only a deposit.

The morning I was on the lake, large black worms worked best. Most of the fish tipped the scales at between 1.5 to 3 pounds, and maintaining a 15-fish-per-hour pace was easy. The fisherman I was with threw Rat'L'Traps and ultimately caught the biggest fish of the day, a 4-pounder.

The jungle near Los Horcones is extremely thick, and as a result, the lake is covered in the kind of ideal cover bass thrive in. Interestingly, when Los Horcones was created, an entire village disappeared under its waterline. Today, where the city once was yields some of the largest lunkers.

Los Horcones may not offer the huge fish many of the other Mexican lakes do, but its strategic location—just outside Mazatlan—means by the next morning I was already afloat in the Pacific, in search of marlin. It's a combination that's hard to beat.

Kids and Fishing — A Healthy Mixture

His contagious grin beamed ear-to-ear excitement.

"I caught him," he proclaimed to the growing shoreline gallery. "He tried to take all my line, but I caught him. See. Here he is. Are we gonna keep him? Can we show Mom?"

Details of the battle were sketchy at first, though they came into focus as he caught his breath. That acrobatic 6-inch sunfish—his first real success without parental intervention—would be permanently etched into his memory and rightfully so.

Everyone's first fish is special. In fact, some of the clearest memories I have of my parents are of uninterrupted quality time fishing in the outdoors. I can almost smell my mother's perfume and hear my father's laugh. It didn't matter if we caught anything, we had good, clean family fun. And now that she's gone, those memories are some of my greatest treasures.

The fish bite best at sunrise, or so I theorized at five or six years old, as I dressed quietly in the tent, grabbed my gear and headed out. I guess my parents thought I was going to stay in camp, which as you can imagine caused quite a stir by the time they discovered me standing at the lake with a newfound friend who, unlike me, was capable of tying proper fishing knots in monofilament. It wasn't a total loss, either, as I did manage to catch a single trout that, true to form, put up a gallant and acrobatic struggle. Its watery explosions are still fresh in my memory, forty years later.

My mother hated handling live worms, so on another trip, when the walleye at Show Low Lake refused to take anything but live night crawlers, I became designated baiter. I could have complained, but the walleye kept biting. Besides, her insistence that the worms maintain a minimum distance forced her into the kind of erratic cast that endangered all within 50 feet. I baited her hook and ran.

My father brought something different to fishing. He understood the sport, and to this day the unspoken lessons he delivered so eloquently at the end of a rod define much of my character—patience, persistence, study and, above all else, integrity.

It's hard not to become fast friends while fishing. It's pure, simple pleasure. Gone is television's clutter. The Internet can no longer overwhelm and who needs mind-numbing video games when you're pitted against Mother Nature? It's fresh air, unencumbered conversation, nature at its finest and hours of hard-to-find companionship with little or no interruption.

It doesn't matter if you catch anything. The real trophy is the time you spend together—fleeting moments we may never recapture but whose memory will last forever. Although my mother didn't live long enough to ring in the new millennium, it seems only yesterday she was squealing at red wigglers and reminding me to savor the wind as it whispers through the pines. "You can hear angels sing," she said. It's the best of memories, a legacy capable of defying time.

Fishing is not as hard as it seems.

Perhaps the most important step for parents is to pick a nearby destination. Not only will this decrease the number of fast-food and bathroom-related stops, but it also reduces the frequency of that often torturous question "Are we there yet?"

Snacks are important for growing youngsters, and regardless how exciting a visit to the lake is, that between-meal hunger pang will come sooner or later. Arm yourself with a generous supply of something healthy—apples, oranges, raisins or granola bars.

Remember too, the majority of the skin's sun damage typically occurs at a young age (before age five). That means parents should apply liberal doses of sunscreen on their youngsters, at regular intervals. Use PABA-free sunscreen for infants or anyone with sensitive skin.

Adults, too, should be wary of Arizona's often relentless sun. Exposure can double near the water, and hats, long-sleeve shirts, zinc oxide and sunscreen are the Arizona angler's unofficial uniform.

Serious anglers usually arrive at sunrise and stay until the only light left is a faint orange glow in the western sky. When you have children along, this is a formula for disaster. For your first couple of trips, arrive mid-morning and leave shortly after lunch.

Pack a picnic and bring a blanket. Break your fishing trip into two distinct periods of time—fishing and a picnic. Try to keep the youngster's interest in fishing, although you'll know when the picnic needs to begin. Arizona's urban lakes are ideal first-time getaways.

Selecting the proper gear for the first trip is critical. The simpler it is, the better.

Start your youngster on a closed-face reel like the one shown here. Open machinery is an invitation for tangled line, sticks, bubble gum, dirt, mud and disassembly. Avoid the problem by using a simple system, and bring a spare reel for the inevitable.

Most people incorrectly think bobbers are designed to keep a child's bait from continually snagging the bottom. However, they're also an extremely convenient method of maintaining bait depth, something I've used successfully on a number of occasions in the White Mountains.

They also happen to be an ideal way to introduce a youngster to fishing. Rig up, toss the line and bobber into the water, and your child can play while keeping an eye on the bait.

Arizona's Sportfishing Education team deliberately uses the smallest hooks possible, and you should too, especially when dealing with novice anglers. The bigger the hook, the greater the chances something other than fish will get snagged. Use a hook big enough to catch your fish, but increase your margin of personal safety by thinking small.

Fishermen who pick up a rod and make a few casts with a lure during the first few outings with a youngster are courting disaster. Children will instantly get excited about the action and insist they too can work the water with the same proficiency as their parents.

Avoid the headache by limiting yourself to simple baits anytime time you're passing on the legacy. Working the shoreline with a live worm on the end of a bobber is a sure hit with bluegills, as is Velveeta cheese or corn for trout. When you get really ambitious, take the bobber off and add a weight and chicken liver for catfish (substitute sliced hot dogs for the liver if you're squeamish, although a hot dog is not quite as effective as bait).

Show that youngster you too can catch fish using that bobber rig and minimize the urge to step up to bigger hooks, lures and potentially disastrous casting and re-casting.

Remember, fish size is relative. That 6-inch bluegill may be a nuisance to a veteran angler, but to a 5 year old it's Jaws. The memory of that "tackle testing" fight will remain crystal clear for years to come, in both your memories. These memories are the cement that binds generations in the kind of heritage found only in the out of doors.

Isn't it time to write some indelible memories of your own? Start someone on a lifetime of good, clean, outdoor fun.

Take 'em fishing—and don't forget the camera!

First, Foremost and Last, Think Safety!

Dozens of jet skiers, boaters, anglers, swimmers and hikers drown or are injured needlessly every year in Arizona. In many cases the accident could have been avoided had they obeyed the first rule of the outdoor: First, foremost and last, think safety!

Boating and alcohol do not mix, and Arizona has a law on the books that makes operating a watercraft under the influence illegal. If you're caught, your boat, vehicle and trailer will be impounded. It makes sense. After all, someone drunk enough to have his or her boat confiscated doesn't need to crawl behind the wheel of a vehicle to drive home.

Anytime you have your boat's big motor running, make sure everyone in the boat has on a properly rated life vest. Do not disable the "kill" switch on your boat. I'm firmly convinced it saved my life on Lake Erie, and it could save yours. It is designed to stop the engine if the driver is thrown overboard, rather than allow the motor's torque to force the craft into increasingly concentric circles that ultimately result in the jettisoned driver and passengers being struck by a propeller—the so-called circle of death. Yes, every time you sit down to take off, it takes an extra second or two to reattach the kill switch, but the life you save may be your own.

Children and adults who can't swim should always wear a life vest. Period. It takes only a few seconds for someone to go under, and if this happens, even an adult who swims well is going to have trouble rescuing anyone in cold water.

Always keep a set of waterproof matches in your tackle box—just in case. Carry a compass, particularly if you're going to hike to the waterway, and always leave behind detailed information on destination, route and equipment you have along. I don't know how many times I've driven into a freak snowstorm in the White Mountains and wondered what might happen if I were to get stranded and no one knew where I was. I spent 12 years with Search and Rescue in Pima County, and two years in charge of Pima County Four Wheel Drive Search and Rescue. On those rare occasions when we had good information, we always got the person out OK. When we didn't, well, it wasn't always a happy ending.

Wear a hat. In the cold, up to 90 percent of body heat loss can be attributed to an unprotected head. In the summer, your nose, ears and face will thank you for the shade and protection from potential sun damage.

Get off the water during thunderstorms. Fiberglass and graphite fishing rods are great conductors of electricity, particularly when they're wet, making you and your fishing partners ideal lightning rods.

Enjoying Arizona's wonderful outdoors is safe, and easy, but first, foremost and last, think safety!

Keep a compass in your tackle box. Sudden storms, lake fog, etc., can make this a very important part of your equipment.

Who to Contact for More Information

The following list is as accurate as humanly possible. For up-to-date water quality and lake levels as well as current fish stocking information, etc., I always recommend that you call ahead. You will also find a number of area chambers of commerce (p. 249). Contact them for an idea of the hotels/motels in the area, restaurants and sights to see along the way.

Call the Arizona Fish and Game 24-hour hotline for current information on all lakes—602-789-3701

Apache-Sitgreaves National Forest
P.O. Box 640
Springerville, AZ 85938
Main Office: 928-333-4301
  District Offices:
    Alpine: 928-339-4384
    Black Mesa: 928-535-4481
    Clifton: 928-687-1301
    Lakeside: 928-368-5111
    Springerville: 928-333-4372
www.fs.fed.us/r3/asnf

Arizona Game & Fish Dept.
Main Office: 602-942-3000
2222 W. Greenway Rd.
Phoenix, AZ 85034
www.azgfd.com.

  Region 1: 928-367-4281
  2878 E. White Mountain Blvd.
  Pinetop, AZ 85935

  Region 2: 928-774-5045
  3500 S. Lake Mary Rd.
  Flagstaff, AZ 86001

  Region 3: 928-692-7700
  5325 N. Stockton Hill Rd.
  Kingman, AZ 86401

  Region 4: 928-342-0091
  9140 E. 28th St.
  Yuma, AZ 85365

  Region 5: 520-628-5376
  555 N. Greasewood Rd.
  Tucson, AZ 85745

  Region 6: 480-981-9400
  7200 E. University Dr.
  Mesa, AZ 85207

Arizona State Parks
1300 W. Washington St.
Phoenix, AZ 85007
602-542-4174
www.pr.state.az.us

Bureau of Land Management
222 N. Central Ave. Ste. 101
Phoenix, AZ 85004
602-417-9200
www.az.blm.gov

Coconino National Forest
2323 E. Greenlaw Lane
Flagstaff, AZ 86001
Main Office: 928-527-3600
  District Offices:
    Mormon: 928-774-1147

Regions used for map location purposes in this book are not the same as those used by the Arizona Game and Fish Department.

Peaks: 928-526-0866
Red Rock: 928-282-4119
Mogollon Rim: 928-477-2255
www.fs.fed.us/r3/coconino

Coronado National Forest
300 W. Congress FB 42
Tucson, AZ 85701
Main Office: 520-670-4552
  District Offices:
    Nogales: 520-281-2296
    Safford: 928-428-4150
    Santa Catalina: 520-749-8700
    Sierra Vista: 520-378-0311
www. fs.fed.us/r3/coronado

Glen Canyon Nat'l Rec. Area
P.O. Box 1507
Page, AZ 86040
928-608-6200
www.nps.gov/glca

Imperial Nat'l Wildlife Ref.
Box 72217
Martinez Lake, AZ 85365
928-783-3371

Kaibab National Forest
800 S. 6th St.
Williams, AZ 86046
928-635-2681
www.fs.fed.us/r3/kai

Lake Mead Nat'l Rec. Area
601 Nevada Way
Boulder City, NV 89005
702-293-8907
www.nps.gov/lame or
canyon-country.com/mead/
  meadinfo.htm

Lake Powell
www.travelwest.net/parks/
lakepowell or www.lakepowell.com

Navajo Nation Fish & Wildlife Service
Box 1480
Window Rock, AZ 86515
928-871-6451
www.navajofishandwildlife.org

Prescott National Forest
344 S. Cortez St.
Prescott, AZ 86303
Main Office: 928-443-8000
  District Offices:
    Chino Valley: 928-567-4121
    Crown King: 928-632-7740
    Verde Valley: 928-777-2216
www.fs.fed.us/r3/prescott

San Carlos Apache Recreation & Wildlife Dept.
P.O. Box 97
San Carlos, AZ 85550
928-475-2343
www.sancarlosrecreationand
  wildlife.com

Tonto National Forest
2324 E. McDowell Rd.
Phoenix, AZ 85006
Main Office: 602-225-5200
  District Offices:
    Cave Creek: 480-595-3300
    Globe: 928-402-6200
    Mesa: 480-610-3300
    Payson: 928-474-7900
    Pleasant Valley: 928-462-4300
    Tonto Basin: 928-467-3200
www.fs.fed.us/r3/tonto

White Mountain Apache Wildlife & Rec. Div.
P. O. Box 220
100 W. Satco Road
Whiteriver, AZ 85941
928-338-4385
www.wmatoutdoors.com

More locations for information, overnight reservations, etc.

Arizona Office of Tourism
1100 West Washington St.
Phoenix, AZ 85007
602-364-3700
www.arizonaguide.com

Lake Pleasant Marina
602-977-7377
www.azmarinas.com

National Recreation Reservation Service
877-444-6777
www.reserveUSA.com

Arizona Fishing Website Sampler

For a wide variety of information regarding lakes, equipment, guides, taxidermists, etc.

www.AZOD.com
www.FishinAZ.com
www.TucsonFishing.com
www.BajaTackleandMarine.com
www.azbasspro.com
www.SaguaroTackle.com

Various Chambers of Commerce

Douglas	520-364-2477
Eagar	928-333-2123
Flagstaff	800-842-7293
Florence	800-437-9433
Globe	800-804-5623
Greer	928-333-2123
Hoover Dam	702-293-2034
Lake Havasau	928-855-4115
Mesa	480-969-1307
Payson	520-474-4515
Phoenix	602-254-5521
Pinetop-Lakeside	800-573-4031
Safford	928-428-2511
Show Low	520-537-4126
Sierra Vista	520-458-6940
Tempe	480-967-7891
Tucson	520-792-1212
Willcox	520-384-2272
Williams	928-635-4061
Winslow	928-289-2434
Yuma	928-782-2567

Did we miss your favorite fishing hole?

If you have a favorite fishing hole that is not covered in this book, drop us a line (get it?) and we'll see if we can include it in the next updated edition of **Fishing Arizona.** If you have a favorite lure, tell us about that, too. If we use your information, we'll send you a free copy of **Fishing Arizona!**

Send your info to:

Golden West Publishers
4113 N. Longview
Phoenix, Arizona 85014

Big Catches

(Listed by species)

The decision not to address state inland or Colorado River records in this book was a conscious decision. Instead we've provided the reader the top five catches as of this printing, per species. While bigger catches are right around the corner, this information is designed to give the reader a synopsis of best times of year and productive waterways. Bear in mind that most big catches go entirely unreported, and therefore may not appear in our abbreviated list.

See updated listing of Big Catches (2003-2004) on Page 252.

Apache Trout
Introduced to Arizona: Native
June 10, 1993, 5 pounds, 15.5 ounces, Hurricane Lake
May 25, 1992, 5.88 pounds, Christmas Tree Lake
1991, 5 pounds, 3 ounces, Christmas Tree Lake
May 1990, 4 pounds, 13 ounces, Christmas Tree Lake
1989, 2 pounds, 1.5 ounces, Hurricane Lake

Arctic Grayling
Introduced to Arizona: 1940
July 10, 1995, 1 pound, 9.76 ounces, Lee Valley Lake

Bigmouth Buffalo
Introduced to Arizona: 1918
March 14, 1995, 36 pounds, 6 ounces, Roosevelt Lake

Black Buffalo
Introduced to Arizona: Unknown
June 19, 2002, 40 pounds, 5 ounces, Apache Lake
May 24, 1995, 35 pounds, 6.72 ounces, Canyon Lake
1998, 31 pounds, 1.8 ounces, Apache Lake

Black Bullhead
Introduced to Arizona: 1920
September 9, 2002, 2 pounds, 6.1 ounces, Parker Canyon Lake
August 22, 1993, 2 pounds, 4.6 ounces, Parker Canyon Lake

Black Crappie
Introduced to Arizona: 1905
1959, 4 pounds, 10 ounces, San Carlos Lake
February 2002, 2.96 pounds, Bartlett Lake
April 2000, 2.9 pounds, Roosevelt Lake
February 2002, 2.79 pounds, Bartlett Lake
March 11, 1996, 2 pounds, 12 ounces, Lake Havasu

Bluegill
Introduced to Arizona: 1932
1965, 3 pounds, 5.0 ounces, San Carlos stock pond
May 27, 1989, 2 pounds, 11.5 ounces, Lake Mead

April 4, 1991, 2.24 pounds, Encanto Lake
April 28, 2002, 1 pound, 11.52 ounces, Mittry Lake

Blue Catfish
Introduced to Arizona: Unknown
July 1970, 31 pounds, Randolph Park, Tucson

Brook Trout
Introduced to Arizona: 1903
March 6, 1982, 5 pounds, 4 ounces, Lee's Ferry
October 20, 1995, 4 pounds, 15.2 ounces, Sunrise Lake
May 1996, 4 pounds, 10.25 ounces, Big Lake
May 1977, 4 pounds, 4.5 ounces, Hawley Lake

Brown Trout
Introduced to Arizona: 1931
August 6, 1999, 22 pounds, 9 ounces, Reservation Lake
May 1, 1971, 17 pounds, Lake Powell
April 22, 1985, 16 pounds, 7 ounces, Horseshoe Cienega Lake
August 1993, 15 pounds, 9 ounces, Pacheta Lake
February 1984, 14 pounds, 5 ounces, Chevelon Canyon Lake

Carp
Introduced to Arizona: 1880
March 1979, 42 pounds, 0 ounces, Lake Havasu
August 8, 1987, 37 pounds, 0 ounces, Bartlett Lake
March 11, 2002, 30 pounds, 0.6 ounces, Encanto Park
April 2, 2001, 27 pounds, 11.04 ounces, Lake Pleasant
May 29, 2002, 27 pounds, 4.16 ounces, Saguaro Lake

Channel Catfish
Introduced to Arizona: 1903
1952, 35 pounds, 4 ounces, Topock Marsh
April 24, 1987, 32 pounds, 4 ounces, Parker Canyon Lake
April 1983, 31 pounds, 10 ounces, Arivaca Lake
June 1991, 29 pounds, Talkalai Lake
July 31, 2000, 18 pounds, 7.52 ounces, Rainbow Lake

Cutthroat Trout
Introduced to Arizona: 1900
August 1979, 9 pounds, 8 ounces, South of Davis Dam
October 1976, 6 pounds, 5 ounces, Luna Lake
June 15, 2000, 4 pounds, 8 ounces, Big Lake
August 15, 2002, 3 pounds, 12 ounces, Big Lake

Flathead Catfish
Introduced to Arizona: 1940s
May 11, 1998, 74 pounds, 0 ounces, Laguna Dam
May 10, 1998, 71 pounds, 0 ounces, Roosevelt Lake
1951, 65 pounds, San Carlos Lake
October 18, 1991, 62 pounds, Bartlett Lake

September 20, 2002, 57 pounds, 0 ounces, Bartlett Lake

Goldfish
Introduced to Arizona: Unknown
January 28, 1997, 5 pounds, 13.0 ounces, Colorado River

Green Sunfish
Introduced to Arizona: 1926
July 27, 1996, 1 pound, 9 ounces, Parker Canyon Lake
May 1, 1989, 1 pound, 8 ounces, Patagonia Lake
July 16, 1997, 1 pound, 5.28 ounces, Lake Havasu

Hybrid Sunfish
Introduced to Arizona: Unknown
October 12, 2000, 3 pounds, 1.28 ounces, Colorado River
July 30, 2001, 2 pounds, 14.88 ounces, Lake Havasu
June 5, 1998, 2 pounds, 2.22 ounces, Patagonia Lake

Largemouth Bass
Introduced to Arizona: 1897
February 21, 2002, 22 pounds, 4.8 ounces, Canyon Lake (C&R)
March 8, 1996, 16 pounds, 14 ounces, Colorado River
April 22, 1997, 16 pounds, 7.68 ounces, Canyon Lake
June 14, 2000, 16 pounds, 1.12 ounces, Canyon Lake
December 29, 2001, 16 pounds, 0.16 ounces, Canyon Lake

Northern Pike
Introduced to Arizona: 1965
November 28, 2002, 29 pounds, 13.76 ounces, Long Lake
May 29, 1999, 24 pounds, 11 ounces, Upper Lake Mary
June 4, 1981, 24 pounds, 3 ounces, Upper Lake Mary
October 26, 2001, 23 pounds, 7.04 ounces, Long Lake
June 23, 2001, 23 pounds, 1 ounce, Long Lake

Pacific Tenpounder
Introduced to Arizona: Unknown
June 13, 1981, 12.6 ounces, Near Pilot Knob

Pacu
September 8, 1999, 5 pounds, .02 oz., Lake Pleasant

Rainbow Trout
Introduced to Arizona: 1898
September 1966, 21 pounds, 5.5 ounces, Willow Beach
April 1979, 11 pounds, 1 ounce, Nelson Reservoir
November 9, 2002, 10 pounds, 3.2 ounces, Oak Creek
April 2002, 10 pounds, Canyon Lake
1992, 10 pounds, White River

Redear Sunfish
Introduced to Arizona: 1946
August 12, 1993, 3 pounds, 9 ounces, Goldwater Lake
June 15, 2000, 3 pounds, 8.64 ounces, Lake Havasu

March 17, 2002, 2 pounds, 14.72 ounces, Colorado River
June 24, 1995, 2 pounds, 14 ounces, Lake Havasu
June 8, 2002, 2 pounds, 11.5 ounces, Colorado River (C&R)

Rock Bass

Introduced to Arizona: Unknown
April 21, 2002, 0 pounds, 8.1 ounces, Oak Creek
June 3, 2001, 0 pounds, 5.33 ounces, Oak Creek

Smallmouth Bass

Introduced to Arizona: 1921
March 18, 1988, 7 pounds, 0.96 ounces, Roosevelt Lake
March 25, 2001, 6 pounds, 2.56 ounces, Fool Hollow Lake (C&R)
January 9, 2002, 5 pounds, 10.88 ounces, Roosevelt Lake
May 10, 2002, 5 pounds, 14.56 ounces, Fool Hollow Lake (C&R)
February 8, 1997, 5 pounds, 2.72 ounces, Colorado River

Striped Bass

Introduced to Arizona: 1959
August 15, 1997, 69 pounds, 1 ounce, Willow Beach
August 15, 1997, 67 pounds, 1 ounce, Lake Mohave
December 2002, 36 pounds, Lake Mead
December 1992, 32.3 pounds, Lake Powell
May 3, 1997, 23 pounds, 8.32 ounces, Alamo Lake

Tilapia

Introduced to Arizona: 1960s
March 31, 2002, 7 pounds, 8.8 ounces, Saguaro Lake
April 16, 2001, 7 pounds, 2.56 ounces, Saguaro Lake
October 14, 2000, 7 pounds, 1 ounce, Saguaro Lake
April 7, 2000, 6 pounds, Saguaro Lake
April 17, 1996, 5 pounds, 8 ounces, Saguaro Lake

Walleye

Introduced to Arizona: 1957
November 18, 2002, 16 pounds, 1.76 ounces, Show Low Lake
September 7, 2001, 13 pounds, 11 ounces, Show Low Lake
October 15, 2000, 12 pounds, 14.4 ounces, Show Low Lake
April 29, 1989, 12 pounds, 12 ounces, Show Low Lake
June 30, 2001, 12 pounds, 11.68 ounces, Show Low Lake (C&R)

White Amur

Introduced to Arizona: Unknown
July 12, 2002, 47 pounds, 1.6 ounces, Encanto Park
July 23, 2000, 44 pounds, 3 ounces, Encanto Park
April 8, 1998, 40 pounds, 3.68 ounces, Encanto Park
February 28, 2000, 39 pounds, Encanto Park

White Bass

Introduced to Arizona: 1960
March 1972, 5 pounds, 5 ounces, Imperial Reservoir
April 1972, 4 pounds, 11.7 ounces, Lake Pleasant
April 15, 2000, 2 pounds, 9.12 ounces, Lake Pleasant
March 30, 2001, 2 pounds, 0.32 ounces, Lake Pleasant

White Crappie
>   Introduced to Arizona: 1903
>   February 22, 1982, 3 pounds, 5.28 ounces, Lake Pleasant

Yellow Bass
>   Introduced to Arizona: 1930
>   May 19, 1995, 1 pound, 15.8 ounces, Upper Lake Mary
>   June 31, 1985, 1 pound, 11 ounces, Canyon Lake
>   June 30, 2002, 1 pound, 3.52 ounces, Saguaro Lake

Yellow Bullhead
>   Introduced to Arizona: 1920
>   July 15, 1989, 4 pounds, 8.1 ounces, Mormon Lake
>   March 24, 1986, 2 pounds, 8.8 ounces, Colorado River
>   March 2000, 1 pound, 13.6 ounces, Apache Lake

Yellow Perch
>   Introduced to Arizona: 1919
>   March 21, 1984, 1 pound, 10 ounces, Stoneman Lake
>   March 24, 1984, 1 pound, 10 ounces, Stoneman Lake

Additional Top Catches (2003-2004)

Inland Waters -- Hook and Line
Bluegill —May 2, 2004, 3 lb. 15.68 oz. 15.75 in., Goldwater Lake
Catfish, Flathead —Jan. 5, 2003, 71 lb. 10.24 oz., 53 in., San Carlos Lake
Mullet —April 24, 2004, 5 lb. 2.24 oz. 23.75 in., Fortuna Pond
Northern Pike —Nov. 5, 2004, 32 lb. 5.6 oz. 49 in., Ashurst Lake
Trout, Rainbow —Dec. 28, 2002, 12 lb. 5.76 oz. 32.25 in., Tempe Town Lake

Inland Waters -- Catch and Release +
Bass, Smallmouth —April 23, 2003, 21 in. Fool Hollow Lake
Bass, Yellow —April 19, 2003, 10 in. Saguaro Lake
Buffalo, Black —April 23, 2003, 41 in. Apache Lake
Carp —April 29, 2003, 35 in. Saguaro Lake
Catfish, Channel —April 29, 2003, 30 in. Saguaro Lake
Catfish, Flathead —April 26, 2003, 47 in. Bartlett Lake
Sunfish, Hybrid —June 19, 2004, 10 in. Papago Ponds #2
Sunfish, Redear —July 3, 2004, 11 in. Papago Ponds #2
Tilapia —October 8, 2003, 17 in. ASU Research Park
Trout, Apache —October 16, 2004, 18 in. Christmas Tree Lake
Walleye —June 27, 2004, 33 in. Fool Hollow Lake
White Amur —September 16, 2004, 41 in. ASU Research Park

Colorado River Waters -- Catch and Release +
Bass, Largemouth —Feb. 17, 2004, 28 in. —Lower Colorado River

Note: C&R denotes the Arizona Game and Fish Department's catch-and-release records. For the catches listed here, anglers were required to photograph their catch and calculate its weight using the formula (Girth)2 X Length/800. As of January 1, 2003, anglers are now required to photograph the fish and measure its length. C&R records, therefore, will now be measured in length instead of weight.

2004 ARIZONA
BIG-FISH-OF-THE-YEAR RECORDS
2004 FINALISTS

Bluegill—3 lb. 15.68 oz., 15.75 in., Goldwater Lake, Christopher Ray Mapes, 05/02
Brook Trout—0 lb. 14.88 oz., 13.31 in., Big Lake, Taylor Wallis, 11/13
Brown Trout—8 lb. 14.4 oz., 29 in., River Reservoir, Lyle Dalby, 06/06
Carp—33 lb. 9.6 oz., 44.5 in., Lower Salt River, Colton J. Bagnoli, 04/15
Channel Catfish—19 lb. 3 oz., 34 in., Kaibab Lake, Kit Kuykendall, 04/29
Flathead Catfish—66 lb. 8.64 oz., 48 in., Roosevelt Lake, Harold M. Chavez, 11/08
Hybrid Sunfish—0 lb. 3.2 oz., 6.75 in., Fortuna Pond, Elaine J. Griswold, 03/25
Largemouth Bass—12 lb. 4.32 oz., 27 in., Canyon Lake, Bill Warman, 05/18
Mullet—9 lb. 1.6 oz., 27.25 in., Salinity Canal, Daniel S. Day, 05/02
Northern Pike—32 lb. 5.6 oz., 49 in., Ashurst Lake, Ronald Needs, 11/05
Redear Sunfish—0 lb. 15.2 oz., 10.5 in., Gila Gravity Canal, Tyler Arnett, 07/16
Tilapia—7 lb. 15 oz., 20.25 in., Saguaro Lake, Michael T. Young, 04/26
Walleye—12 lb. 7.04 oz., 30.63 in., Show Low Lake, James Churchill, 06/07
Yellow Bass—1 lb. 8 oz., 14 in., Apache Lake, Charlie Prince, 03/24

CATCH and RELEASE RECORDS*

Apache Trout—18 in., Christmas Tree Lake, Jeff Senn, 10/16
Carp—33 in., Saguaro Lake, Ron Nuss Jr., 05/18
Channel Catfish—20 in., Tempe Town Lake, Edward S. Zalig, 03/31
Flathead Catfish—37 in., Bartlett Lake, Laurie Lingreen, 03/20
Largemouth Bass—28 in., Lower Colorado River, David Percell, 02/17
Redear Sunfish—10 in., Lake Pleasant, Mary Moore, 05/12
Smallmouth Bass—19 in., Roosevelt Lake, Gregg Munck, 04/20
Walleye—33 in., Fool Hollow Lake, Gregg Munck, 06/27
White Amur —41 in., ASU Research Park, Stuart Black, 09/16

URBAN LAKE RECORDS

Carp—15 lb. 1.6 oz., 31 in., Alvord Lake, Russell J. McMillan, 09/29
Channel Catfish—10 lb. 8.32 oz., 25 in., Chaparral Lake, Kevin Collins, 03/20
Rainbow Trout—2 lb. 10 oz., 17.38 in., Encanto Park Lake, Luis Bermudes, 02/12
White Amur—32 lb. 15.04 oz., 40 in., Kiwanis Lake, Duane Halvorson, 03/17

URBAN LAKE CATCH and RELEASE RECORDS

Hybrid Sunfish—10 in., Papago Ponds #2, Mack Hollen Jr., 06/19
Largemouth Bass—20 in., Papago Ponds #1, Louis Hoeniger, 05/15
Redear Sunfish—11 in., Papago Ponds #2, Warren Hollen, 07/03

* Based on length only and rounded down to nearest inch. New entries must exceed existing entry by at least 1 inch.

Arizona Fishing License Vendors
(Names, addresses and telephone numbers subject to change)

Amigo Liquor/Party	750 N. Second	Ajo	520-387-6966
Amigo Liquor/Party	750 N. Second	Ajo	520-387-6966
Luna Lake Yacht Club	P.O. Box 761	Alpine	928-520-4518
The Tackle Shop LLC	P.O. Box 109	Alpine	928-339-4338
Wal-Mart	10603 E. Apache Trail	Apache Jnctn	480-380-3800
Straight Shooter Guns	517 W. Western	Avondale	623-925-0988
Wal-Mart	955 E. Rancho-Santa Fe	Avondale	623-935-4010
Bashas	105 Main St.	Bagdad	928-633-4599
Benson Ace Hardware	P.O. Box 265	Benson	520-586-7345
Safeway	101 Naco Hwy.	Bisbee	520-432-3038
The Stage Stop	18740 School House Rd.	Black Cnyn Cty	623-374-0252
Big K Discount Food	101 E. Monroe	Buckeye	623-386-5047
Buckeye Feed & Co.	24100 W. Hwy 85	Buckeye	623-386-6122
Big 5 Sporting Goods	1835 Hwy 95	Bullhead City	928-763-0608
Lake Mohave Resort	Katherine Landing	Bullhead City	928-754-3245
K Mart	2250 Hwy 95	Bullhead City	928-763-7878
Wal-Mart	2840 Hwy 95	Bullhead City	928-758-7222
Alco Discount	522 Finnie Flat Rd.	Camp Verde	928-567-1968
Bashas	7th St. & Finney Flat	Camp Verde	928-252-5385
Camp Verde Feed	4201 E. Hwy 260	Camp Verde	928-567-3351
Bashas	36889 Tom Darlington	Carefree	480-488-1797
Big 5 Sporting Goods	1320 E. Florence Blvd.	Casa Grande	520-836-6471
K mart	1214 E. Florence Blvd.	Casa Grande	520-836-3466
Wal-Mart	1325 E. Florence Blvd.	Casa Grande	520-421-1200
TJ's Hardware	6140 E. Cave Creek Rd.	Cave Creek	480-488-1520
Archery Headquarters	6401 W. Chandler Blvd.	Chandler	480-961-3100
Big 5 Sporting Goods	2050 N. Arizona Ave.	Chandler	480-821-9226
Chandler Liquors	554 N. Arizona Ave.	Chandler	480-963-5100
Popular Outfitters	2050 N. Alma School	Chandler	480-899-3662
Tempe Marine Ltd.	1800 N. Arizona Ave.	Chandler	480-782-6813
Wal-Mart	800 W. Warner Rd.	Chandler	480-786-0062
Alco Discount	1950 N. Hwy 89	Chino Valley	928-636-8603
Buckaroo Roundup Mkt.	1496 N. Hwy 89	Chino Valley	928-636-2232
Cibola Sportsmens Club	Rt. 2 Box 105	Cibola	928-857-3531
Rick Francis Guide SVC	65891 N. Melody Ln.	Cibola	928-857-3581
Wal-Mart	100 S. Ragus Rd.	Claypool	928-425-7171
Coles Sporting	3-Way Intersection	Clifton	928-687-1111
Jiffy Store	Commercial Drive	Concho	928-337-2616
Bottle Stop Inc.	474 S. Arizona Blvd.	Coolidge	520-723-3852
Wal-Mart	1695 N. Arizona Blvd.	Coolidge	520-723-0945
Wal-Mart	1100 W. Hwy 279	Cottonwood	928-634-0444
J-J Supply co.	1661 Ave. 64 E	Dateland	928-454-2263
Davis Monthan AFB	5465 E. Nuggat St.	Davis Mnthn	520-228-4491
Wal-Mart	204 W. 5th Ave.	Douglas	520-364-1281
Bashas	150 N. Main St.	Eagar	928-333-0177
River Lagoon Resort	Parker Poston Rd.	Ehrenberg	928-923-7942
Desert Videoland Oasis	10338 N. Hwy 191	Elfrida	520-642-3819
Fish Haven Inc.	HC 1 Box 372	Elgin	520-455-5847

Babbits Fly Fishing	15 E. Aspen Ave.	Flagstaff	928-779-3253
Bashas	2700 S. Woodlands Vlg.	Flagstaff	928-252-1523
Big 5 Sporting Goods	2775 S. Woodlands Vlg.	Flagstaff	928-214-0590
Express Stop	4525 N. Hwy 89	Flagstaff	928-526-2959
*AZ Dept. Game/Fish	3500 S. Lake Mary Rd.	Flagstaff	928-774-5045
Lake Mary Co. Store	480 Lake Mary Rd.	Flagstaff	928-774-1742
Peace Surplus Inc.	14 W. Santa Fe	Flagstaff	928-779-4521
Popular Outfitters	901 S. Milton Rd.	Flagstaff	520-774-0598
Ruffs Liquor/Sporting	2 S. Milton Rd.	Flagstaff	928-774-6051
Silver Saddle Trading	9001 N. Hwy 89	Flagstaff	928-527-1672
Wal-Mart	2750 S. Woodlands Blvd.	Flagstaff	928-773-1117
Florence True Value	290 N. Main St.	Florence	520-868-0410
The Bottle Shoppe	231 N. Main St.	Florence	520-868-4281
Campers Ctry Corner	Hwy 260 & Spring Loop	Forest Lakes	928-535-4716
Keen's Store	15560 W. Hwy 70	Fort Thomas	928-485-2261
Judd Auto Service	623 S. Main	Fredonia	928-643-7107
Lawrence Reese	395 N. Main	Fredonia	928-643-7274
ATZS-US Army	Sportsman Center	Fort Huachuca	520-533-7085
Henry/Davis Inc.	619 W. Pima	Gila Bend	928-683-2468
Papago Hardware	110 N. Martin	Gila Bend	928-683-2457
K Mart	6761 W. Bell Rd.	Glendale	623-412-2539
Lone Wolf Trading Co.	4977 W. Peoria Ave.	Glendale	623-939-0668
The Sports Authority	7360 W. Bell Rd.	Glendale	623-412-0416
Wal-Mart	5845 W. Bell Rd.	Glendale	623-978-8205
Waterdog Willy's West	4360 W. Olive	Glendale	623-435-1533
Express Stop	1501 E. Ash St.	Globe	928-425-3911
**Killmer's Kountry Store	Hwy. 88 Apache Trail	Globe	928-425-1142
Sir Alberts Ctry Store	3685 Hwy 68	Golden Valley	928-565-4632
General Store	Mathers Bus Center	Grand Canyon	928-638-2262
Wal-Mart	18705 S. I-19 Frntge Rd.	Green Valley	520-625-3808
Circle B. Market & Motel	38940 Hwy 373	Greer	928-735-7540
Long Valley Service	MP 290/Hwy 87	Happy Jack	928-477-2211
Rim Resort	985 A AZ Hwy 260	Heber	Seasonal
Alco Discount	1515 Navajo Blvd.	Holbrook	928-524-3078
Walts Western Hdwr.	516 W. Hopi Dr.	Holbrook	928-524-6946
Jacob Lake Inn	Int. Hwy 89A & 67	Jacob Lake	928-643-7232
Speedy's	4526 Main	Joseph City	928-288-3490
Kayenta Trading Post	1000 Main St.	Kayenta	928-697-3541
Ace Hardware	346 Alden Rd.	Kearny	928-363-7346
Byers Northern Liquor	3019 Northern Ave.	Kingman	928-757-8631
*AZ Dept. Game/Fish	5325 N. Stockton Hill	Kingman	928-753-3300
Garland Fishing Products	602 1/2 Andy Devine	Kingman	928-753-5242
K Mart	3340 E. Andy Devine	Kingman	928-757-3202
Wal-Mart	3320 Stockton Hill	Kingman	928-692-0555
*Anglers Pro Shop	251 London Bridge Rd.	Lake Havasu	928-854-2277
Big 5 Sporting Goods	251 S. Lake Havasu Ave.	Lake Havasu	928-536-0611
Hidden Shores RV Vlg.	2410 Demaret Dr.	Lake Havasu	928-783-1448
K Mart	1870 Mc Culloch Blvd.	Lake Havasu	928-453-5919
Lake Havasu Marina	1100 Mc Culloch Blvd.	Lake Havasu	928-855-6525
Sandpoint Marina	P.O. Box 1469	Lake Havasu	928-855-0549

Vendor	Address	City	Phone
Wal-Mart	1795 N. Kiowa Blvd.	Lake Havasu	928-453-565
Bobs Bang Room	3973 Hwy 260	Lakeside	928-368-504
Lyman Lake Store	Hwy. 180 & Hwy. 191	Lakeside	928-537-888
Pinetop Sporting Goods	747 E. White Mntn. Blvd.	Lakeside	928-367-505
Rainbows End Resort	2677 Trout Rd.	Lakeside	928-368-900
Ambassador Guide Ser.	MP541 1/2 Hwy 89A	Marble Cnyn	928-355-235
Lees Ferry Anglers Inc.	MP 541 1/2 Hwy 89A	Marble Cnyn	928-355-226
Marble Canyon Co. Inc.	MP 547 1/2 Hwy 89A	Marble Cnyn	928-355-222
Martinez Lake Resort	St. Rt. 4	Martinez Lake	928-783-958
Meadview Market	110 Meadview	Meadview	928-564-229
*AZ Dept. Game/Fish	7200 E. University	Mesa	480-981-9400
Arizona Sportsman	1232 E. Southern	Mesa	480-844-0802
Bear Mountain Sports	899 E. Southern	Mesa	480-926-7161
Big 5 Sporting Goods	2930 N. Power Rd.	Mesa	480-854-1889
K Mart	1920 W. Broadway	Mesa	480-833-1291
K Mart	2840 E. Main St.	Mesa	480-832-2650
K Mart	1445 Power Road	Mesa	480-985-8448
K Mart	5833 E. McKellips Rd.	Mesa	480-396-2891
Larada Army Surplus	764 W. Main St.	Mesa	480-834-7047
*Liar's Korner	9529 E. Apache Trail	Mesa	480-986-2515
Mesa Gun Shop	915 E. Broadway	Mesa	480-962-9802
Popular Outfitters	202 E. Southern	Mesa	480-844-1153
Popular Outfitters	1845 S. Power Rd.	Mesa	480-654-0755
Popular Outfitters	5916 E. McKellips Rd.	Mesa	480-325-3944
*Saguaro Lake Marina	14011 Bush Highway	Mesa	480-986-0969
The Sports Authority	7022 E. Hampton Ave.	Mesa	480-654-6888
The Sports Authority	1308 S. Country Club Dr.	Mesa	480-649-1495
U Stop Conv. Store	5207 E. Main St.	Mesa	480-985-4231
Wal-Mart	1955 S. Stapley Dr.	Mesa	480-892-9009
Wal-Mart	1305 W. Main St.	Mesa	480-962-1162
Wal-Mart	6131 E. Southern Ave.	Mesa	480-830-3919
The Beverage House	2250 US Hwy 60	Miami	928-425-2912
Phelps Dodge Merc	Plantsite Shop Ctr	Morenci	928-865-4121
Mormon Lake Lodge	P.O. Box 38012	Mormon Lake	928-354-2227
City Concession	423 Lake Patagonia Rd.	Nogales	520-391-0753
K Mart	300 W. Mariposa Rd.	Nogales	520-761-4844
Wal-Mart	351 W. Mariposa Rd.	Nogales	520-281-4974
Guyton's Feed	1210 W. American Ave.	Oracle	520-896-2158
Al's Rim Auto & Sports	1884 Hwy 260	Overgaard	928-535-4256
Bashas	687 S. Lake Powell Rd.	Page	928-645-3291
Fred's Liquor Store	902 N. Navajo Dr.	Page	928-645-3575
Lake Powell Conv. Ctr.	P.O. Box 3910	Page	928-645-5998
Southwest Sport	100 Lakeshore Dr.	Page	928-645-1051
Stix Market	5 S. Lake Powell Blvd.	Page	928-645-2666
Wahweap Lodge	100 Lakeshore Dr.	Page	928-645-2433
Wal-Mart	655 S. Lake Powell Blvd.	Page	928-645-2622
Blue Water Resort	11300 Resort Dr.	Parker	928-669-7000
Doodlebug Bait Shop	10221 Harbor Dr.	Parker	928-667-1121
*June's Unique	809 K of A Ave.	Parker	928-669-8883
Lake Havasu Spr. Resort	2581 Hwy 95	Parker	928-667-3361

Woodys	1001 Fiesta Dr.	Parker	928-669-8792
**Marina Cove Store	Patagonia Lake State Park		520-287-6063
Bashas	142 E. Hwy. 260	Payson	928-258-0358
Express Stop	401 S. Beeline Hwy	Payson	928-474-4736
Jake's Corner Store	HC-1 Box 5276V	Payson	928-474-4675
Payson Market Place	1116 N. Beeline Hwy	Payson	928-474-2810
Tall Pines Market	HC-2 Box 121L	Payson	928-478-4550
Wal-Mart	300 N. Beeline Hwy	Payson	928-474-0031
Webers IGA Food	107 E. Hwy 260	Payson	928-474-2922
Woods Canyon Store	Rt. 105 Hwy 260	Payson	928-521-3101
Big 5 Sporting Goods	10030 N. 91st Ave.	Peoria	623-878-0399
Big K Mart	10140 N. 91st Ave.	Peoria	623-486-1830
Campbell Mercantile	9098 W. Pinnacle Peak	Peoria	623-972-6133
Oshmans	7555 West Bell Rd.	Peoria	623-979-5900
Pleasant Harbor Marina	40202 N. 87th Ave.	Peoria	602-977-7377
Popular Outfitters	6750 W. Peoria	Peoria	623-979-5450
Wal-Mart	8200 W. Peoria Ave.	Peoria	623-878-9907
**AZ Dept. Game/Fish	2222 W. Greenway Rd.	Phoenix	602-942-3000
AZ Public Land Info.	222 N. Central Ave.	Phoenix	602-417-9800
Arizona Sportsman	2314 E. Bell Rd.	Phoenix	480-844-0802
Alta Vista Classic Angler	4730 N. 7th Ave.	Phoenix	602-277-3111
Arizona Sportsman	525 W. Camelback Rd.	Phoenix	602-264-1970
Big 5 Sporting Goods	3560 E. Thomas Rd.	Phoenix	602-955-9601
Big 5 Sporting Goods	1919 W. Bell Rd.	Phoenix	602-863-1309
Big 5 Sporting Goods	4623 E. Cactus Rd.	Phoenix	602-953-0305
Del Re Western Outdoor	5437 S. Central Ave.	Phoenix	602-276-1409
Desert Hills Mail Box	515 E. Carefree Hwy	Phoenix	623-780-7692
Fisherman's Choice Pro	13616 N. 35th Ave.	Phoenix	602-993-1139
Honeywell Empl. Club	3401 E. Airlane	Phoenix	602-231-7406
K Mart	4225 W. Indian School	Phoenix	602-272-1317
K Mart	2526 W. Northern Ave.	Phoenix	602-995-8867
K Mart	801 E. Bell Rd.	Phoenix	602-863-6774
K Mart	1602 E. Roosevelt St.	Phoenix	602-258-6957
K Mart	3401 W. Greenway Rd.	Phoenix	602-993-8050
K Mart	12025 N. 32nd St.	Phoenix	602-996-4950
K Mart	335 E. Baseline Rd.	Phoenix	602-276-1181
Phoenix Arms	717 W. Union Hills Dr.	Phoenix	602-993-2389
Popular Outfitters	3536 W. Glendale	Phoenix	602-841-2811
Popular Outfitters	2814 W. Bell Rd.	Phoenix	602-863-2462
Popular Outfitters	15230 N. 32nd St.	Phoenix	602-493-3223
Popular Outfitters	4025 N. 16th St.	Phoenix	602-264-3535
Popular Outfitters	4525 E. Ray Rd.	Phoenix	480-705-9513
The Sports Authority	12869 N. Tatum Blvd.	Phoenix	602-494-7715
The Sports Authority	9610 Metro Pkwy	Phoenix	602-870-3620
Sportmart	7000 E. Mayo Blvd.	Phoenix	480-563-4009
Wal-Mart	3721 E. Thomas Rd.	Phoenix	602-685-0555
Wal-Mart	1606 W. Bethany Home	Phoenix	602-246-1700
Wal-Mart	330 W. Bell Rd.	Phoenix	602-942-4138
Wal-Mart	4617 E. Bell Rd.	Phoenix	602-482-7575
Wal-Mart	2020 N. 75th Ave.	Phoenix	623-849-1030

**Waterdog Willy's	18617 N. Cave Crk Rd.	Phoenix	602-867-0314
Minit Mart	325 E. Hwy 70	Pima	928-485-3040
Uncle Toms Kwik Stop	Hwy 87 @ Pine Crk Rd.	Pine	928-476-4105
*AZ Dept. Game/Fish	2878 E. White Mt. Blvd.	Pinetop	928-367-4281
Bashas	1753 E. White Mt. Blvd.	Pinetop	928-367-2161
Mountain Outfitters	560 W. White Mt. Blvd.	Pinetop	928-367-6200
White Mntn Pawn Co.	HC 62 Box 50403	Pinetop	928-367-1221
High Country Guns	555 White Spar Rd.	Prescott	928-445-7704
K Mart	1048 Willow Creek	Prescott	928-778-5800
Lynx Creek Unlimited	130 W. Gurly St.	Prescott	928-776-7088
Lynx Lake Store	HC 31 P.O. Box 475	Prescott	928-776-4200
Popular Outfitters	1841 E. Hwy 69	Prescott	928-445-2430
Twin Lakes Market	3122 N. Hwy 89	Prescott	928-778-9686
Wal-Mart	1801 E. Hwy 69	Prescott	928-445-1113
Big 5 Sporting Goods	6101 Hwy 69	Prescott Valley	928-759-0013
K Mart	7550 E. Hwy 69	Prescott Valley	928-772-0017
Prescott Valley Archery	6330 E. Hwy 69	Prescott Valley	928-772-0255
Quartzsite General Store	I-10 Business Loop	Quartzsite	928-927-6310
Roadrunner Market	Main St.	Quartzsite	928-927-6326
Gonzo's Country Store	5154 Ave. 38 E.	Roll	928-785-4504
Minit Market	6565 E. Grant Rd.	Roosevelt	928-467-2468
Roosevelt Marina	Highway 88	Roosevelt	928-230-9000
B & M Guns & Archery	10221 1st Ave.	Safford	928-428-0305
Beverage House	1930 Thatcher Blvd.	Safford	928-428-6516
Gila Outdoor	410 Main St.	Safford	928-348-0710
Mt. Graham Market	1000 W. Swift Trail	Safford	928-428-7249
Pinkys Bait & Tackle	4656 S. 12th Ave.	Safford	928-428-0056
Thriftee Food & Drug	755 Central Ave.	Safford	928-428-1844
T Bar B Feed	66952 Hope St.	Salome	928-859-3335
The Outdoorsman Inc.	136 8th Ave.	San Manuel	520-385-4646
Bear Mountain Sports	8459 E. McDonald Rd.	Scottsdale	480-607-2838
Don's Sport Shop	7803 E. Mc Dowell Rd.	Scottsdale	480-946-5313
K Mart	7902 E. Mc Dowell Rd.	Scottsdale	480-947-5761
Paul's Fountain Hills	2845 N. Scottsdale Rd.	Scottsdale	480-947-7281
Popular Outfitters	7214 E. Thomas	Scottsdale	480-423-5121
Popular Outfitters	8734 E. Shea Blvd.	Scottsdale	480-948-2323
Props Plus Ltd.	8625 E. Mc Dowell Rd.	Scottsdale	480-949-0840
The Sports Authority	9009 E. Indian Bend Rd.	Scottsdale	480-922-8811
Wal-Mart	15355 N. Northsight Blvd.	Scottsdale	480-348-5505
Wal-Mart	4915 N. Pima Rd.	Scottsdale	480-941-0333
Bashas	160 Coffee Pot Dr.	Sedona	928-257-1470
On The Creek Sedona	274 Apple Ave.	Sedona	928-203-9973
Recreation Resource	30 Walapai Dr.	Sedona	928-282-1629
Rite Aid	2350 W. Hwy 89A	Sedona	928-282-9577
Sedona Sports	251 Hwy 179	Sedona	928-282-1317
Historic Rt. 66 Gen Store	506 W. Hwy 66	Seligman	928-422-3549
K Mart	750 W. Deuce of Clubs	Show Low	928-537-3192
Popular Outfitters	4201 S. White Mountain	Show Low	928-537-0130
Silver Creek Gnrl Store	8472 Silver Creek Dr.	Show Low	928-532-0175
Wal-Mart	5401 S. White Mountain	Show Low	928-537-3141

All Custom Firearms	498 W. Fry Blvd.	Sierra Vista	520-459-3450
Big 5 Sporting Goods	135 E. Hwy 92	Sierra Vista	520-459-1801
*KH Outdoors (scale only)	430 N. 7th St.	Sierra Vista	520-459-8095
K Mart	2011 E. Fry Blvd.	Sierra Vista	520-459-0345
Wal-Mart	657 St. Hwy 90/Vis Plaza	Sierra Vista	520-458-8790
Coast to Coast	791 S. Main St.	Snowflake	928-536-4756
Hunters Paradise	481 S. Main St.	Snowflake	928-536-3343
Alco Discount	207 S. Mountain Ave.	Springerville	928-338-4371
Big Lake Tackle	253 S. Burk St.	Springerville	928-333-2896
Safeway	203 S. Mountain Ave.	Springerville	928-333-4165
The Speckled Trout	224 E. Main St.	Springerville	928-333-0852
Sport Shack	329 E. Main St.	Springerville	928-333-2222
Western Drug Inc.	105 Main St.	Springerville	928-333-4321
Express Stop	Hwy 80	St. David	520-720-4180
Pera Club-Coronado	1190 W. Cleveland	St. Johns	928-337-2072
St. John's United Drug	1155 W. Cleveland	St. Johns	928-337-2229
Strawberry Market	Rt. 87 & Fossil Sprgs Rd.	Strawberry	928-476-3040
Express Stop	Hwy 70 & Western Ave.	Superior	520-689-5554
Guns Plus	16551 N. Dysart Rd.	Surprise	623-583-1570
Wal-Mart	13770 W. Bell Rd.	Surprise	623-544-2200
Wells Country Store	23811 N. 193rd. Ave.	Surprise	623-584-1301
Alco Discount	640 N. Main St.	Taylor	928-263-3350
Bashas	650 E. Main	Taylor	928-258-3972
Big 5 Sporting Goods	921 E. Southern Ave.	Tempe	480-491-4511
Honeywell Emp. Club	1300 W. Warner	Tempe	480-592-5984
K Mart	1330 W. Baseline Rd.	Tempe	480-839-3304
Oshmans	5000 Arizona Mills Circle	Tempe	480-831-6161
Popular Outfitters	1036 E. Baseline Rd.	Tempe	480-820-6362
Shooting Star	5861 S. Kyrene Rd.	Tempe	480-345-7827
The Sports Authority	7760 S. Priest Dr.	Tempe	480-496-8622
Wal-Mart	1380 W. Elliott Rd.	Tempe	480-345-8686
Waterdog Willy's	1805 E. Baseline Rd.	Tempe	480-897-4981
Temple Bar Resort	1 Main St.	Temple Bar	928-767-3211
Wal-Mart	2281 W. 190 N Hwy 70	Thatcher	928-428-7990
K Mart	8701 W. Mc Dowell Rd.	Tolleson	623-936-1284
Butcher Hook Bait	Hwy 188	Tonto Basin	928-479-2226
Old Western Trader	12994 Golden Shore	Topock	928-768-4954
*Apache Lake Marina	P. O. Box 15627	Tortilla Flat	928-467-2511
*Canyon Lake Marina	16802 NE Hwy 88	Tortilla Flat	928-983-1002
CSWTA Inc.	1 S. Main St.	Tuba City	928-283-4323
*AZ Dept. Game/Fish	555 N. Greasewood	Tucson	520-628-5376
Archery Center	5743 E. Speedway	Tucson	520-298-2626
*Baja Tackle & Marine	1293 W. Miracle Mile	Tucson	520-620-6454
Big 5 Sporting Goods	4646 N. Oracle Rd.	Tucson	520-292-2778
Big 5 Sporting Goods	5695 E. Speedway	Tucson	520-296-3326
Big 5 Sporting Goods	6441 S. Midvale Prk Rd.	Tucson	520-573-4135
Cash Box	2014 S. Craycroft	Tucson	520-790-7404
Jensens Sportsman	1280 W. Prince Rd.	Tucson	520-293-8516
Jensens Sportsman	5146 E. Pima	Tucson	520-325-3346
K Mart	7055 E. Broadway	Tucson	520-643-1771

K Mart	4075 W. Ina Rd.	Tucson	520-744-6900
K mart	1800 W. Valencia Rd.	Tucson	520-294-4200
Popular Outfitters	6314 N. Oracle	Tucson	520-575-1044
Popular Outfitters	6315 E. Broadway	Tucson	520-290-1644
Popular Outfitters	2820 N. Campbell	Tucson	520-326-2520
Precision Shooting	2727 N. Fairview	Tucson	520-884-9201
Saguaro Tackle & Bait	5552 E. Speedway Rd.	Tucson	520-745-0003
The Sports Authority	4225 N. Oracle Rd.	Tucson	520-292-6955
Wal-Mart	455 E. Wetmore	Tucson	520-292-2994
Wal-Mart	1650 W. Valencia	Tucson	520-573-3777
Wal-Mart	7150 W. Speedway	Tucson	520-751-1882
Wal Mart	7635 N. La Cholla Blvd.	Tucson	520-297-0840
*Alamo Lake Store	P.O. Box 304	Wenden	928-925-0133
Jim & Beas Bait /Tackle	2nd & Santa Fe	Wenden	928-859-3819
Alco Discount	2031 W. Wickenburg Wy	Wickenburg	928-684-2231
Gun Trader	36 E. Yavapai	Wickenburg	928-684-2149
Safeway	2031 W. Wickenburg Wy	Wickenburg	928-684-7775
Alco Discount	510 N. Bisbee Ave.	Willcox	520-384-0159
Browns Co. General	Ft. Grand Rd.	Willcox	520-384-2879
Safeway	630 N. Bisbee Ave.	Willcox	520-384-1311
Stronghold Feed/Supply	401 N. Railroad Ave.	Willcox	520-384-4113
Sportway Supplies	400 W. Route 66	Williams	928-635-4571
**Willow Beach Harbor	Willow Beach/HC 37	Willow Beach	928-767-4747
Wal-Mart	700 Mikes Pike Blvd.	Winslow	928-289-4641
*AZ Dept. Game/Fish	9140 E. 28th St.	Yuma	928-342-0091
Big 5 Sporting Goods	505 Catalina	Yuma	928-726-2884
**Fisher's Landing	Rural Rt. 4 Box 45	Yuma	928-782-7049
Gonzos EZ Market	1334 S. 4th Ave.	Yuma	928-782-6339
Gonzos EZ Market	3198 S. Ave B.	Yuma	928-783-0405
K Mart	2375 W. 32nd St.	Yuma	928-344-0124
Marine Corps Rec.	Box 99119	Yuma	928-783-3422
Marine Corps Rec.	Marine Corp Bldg. 692	Yuma	928-341-2016
**Mesa Sport Shop Inc.	1314 4th Ave.	Yuma	928-783-3850
Spragues Sports & RV	345 W. 32nd St.	Yuma	928-726-0022
Wal-Mart	2900 S. Pacific Ave.	Yuma	928-344-0922
Hurst Ace Hardware	953 Red Cliff Dr.	Washington UT	435-652-1111

Navajo Nation Permit Vendors

C.S.W.T.A., Inc.	Box 790	Tuba City	928-283-4323
Kayenta Trading Post	Box 1218	Kayenta	928-697-3541
Navajo Fish & Wildlife	Box 1480	Window Rock	928-871-6451
Shirley's Trading Post	Box 44	Lupton	928-888-2690
Tse Bonito Mustang	Box 1944	Window Rock	505-371-5566
Wilkinson's Trading Post	Box 66	Tsaile	928-724-3484
Wal-Mart	700 Mikes Pike Blvd.	Winslow	928-289-4741

San Carlos Reservation Permit Vendors

Tempe Marine	1800 N. Arizona Ave.	Chandler	480-782-6813
Bob Keen's Store	15560 W. Hwy 70	Fort Thomas	928-485-2261
Circle K	1915 E. Ash St.	Globe	928-425-5942
Express Stop	1501 E. Ash St.	Globe	928-425-3911
San Carlos Lake Store	HCR 1, Box 24	Peridot	928-475-2756
Mini-Market	325 E. Hwy 70	Pima	928-485-3040
Pinkys Bait & Tackle	4656 S. 12th Ave.	Safford	928-428-0056
Apache Gold Casino	P.O. Box 1210	San Carlos	928-475-7800
Waterdog Willys	1805 E. Baseline	Tempe	480-897-4981
Ba-Ha Tackle	1293 W. Miracle Mile	Tucson	520-620-6454
Bashas	US Hwy 70 /SR 170	Peridot	928-475-2391
San Carlos Wildlife	Hwy 70 E. Old Moonbase	Peridot	928-475-2343

White Mountain Apache Reservation Permit Vendors

Canyon Day Store	Canyon Day Community	Canyon Day	928-338-1326
Carrizo Station	Jct. 60 & Hwy 73	Carrizo	928-332-2404
Tempe Marine	1800 N. Arizona Ave.	Chandler	480-782-6813
Circle B Market	38940 Main St.	Greer	928-735-7540
Hon Dah Sport	Jct. Hwy 260 & Hwy 73	Hon-dah	928-369-7669
Hon Dah Service Station	3 Mi. S. of Pinetop	Hon-dah	928-369-4311
Bob's Bang Room	3973 Hwy 260	Lakeside	928-368-5040
Pinetop Sporting Goods	747 E. White Mountain	Pinetop	928-367-5050
K mart	750 W. Deuce/Clubs	Show Low	928-537-3192
Western Drug	105 Main St.	Springerville	928-333-4321
North Fork Foods	Hwy 73	Whiteriver	
7-Mile Store	3 Mi. S. of Whiteriver	Whiteriver	928-338-1100
Wildlife/Outdoor Rec.	1205 S. Chief Ave.	Whiteriver	928-338-4385
Apache Shell Service	Hwy 73	Whiteriver	928-338-4315
Salt River Cnyn. Inn	Salt River Canyon		
Sunrise Marina	Sunrise Lake		928-735-7335
Sunrise Serv. Station	Sunrise Lake		928-735-7335
Horseshoe Marina	Horseshoe Lake		928-521-2613
Reservation Marina	Reservation Lake		928-521-7458
Hawley Lake Store	Hawley Lake		928-335-7511

Out of State Arizona License Vendors

Systems Consultants	185 N. Main St.	Fallon	NV	775-423-1345
Jadde Sporting Goods	223 Sandhill Blvd.	Mesquite	NV	702-346-6636
Mesquite Outdoors	300 N. Sandhill Blvd.	Mesquite	NV	702-345-3120
Hurst Stores Inc.	165 S. Main St.	Cedar City	UT	435-865-9335
CJ's	625 N. State St.	Hildale	UT	435-874-2437
Hurst Sales Corp	489 W. State St.	Hurricane	UT	435-635-4449
Hurst Ace Hardware	160 N. 500 W.	St. George	UT	435-673-6141
The Locker Room	1062 E. Tabernacle	St. George	UT	435-674-4008
Red Rock Fly Shop	2 W St. George Blvd.	St. George	UT	435-656-4665
Wal-Mart	1850 E. Red Cliff Dr.	St. George	UT	435-628-2802

Indicates a 30-pound scale capacity
Indicates a 120-pound scale capacity
You can also purchase Arizona fishing licenses online: www.azgfd.com
or by phone: 1-866-462-0433

Index

Note: All fish types are listed under **fish;** all bodies of water are listed under **lakes, reservoirs, ponds, tanks** or **rivers, creeks and streams.**

Epilogue

Look into a child's eyes and witness the crystal-clear vision that is our future. Teach him an appreciation for the out of doors, and you ensure his ability to focus on, and understand, all that is natural.

Author on the way to Apache Lake

About the Author

Guy J. Sagi, author of *Fishing Arizona* and *Hunting Small Game in Arizona,* was born and raised in Tucson. For a dozen years he served with the Southern Arizona Rescue Association and was twice elected Captain of Pima County Four Wheel Drive Search and Rescue.

He has served as editor in chief of Safari Club International's *Safari Times, Mule Deer* magazine and is currently Executive Editor for NRA's *Insights, Shooting Sports USA* and *Shooting Illustrated* magazines. He is a former president of the Society of Outdoor Magazine Editors, served twice as president of the Communicators of Hunting's Heritage and is a member of the Western Outdoor Writers, Southeast Outdoor Press Association and the Outdoor Writers Association of America. His byline has appeared in many major outdoor publications and includes dailies like the *Washington Post, San Francisco Chronicle* and *Cleveland Plain Dealer.*

His most important roles, however, are that of husband, father and grandfather.

More Books from Golden West Publishers

EXPLORE ARIZONA!

Where to find old coins, bottles, fossil beds, arrowheads, petroglyphs, waterfalls, ice caves, cliff dwellings. Detailed maps to 59 Arizona wonders. By Rick Harris.

5 1/2 x 8 1/2—128 pages . . . $6.95

DISCOVER ARIZONA!

Enjoy the thrill of discovery! Prehistoric ruins, caves, historic battlegrounds, fossil beds, arrowheads, waterfalls, rock crystals and semi-precious stones! By Rick Harris.

5 1/2 x 8 1/2 — 112 pages . . . $6.95

GHOST TOWNS
and Historical Haunts in Arizona

Visit cities of Arizona's golden past, browse through many photographs of adobe ruins, old mines, cemeteries, ghost towns, cabins and castles! Come, step into Arizona's past! By prize-winning journalist Thelma Heatwole.

5 1/2 x 8 1/2—144 pages . . . $6.95

HORSE TRAILS IN ARIZONA

Complete guide to over 100 of Arizona's most beautiful equestrian trails, from the desert to the high country. Maps, directions to trailheads, water availability and more to ensure an unmatched experience for all. Lodging and "hitchin' post" restaurant information, too!

5 1/2 x 8 1/2 — 160 pages . . . $12.95

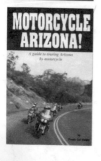

MOTORCYCLE ARIZONA!

Detailed guide (with maps) of more than 70 motorcycle trips ranging from day-rides to two-week tours! From the Grand Canyon to Bisbee and with cross-overs into Colorado, Utah and Nevada by way of the most scenic motorcycling roads in the southwest! Arizona attractions, lodging, tips on clothing, safety, weather and more! By Frank Del Monte.

5 1/2 x 8 1/2 — 160 pages . . . $9.95

ORDER BLANK

GOLDEN WEST PUBLISHERS

☼ 4113 N. Longview Ave. • Phoenix, AZ 85014

www.goldenwestpublishers.com • 1-800-658-5830 • FAX 602-279-6901

Qty	Title	Price	Amount
	Arizona Adventure—*Arizona Trilogy Vol. 1*	9.95	
	Arizona Legends and Lore	9.95	
	Arizona Trails & Tales	9.95	
	Arizona Trivia	8.95	
	Arizoniana—*Arizona Trilogy Vol. 3*	9.95	
	Arrows, Bullets and Saddle Sores	9.95	
	Discover Arizona!	6.95	
	Easy Recipes for Wild Game and Fish	6.95	
	Easy RV Recipes	6.95	
	Explore Arizona!	6.95	
	Fishing Arizona	14.95	
	Ghost Towns in Arizona	6.95	
	Haunted Arizona	12.95	
	Hiking Arizona	6.95	
	In Old Arizona—*Arizona Trilogy Vol. 2*	9.95	
	Motorcycle Arizona	9.95	
	Scorpions & Venomous Insects of the Southwest	9.95	
	Sleeping with Ghosts: (Arizona)	12.95	
	Snakes and other Reptiles of the Southwest	9.95	
	Tales of Arizona Territory	9.95	

Shipping & Handling Add: (Shipping to all other countries see website.)	1-3 Books $5.00	
	4+ Books $7.00	
Arizona residents add 8.1% sales tax		

Total $ _____
(Payable in U.S. funds)

☐ My Check or Money Order Enclosed
☐ MasterCard ☐ VISA

Acct. No. _____ Exp. Date _____

Signature _____

Name _____ Phone_____

Address _____

City/State/Zip _____

11/05   **Call for a FREE catalog of all of our titles**   Fishing AZ